Greater Heights

Scan the QR code to see all the titles in this series.

EUROPE AND CENTRAL ASIA STUDIES

Greater Heights

Growing to High Income in Europe and Central Asia

Leonardo Iacovone
Ivailo V. Izvorski
Christos Kostopoulos
Michael M. Lokshin
Richard Record
Iván Torre
Szilvia Doczi

WORLD BANK GROUP

Europe and Central Asia Studies

The Europe and Central Asia Studies series features analytical reports on main challenges and opportunities faced by countries in the region, with the aim to inform a broad policy debate. Titles in this series undergo extensive internal and external review prior to publication.

Previous Books in This Series

2024

The Journey Ahead: Supporting Successful Migration in Europe and Central Asia (2024), Laurent Bossavie, Daniel Garrote Sánchez, Mattia Makovec

2018

Toward a New Social Contract: Taking on Distributional Tensions in Europe and Central Asia (2018), Maurizio Bussolo, Vito Peragine, Ramya Sundaram

Critical Connections: Promoting Economic Growth and Resilience in Europe and Central Asia (2018), David Michael Gould

2017

Reaping Digital Dividends: Leveraging the Internet for Development in Europe and Central Asia (2017), Tim Kelly, Shawn W. Tan, Hernan Winkler

Risks and Returns: Managing Financial Trade-Offs for Inclusive Growth in Europe and Central Asia (2017), David Michael Gould, Martin Melecky

2015

Golden Aging: Prospects for Healthy, Active, and Prosperous Aging in Europe and Central Asia (2015), Maurizio Bussolo, Johannes Koettl

2014

Shared Prosperity: Paving the Way in Europe and Central Asia (2014), Maurizio Bussolo, Luis F. Lopez-Calva

All books in the Europe and Central Asia Studies Series are available free at https://hdl.handle.net/10986/2155.

Contents

Boxes

Figures

Tables

Foreword

The countries of Europe and Central Asia (ECA) embarked on a remarkable journey more than three decades ago. In the early 1990s, they began transitioning from planned to market economies, supported by broad and deep structural reforms. This transformation was bolstered by integration into global markets; the emergence of private initiative as the main driver of growth; and, for some of the countries, entry into the European Union. As a result, 10 ECA economies had achieved high-income status by 2024.

Another 20 ECA economies are still middle income, as they and the region face the challenges of accelerating economic growth while creating well-paying jobs. In these middle-income countries (MICs), it has been found that the transition to high-income status requires not only continued foundational reforms but also new transformative measures to unleash business dynamism, nurture talent and reduce its misallocation, and ensure secure and affordable energy.

This report provides a comprehensive assessment of the prospects for ECA countries to reach and maintain high-income status. It offers detailed recommendations about how to escape the middle-income trap. These ECA countries need to undergo not one, but two, transitions. One transition requires a shift from a strategy driven largely by investment to a strategy augmented by the importation and diffusion of global capital, technology, and knowledge (infusion). The other transition is to a stage that adds the dimension of innovation. An emphasis on the overall strategy driven by investment, infusion, and innovation is even more important in countries that have already attained high-income status, because they must avoid becoming stuck in what may be termed "low high-income status."

Productivity growth among the ECA MICs has lagged. While structural shifts and resource reallocation have contributed to gains, within-firm productivity driven by innovation and technological upgrading remains insufficient. The prevalence of state-owned enterprises (SOEs) and restricted competition have stifled entrepreneurial dynamism and productivity. It is essential to strengthen competition frameworks, attract knowledge-intensive foreign direct investment, and improve capacities and managerial skills. Additionally, incentivizing R&D and addressing credit misallocation are critical steps to enhancing productivity.

Furthermore, intergenerational mobility in education is declining. Younger generations in ECA are now less likely to surpass the educational attainment of their parents. The deterioration in the quality of education poses a significant risk to long-term growth prospects. Addressing these challenges requires strengthening the teaching of foundational skills, revamping vocational education, improving the management and accountability of universities, and integrating research with teaching. Equal access to higher education must be preserved, while emphasizing merit-based graduation. Facilitating the broader participation of women in the labor market and managing talent flows across borders are also crucial.

The ECA MICs have made progress in reducing energy and emissions intensity, but the region remains one of the least energy efficient. Ensuring secure, abundant, and affordable energy presents a significant growth opportunity, but policy, market, and regulatory barriers, along with inefficiencies in incumbent SOEs, are hindering progress. Creating competitive markets and rationalizing energy prices, phasing out fossil fuel subsidies, and introducing carbon pricing are essential measures. Promoting energy efficiency, including in SOEs, while creating new opportunities for workers in affected sectors are vital for a sustainable energy future in the region.

As we look ahead, the ECA region has the potential to continue its remarkable progress. This will not be easy, but by embracing the necessary reforms and leveraging its unique strengths, the region can achieve strong, job-rich growth, ensuring a prosperous future for all its citizens.

Antonella Bassani
Regional Vice President
Europe and Central Asia Region
The World Bank

Acknowledgments

The report was prepared by a World Bank team led by Ivailo V. Izvorski that included Leonardo Iacovone, Christos Kostopoulos, Michael M. Lokshin, Richard Record, Iván Torre, and Szilvia Doczi.

The extended team included Matias Belacin, Nicholas David Elms, Tom Farole, Gentian Gashi, Julia Norfleet, and Fabian Alexander Scheifele. Substantial inputs were received from Stefan Apfalter, Donato De Rosa, Zuzana Dobrotkova, Sergiy Kasyanenko, Harry Patrinos, Francis Ralambotsiferana Ratsimbazafy, and Gregor Semieniuk.

The work benefited from the guidance of Antonella Bassani, Vice President of the Europe and Central Asia region; Indermit Gill, Chief Economist of the World Bank Group and Senior Vice President for Development Economics (DEC); and Somik Lall, Senior Advisor in DEC.

The team is grateful for comments, suggestions, and inputs from Elcin Akcura, Asad Alam, Ani Balabanyan, Sudeshna Ghosh Banerjee, Roberta Bassett, Gunhild Berg, Manuel Berlengiero, Maurizio Bussolo, Pietro Calice, Piotr Charewicz, Alexandru Cojocaru, Charles Cormier, Rafael de Hoyos, Rocco De Miglio, James Foster, Katharina Gassner, Koen Geven, Mariano Gonzalez, Joern Hunteler, Jonathan Karver, Tatyana Kramskaya, Nathalie Lahire, Alan David Lee, Luis Felipe López-Calva, Magda Malec, Lukasz Marek Marc, Silvia Martinez Romero, Farah Nadeem, Naveed Naqvi, Claire Nicholas, Sergio Perilla, Claudio Protano, Miguel Purroy, Angelica Rivera-Olvera, Michal Rutkowski, Maksud Safarov, Gulnaz Sharafutdinova, Maria Vagliasindi, and Sameh Wahba.

The team is grateful for the guidance and comments provided by a group of advisors, including Ufuk Akcigit (University of Chicago), Vache Gabrielyan (American University of Armenia), André Sapir (Bruegel), and Kori Udovički (Center for Advanced Economic Studies, Serbia). The report benefited from the presentations and discussions organized by Peter Berkowitz at DG REGIO and Alexandr Hobza at DG RTI, both at the European Commission; Jesus Crespo of the Department of Economics at Vienna University of Economics and Business; Jan Hagemejer at the Center for Social and Economic Research; Mario Holzner from the Vienna Institute for International Economic Studies; Robert Jeszke from the Centre for Climate and Energy Analyses in Poland; Piotr Lewandowski at the

Institute for Structural Research in Poland; Professor Piotr Maszczyk and Professor Mariusz Próchniak at the Warsaw School of Economics; André Sapir and Nicolas Veron at Bruegel and the Center for Advanced Economic Studies, Serbia; and Julia Woerz from the Austrian National Bank.

Special thanks go to the National Statistics Office of Georgia (GEOSTAT), the Bureau of National Statistics of Kazakhstan, the Kosovo Agency of Statistics (KAS), the National Statistical Committee of the Kyrgyz Republic, the Statistical Office of Montenegro (MONSTAT), the Statistical Institute of North Macedonia, Statistics Poland, the Ministry of Finance of Romania, and the Statistical Office of the Republic of Serbia for their collaboration in providing access to firm-level data.

The communications strategy was led by a team comprising Indira Chand, Nicole Frost, Aaron Wesley Korenewsky, Marcelo Gonzales Montoya, and Nina Vucenik.

A team at Communications Development—led by Bruce Ross-Larson and including Joe Caponio, Mike Crumplar, and Chris Trott—edited the report. Robert Zimmermann copyedited the report. Special thanks are extended to the World Bank's Formal Publishing Program, including Cindy Fisher, Patricia Katayama, Devika Seecharran Levy, and Stephen Pazdan. Ekaterina Ushakova coordinated the full preparation and publication of the report. Suzette Dahlia Samms-Lindsay provided continued support.

About the Authors

Szilvia Doczi, a Senior Energy Economist at the World Bank, leads the development of energy system models for Europe and Central Asia. These models are used in energy security assessments; the regional Net-Zero Energy by 2060 analysis; and Country Climate and Development Reports for Croatia, the Kyrgyz Republic, Poland, Tajikistan, and Uzbekistan. Before joining the World Bank in 2022, she spent 16 years in the public and private energy sectors, including roles at the International Energy Agency, Arup's Transaction Advisory Services team, the UK energy regulator, and MAVIR (the Hungarian transmission system operator). She has been involved in more than 20 energy sector transactions and projects in the Americas, Asia, and Europe. Szilvia holds an MSc in economics from Corvinus University of Budapest.

Leonardo Iacovone, Lead Economist in the Europe and Central Asia region, works on productivity, firm dynamics, innovation, and entrepreneurship. He studied at Bocconi University, Torcuato Di Tella University, and the University of Sussex. Leonardo is Adjunct Professor at the Hertie School and is affiliated with the Abdul Latif Jameel Poverty Action Lab and the Small and Medium Enterprise Initiative of Innovations for Poverty Action. He has published in *American Economic Review: Insights; Economic Journal; Journal of Development Economics; Journal of International Economics; PNAS; Review of Economic Studies; Science; World Bank Economic Review;* and *World Development.* In 2009, he received the Paul Geroski Prize, awarded by the European Association for Research in Industrial Economics for the most significant policy contribution by young economists.

Ivailo V. Izvorski is the Chief Economist in the Europe and Central Asia region of the World Bank. Over the past 25 years, he has worked in technical and management positions covering the countries of Africa, East Asia and the Pacific, and Europe and Central Asia at the World Bank, the Institute of International Finance, and the International Monetary Fund. Before his current position, Ivailo was the Manager of the World Bank Global Debt, Macro, and Growth Unit and, before that, a manager of macroeconomists for Europe and Central Asia. He holds MA and PhD degrees in economics from Yale University. Ivailo is coauthor of *Diversified Development: Making the Most of Natural Resources in Eurasia* and of "Reinvigorating Growth in Resource-Rich Sub-Saharan Africa."

Christos Kostopoulos is a Lead Economist for the Western Balkans at the World Bank. Earlier, he was a Lead Country Economist based in Beirut for the Middle East Department, covering Iran, Iraq, Jordan, Lebanon, and Syria from 2017 to 2022. Before that assignment, Christos worked in a similar capacity in Central Asia, based in Almaty, Kazakhstan, from 2014 to 2017, where he focused on operations and analytical work on Kazakhstan and Uzbekistan. Christos has also worked in Washington, DC, in corporate business and as an economist on Azerbaijan and Brazil. He was a country economist for the Indian Ocean countries, particularly Madagascar, Mauritius, and the Comoros, based in Antananarivo, Madagascar. He holds a PhD in economics from the University of Maryland at College Park.

Michael M. Lokshin is a Lead Economist in the Office of the Chief Economist for Europe and Central Asia at the World Bank. He joined the Development Research Group of the World Bank with the Young Economist Program. He has worked in more than 40 countries. His research focuses on poverty, inequality, labor, social protection, migration, and aging. He received his PhD in economics from the University of North Carolina at Chapel Hill. Michael has published more than 70 papers in *Economic Policy, European Economic Review, Journal of Development Economics, Journal of Economic Behavior and Organization, Journal of Human Resources, Journal of Public Economics,* and *World Bank Economic Review,* among others. He is ranked in the top 3 percent of world economists by Research Papers in Economics.

Richard Record is the World Bank's Lead Country Economist for the Western Balkans. Based in Vienna, he coordinates the World Bank's engagement on economic policy, finance, and institutions across Albania, Bosnia and Herzegovina, Kosovo, Montenegro, North Macedonia, and Serbia. Richard previously worked across several countries in the Africa, East Asia and Pacific, and Europe and Central Asia regions, managing programs on macroeconomics, fiscal policy, trade, and private sector development, including assignments based in Hanoi, Kuala Lumpur, Lilongwe, and Vientiane. He holds bachelor's, master's, and doctoral degrees in economics from, respectively, the London School of Economics, the School of Oriental and African Studies, and the University of Manchester.

Iván Torre is a Senior Economist in the World Bank's Office of the Chief Economist, Europe and Central Asia region. Before joining the World Bank, he worked as a consultant for the Inter-American Development Bank. His work focuses on inequality, human development, and political economy. He has a bachelor's degree in economics from Universidad de Buenos Aires and holds a PhD in economics from Sciences Po, Paris. His research has been published in peer-reviewed journals, such as *Economics & Politics, Journal of Comparative Economics, Journal of International Economics, Review of Development Economics, Review of Income and Wealth, World Bank Economic Review,* and *World Development.*

Main Messages

Chapter 1: Transitioning to High Income—or Not

- Since 1990, 27 countries across the globe have reached high-income status; of these, 10 are in the Europe and Central Asia (ECA) region and have joined the European Union. Another 20 ECA countries have become more prosperous since the 1990s. However, these middle-income countries (MICs) have found that their prospects for growing to high income have become troubled. This partly reflects the slowing pace of progress on structural reforms at home. The challenges are also partly linked to the deteriorating global environment.

- Concern is growing that many ECA countries may have become caught in a middle-income trap, a development phase of repeated growth slowdowns, with per capita incomes systematically below the high-income threshold. On current trends, it is unlikely that any of the ECA MICs will cross the high-income threshold in the next few years.

- To ensure that these countries overcome recent growth slowdowns and the challenges associated with the wobbly global environment, policy makers need to focus on two transitions. One transition is from a strategy driven largely by investment to a strategy augmented by the importation and diffusion of global capital, technology, and knowledge (infusion). The other transition is from the latter infusion stage to a stage that adds the dimension of innovation. The emphasis on the overall strategy driven by investment, infusion, and innovation is even more important in countries that have already attained high-income status because these countries must avoid becoming stuck in what may be termed "low high-income status."

- Unleashing the Schumpeterian forces of creative destruction is essential to the transition to high-income status in the years ahead. In the 1990s, the early years of transition from a planned to a market economy, the forces of destruction dominated the economies of the ECA MICs. For those countries that advanced the most quickly, the forces of preservation were muted, while the forces of creation were emerging. Fast forward three decades. Now, the forces of preservation have the upper hand. Countries must help balance more evenly the forces of creation, destruction, and preservation to reach high-income status and sustain progress.

Chapter 2: Enterprises and Productivity

- The ECA MICs can reach high-income status only if firms are able to grow, innovate, and compete. Within Europe and outside the region, successful transitions to high income have been driven by private sector transformation. Policy makers need to shift from protecting incumbents to enabling business dynamism, rewarding merit, and facilitating innovation. With the proper reforms, the ECA MICs can foster the enterprise-driven growth needed to sustain long-term prosperity.

- Traditional policies centered on supporting small and medium enterprises (SMEs) alone frequently prove misguided because they result in an excess of SMEs and do little to promote cumulative growth in jobs and output. Startups and young firms, rather than SMEs in general, drive job dynamism both in the ECA region and around the world. MICs must abandon overly broad support for enterprises based on size and focus on the value added by supporting dynamic, high-growth firms that create jobs and innovate. The ECA MICs suffer from a "missing large" problem: there are too many small, unproductive firms that do not grow and too few businesses that are industry leaders.

- Domestic competition should be reinvigorated to allow new, dynamic firms to emerge. The enduring presence of state-owned enterprises (SOEs) in the ECA region dulls the impact of market competition on creative destruction. Wherever SOEs are more prominent, the broader economy-wide impacts involve reduced entrepreneurial activity, less business entry and exit, and lower investment. Governments must strengthen competition authorities, discipline SOEs, and help ensure that new entrants are not blocked from gaining access to markets and finance.

- Access to finance, especially long-term credit and risk capital, must greatly improve. Limited access to finance is often linked to lingering macro risks and an uncompetitive financial system reliant on government direction and support. Venture capital and other forms of long-term financing remain underdeveloped in the ECA MICs, limiting the ability of firms to invest in innovation and scale up. Governments should facilitate access to risk capital, deepen financial markets, and reduce distortions caused by state-directed lending that often benefits less productive firms.

Chapter 3: Talent and Social Mobility

- The shortage and misallocation of talent are becoming a binding growth constraint on ECA countries. This limits the ability of firms to invest; to infuse technologies, capital, and expertise from abroad; and to innovate.

- Social mobility is the most important measure of the extent to which the talents of children are utilized well and, thus, whether societies have embraced a pro-growth focus. The expectation of social mobility matters because it confirms the possibility of progress and dynamism and ultimately fosters public support for structural reforms, including in education. Social mobility has been declining among younger generations in the ECA region. The probability that children are more highly educated than their parents is lower today than in the past. Family circumstances are now playing a larger role in determining children's educational attainment.

- The quality of education across the ECA MICs has deteriorated substantially in recent decades. Over the past decade, lower education quality has meant that children have lost the equivalent of a full year of schooling. One of the most pressing issues in the region is the effectiveness of vocational education and training (VET). While VET programs are often touted as a viable pathway to enhancing employability, they frequently fail to equip students with the skills to thrive in a rapidly evolving job market. The picture is even gloomier at universities. Obtaining a diploma has become more important than receiving knowledge or acquiring skills. Academic capture, inadequate funding, outdated curricula, a lack of modern infrastructure, and the proliferation of tertiary institutions are among the leading causes of the poor quality of tertiary education.

- To bolster social mobility and foster innovation, ECA countries must dramatically overhaul education systems, particularly vocational and university education. Vocational education should be deeply reformed by delaying the placement of students in separate academic tracks, boosting links with the private sector for relevance, and ensuring that foundational skills are also learned. Universities should be consolidated, research centers should be integrated into universities, and graduation on merit should once again become entrenched in the practice of education.

Chapter 4: Energy

- The ECA MICs are on the verge of decoupling energy intensity and growth in emissions from growth in output, a feat accomplished thus far mostly by high-income countries. Nonetheless, ECA remains the most energy-intensive developing world region, with a substantial prevalence of SOEs and some of the world's highest energy subsidies.

- The transition to lower energy intensity and lower emissions can become a transition to high-income status, but this link is not automatic and will require deliberate, well-sequenced steps. Reaching and sustaining high-income status depend crucially on the ECA countries tackling substantial energy inefficiencies, reducing energy intensity, and adopting lower-cost energy production. As an important step, countries need to discipline the incumbent SOEs that control 100 percent of transmission, more than 80 percent of fossil fuel power generation (double the global average), and more than 65 percent of electricity distribution. A large share of the ECA SOEs are loss making, preventing them from upgrading their infrastructure and infusing global knowledge and expertise.

● Transmission networks urgently need to be upgraded, and adequate battery storage created so that the energy generated by the new entrants to the market is not wasted. A large majority of private companies deem grid access a high or remarkably elevated risk. They expect most ECA countries to encounter issues in integrating the planned solar and wind volumes if these countries do not also undertake substantial investment in transmission and distribution networks.

● The ECA MICs need to establish the proper price signals, make sure energy markets work, and ensure that startups can connect to the transmission grid and not be blocked by incumbents. Energy prices should reflect economic and social costs. Realizing this adjustment requires the elimination of energy subsidies and the introduction of carbon taxes to internalize externalities. Economic merit dispatch needs to be observed. Energy efficiency standards also need to become appropriately stringent.

● The transition to more efficient and lower carbon emissions creates losses among consumers, workers, and businesses and, so, encounters resistance. Affected groups will push back against well-intentioned reform. Addressing such political economy concerns requires careful policy sequencing so that reforms impose no unbearable burdens on any group. But focusing only on low-hanging fruit that is unlikely to create a backlash may not lead to the emergence of new firms and the destruction of inefficient practices and enterprises. Reductions in fossil fuel subsidies among vulnerable groups can be balanced by targeted income support, and money can be saved.

Abbreviations

BOS	businesses of the state
ECA	Europe and Central Asia
ETS	emissions trading system
EU	European Union
GDP	gross domestic product
GNI	gross national income
HIC	high-income country
IEA	International Energy Agency
LIC	low-income country
LMIC	lower-middle-income country
MIC	middle-income country
NACE	statistical classification of economic activities in the European Community
OECD	Organisation for Economic Co-operation and Development
PISA	Programme for International Student Assessment (OECD)
PPP	purchasing power parity
R&D	research and development
SD	standard deviation
SMEs	small and medium enterprises
SOE	state-owned enterprise
TFP	total factor productivity
UMIC	upper-middle-income country
VET	vocational education and training

Country Classifications Used in This Report

Europe high-income countries (Europe HICs): Andorra, Austria, Belgium, Cyprus, Denmark, Finland, France, Germany, Iceland, Ireland, Italy, Liechtenstein, Luxembourg, Monaco, Netherlands, Norway, San Marino, Spain, Sweden, Switzerland, and United Kingdom.

Convergers: Croatia, Czech Republic, Estonia, Greece, Hungary, Latvia, Lithuania, Malta, Poland, Portugal, Romania, Slovak Republic, and Slovenia.

Europe and Central Asia high-income countries (ECA HICs): This is a subset of the Convergers and includes the three HICs in Europe that are World Bank member countries, that is, Croatia, Poland, and Romania.

ECA middle-income countries (ECA MICs): Albania, Armenia, Azerbaijan, Belarus, Bosnia and Herzegovina, Bulgaria, Georgia, Kazakhstan, Kosovo, Kyrgyz Republic, Moldova, Montenegro, North Macedonia, Russian Federation, Serbia, Tajikistan, Türkiye, Turkmenistan, Ukraine, and Uzbekistan.

Overview

Introduction

Twenty-seven countries across the globe have reached high-income status since 1990. Ten of these countries are in the Europe and Central Asia (ECA) region, and all of them have joined the European Union (EU). These countries saw their economic growth peak in the 2000s because of the transition from a planned economy to a market economy that began in the early 1990s, the accompanying broad and deep structural reforms, and the emergence of private initiative as the main driver of growth. The success of these countries in their embrace of EU-integrated markets, robust institutions, and reformed and realigned production structures resulted in the transition to high-income status (refer to figure O.1).[1]

Another 20 ECA countries have become more prosperous since the 1990s, but their transition to high-income status has been delayed. These middle-income countries (MICs) have found that their prospects for achieving high-income status have become more complicated since the global financial crisis in 2007–09. The problems have arisen partly because of slow progress in advancing domestic structural reforms, notably, in reducing the role of the state in the economy and establishing effective competition policies to support the emergence and growth of efficient, innovative enterprises.[2] Another factor is rapid population aging and the dramatic declines in birth rates in most of these countries, except in Türkiye and in Central Asia, combined with large outward migration, that have resulted in reductions in the size of working-age populations and downward pressure on economic growth. The deteriorating global environment has also played a role. These countries have been battered by a succession of crises, including the global financial crisis, the European debt crisis, the COVID-19 pandemic, and Russia's

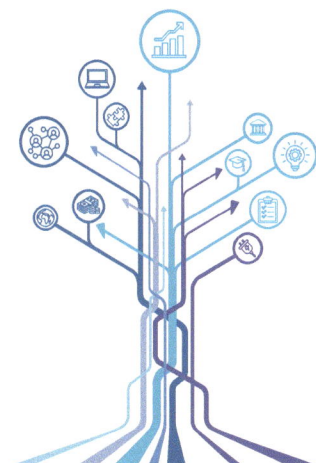

FIGURE O.1 **Ten ECA countries have achieved high-income status since 1990**

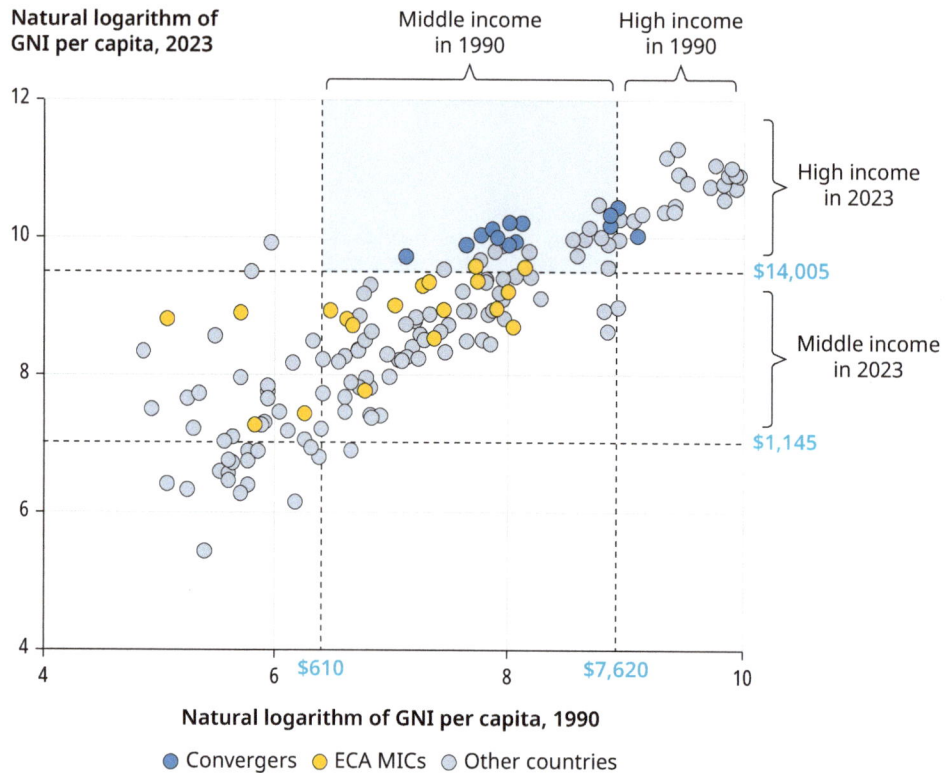

Source: WDI (World Development Indicators) (dashboard), World Bank, Washington, DC, https://
datatopics.worldbank.org/world-development-indicators/.

Note: The shaded area indicates countries that transitioned from middle-income to high-income
status in 1990–2023. The countries of the ECA region in 1990 are shown in dark blue. GNI = gross
national income; MICs = middle-income countries.

invasion of Ukraine. Global economic growth is weaker today than it has been since
the mid-1990s. The pace of economic expansion in the EU, the largest trading and
investment partner of the ECA countries, has dropped significantly. Global value
chains are becoming more fragmented as geopolitical tensions have increased.
Populism and protectionism have acquired more support, resulting in a shift away
from an outward-looking focus in many countries.

With these challenges, per capita economic growth in the MICs in the region
weakened from an annual average of 4.8 percent during 2000–09 to 3.6 percent
during 2010–19 and 2020–25, about one percentage point less than in East Asia
and the Pacific (refer to figure O.2). Average gross domestic product (GDP) per
capita in purchasing parity prices in the ECA region increased from 22 percent of
the US level in 1999 to more than 33 percent by 2009, but only rose to 38 percent
by 2022. Thus, the income convergence of the MICs in the region with the

FIGURE O.2 Economic growth in the middle-income countries of ECA has stagnated, 2000–25

Percent, period average

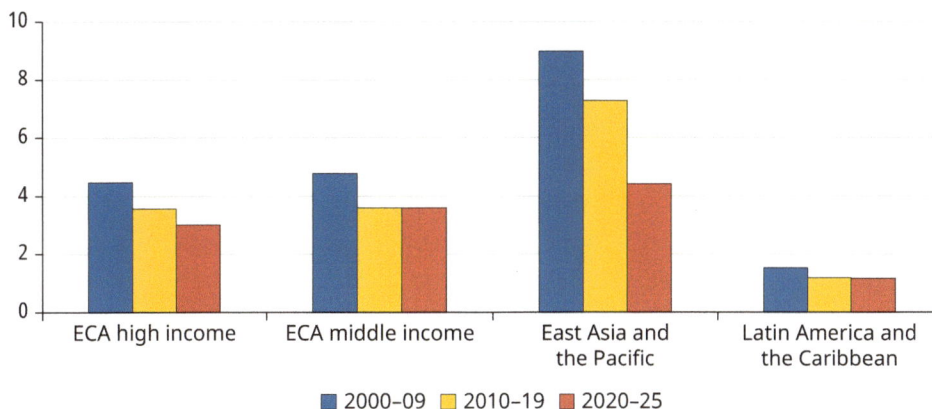

Source: WDI (World Development Indicators) (dashboard), World Bank, Washington, DC, https://datatopics.worldbank.org/world-development-indicators/.

Note: ECA high-income countries include Croatia, Poland, and Romania.

high-income countries (HICs) slowed, and diminishing returns appeared to have become the norm. Although the slowdown mirrored global trends, and the average ratios to the United States were higher in the ECA countries than in other countries, the slowdown in the ECA region was much steeper. Based on average 15-year per capita growth rates, only a couple of MICs in the region seemed likely to reach the high-income threshold (currently $14,005) by 2040.

The concern is growing that many ECA countries may have become caught in a middle-income trap, a phase of development characterized by recurring slowdowns in growth and by per capita incomes that are systematically below the high-income-country threshold. To overcome the string of growth slowdowns and the challenges of the wobbly global environment and to shift to a path to high-income status, these countries need to make the transition from strategies driven largely by investment to strategies that are supported by the importation and diffusion of global capital and the infusion of technology and knowledge and that take advantage of the dimension of innovation. Such a transition will require sustained foundational reform to fuel the engines of economic growth, while pivoting to new transformative reforms aimed at developing the more complex economic structures and institutions that can enable firms to accumulate human and physical capital, infuse fresh expertise and technology, and implement innovations that expand the frontier of products and processes. The emphasis on a strategy driven by innovation is also important for countries that have already attained high-income status to ensure that they do not become stuck at a low level of high-income status.

Investment, Infusion, and Innovation to Achieve and Sustain High-Income Status

This report follows the approach of *World Development Report 2024* on the middle-income trap to assess the prospects of the ECA countries and provide policy options on how they might achieve high-income status (World Bank 2024). This study concludes that the transition to high-income status among the ECA MICs is possible but will require reforms supplemented by measures to raise competition, unleash private enterprise, and cut inefficiencies. Reform will also be needed to reduce the waste and misallocation of talent and harness lower energy intensity to transition, ultimately, to net zero emissions to bolster productivity growth. Following *World Development Report 2024*, this report relies on the 3*i* strategy to articulate that the MICs in the region must navigate two key development transitions on the path to high income (refer to figure O.3), as follows.

- *From investment to investment and infusion.* The first transition is the shift from mostly investment-driven growth—the 1*i* strategy (often called accumulation in the economic literature)—to a strategy focused on both investment and infusion or integration in the global economy (the 2*i* strategy). The 2*i* strategy involves adopting new technologies, ideas, capital, and expertise from abroad and diffusing them domestically. Of the 20 MICs in the region, 17 are upper-middle-income countries in which the 2*i* strategy is being implemented. Governments and stakeholders in these countries should not ignore the need to boost investment in both human and physical capital.

FIGURE O.3 **Reaching high-income status requires two transitions: from 1*i* to 2*i* and then to 3*i***

Relative contribution to growth

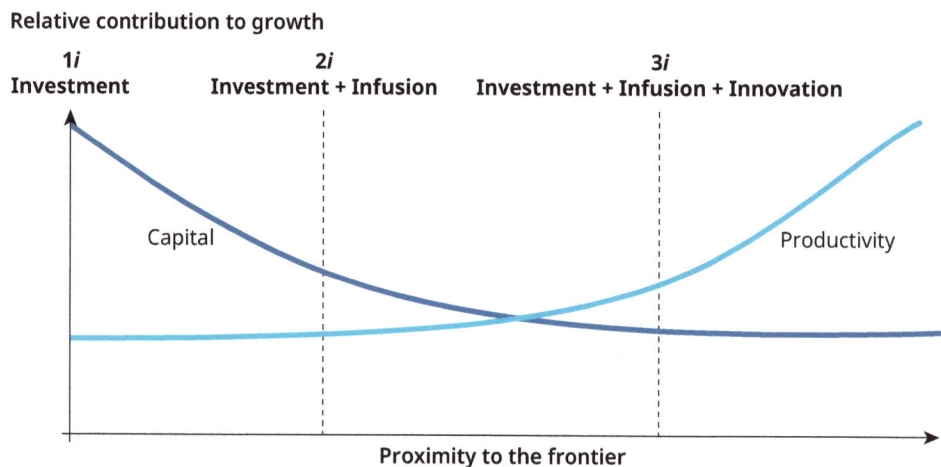

Source: World Bank 2024.

Note: The curves illustrate the relative contributions of capital and productivity to economic growth (*y*-axis) according to countries' proximity to the frontier (represented by leading economies). Countries farther out on the *x*-axis are closer to the frontier.

- *From investment and infusion to investment, infusion, and innovation.* The second transition involves the shift to the 3*i* strategy, whereby firms not only accumulate capital and infuse foreign expertise and technology but also advance innovation. This is challenging in most MICs in the region. Even enterprises in countries close to the high-income threshold are largely only production facilities that are linked through value chains to firms in the EU. They do not spend much on research and development (R&D), and they produce few innovations.

While these two transitions are essential if MICs in the region are to achieve high-income status, governments and stakeholders in the HICs in the region need to persevere in their efforts to realize the second transition to make economies more innovative and able to sustain growth within the challenging global context. The HICs in the region have benefitted tremendously from their participation in EU global value chains and the infusion of expertise and advanced technology. The HIC economies have prospered by being open to foreign trade and investment and, thanks to competitive wages and good skills, acting largely as production facilities for large European firms. Although these HICs are implementing the 3*i* strategy, their R&D spending and patenting performance are modest compared with European HICs, and their shift to an innovation-driven economy is still at an early stage. Accelerating this progress should help the ECA HICs strengthen productivity and growth despite the challenges faced by their main trading and investment partners.

Understanding Growth Through the Lens of Schumpeterian Creative Destruction

A key feature of the analysis in *World Development Report 2024* is the Schumpeterian lens on development that helps clarify the path the MICs in the region need to take to achieve high-income status (Schumpeter 1942; World Bank 2024). In the early years of the transition from a planned economy to a market economy in the 1990s, the forces of destruction dominated in the economies of the MICs in the region. Among the countries that advanced the most rapidly, the forces of preservation were muted, and the forces of creation were emerging. Fast forward three decades: the forces of preservation now have the upper hand in the MICs. The forces of creation, destruction, and preservation must become more well balanced if these countries are to become HICs and achieve sustained economic progress (refer to figure O.4):

- *Creation.* Economic progress is driven by firms or entrepreneurs that take risks and incur costs to accumulate capital, infuse new technologies, and innovate. Incumbents and new entrants—whether firms or entrepreneurs—are both central to creative destruction. But incumbents tend to adopt technology and

FIGURE O.4 **Balance creation, preservation, and destruction to reach high-income status**

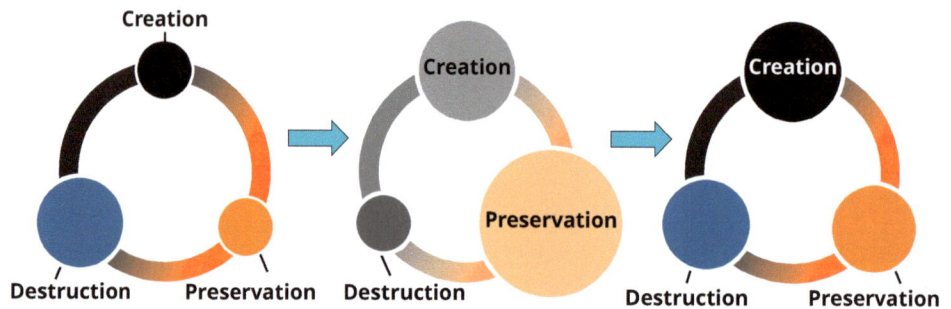

Source: Adapted from World Bank 2024.

innovate more slowly. In the ECA region, there are too many small, low-productivity firms; few large companies other than large, legacy state-owned enterprises (SOEs); and even fewer global innovators. Creation is weak, and productivity growth is mostly driven by the reallocation of resources, not by innovation. A competitive environment that levels the playing field and allows the access of new entrants to the market is crucial.

- *Preservation.* Incumbents have often successfully driven the transition from a 1*i* strategy to a 2*i* strategy and are keen to preserve their positions by limiting the market access of new entrants. The key issue is the extent to which governments facilitate or blunt the natural force of creation represented by the entry and growth of new businesses. For example, the dominant SOEs in the region benefit from some of the world's highest subsidies on fossil fuels. Such subsidies hamper the scale-up of low-carbon technologies and incentivize the inefficient use of energy.

- *Destruction.* This allows scarce resources to be reallocated to the most efficient uses and often occurs during or after an economic crisis. Although it is a necessary process, governments often limit the extent to which destruction may take place, thus restricting the scope for creation. For instance, in MICs in the region, academic capture—whereby universities prioritize political or business interests over academic excellence—is a major reason for the poor quality of university education. Such inefficient structures and policies persist rather than being reformed or destroyed, resulting in the waste and misallocation of the talent needed to achieve high-income status. Another example is the dominant role of SOEs in several countries even in sectors with an abundance of competitive firms.

The Three Fundamental Drivers of Economic Growth

The process of creative destruction involves three fundamental drivers of economic growth: enterprises, talent and social mobility, and energy. The main difference between the MICs and the HICs in the ECA region is not the quantity of the inputs used by these drivers, but the efficiency—the productivity—of the use. Measured in purchasing power parity, the average amount of physical and human capital per worker used by enterprises in the ECA MICs is about 71 percent of the amount in the United States. This compares with about 80 percent in the ECA HICs. However, GDP per capita in the ECA MICs is only 38 percent of US GDP per capita. This difference is staggering and is the main reason many countries have become trapped in middle-income status. If they are to reach and sustain high-income status, the ECA countries must tackle the inefficiencies and make the best use of resources.

Enterprises

Business dynamism based on more productive and efficient resource use is critical to achieving stronger economic growth and creating jobs. Most governments and stakeholders in the ECA MICs rely on the 2*i* strategy, that is, a combination of investment and the infusion of technology and expertise from abroad. Measured at the firm level, productivity growth in the MICs is almost wholly driven by the reallocation of resources to more productive uses and improvements in the functioning of factor and product markets. Investment in R&D is low (around 0.2 percent of GDP in the Caucasus and Central Asia, for example), and innovation is mostly absent.

Frontier innovation, the key component of the 3*i* strategy, is challenging and requires good skills, substantial management capacity, and strong incentives. These inputs are in short supply in the MICs relative to the HICs in the region and take time to develop. Because of more sluggish structural transformation in some countries, the MICs innovate even less than what might be expected based on income levels. In the ECA HICs, by contrast, firm upgrading and more effective management play a greater role. Within-firm productivity rather than reallocation thus drives expansion in these countries (refer to figure O.5). However, even these countries are behind the European HICs in R&D spending, innovation, and patenting performance.

The enduring presence of SOEs in the region dulls the impact of market competition on creative destruction. If SOEs are more prominent, the broader economy-wide impacts include reduced entrepreneurial activity, lower business entry and exit, and reduced investment. In sectors in which SOEs are present, especially in competitive sectors, there is substantial labor hoarding and more modest job creation and destruction.

FIGURE O.5 Drivers of productivity growth: between-firm reallocation and within-firm upgrading

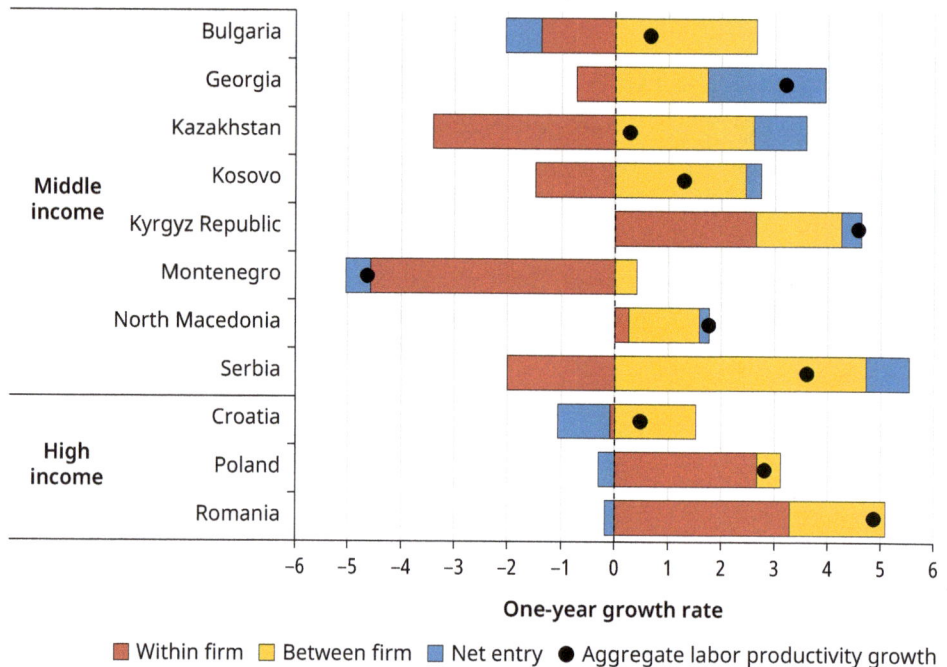

Sources: World Bank elaboration based on data of national statistical institutes; Melitz and Polanec 2015; Orbis (portal), Moody's, New York, https://www.moodys.com/web/en/us/capabilities /company-reference-data/orbis.html.

Note: The data reported are one-year arithmetic averages. A dynamic Olley-Pakes decomposition was performed at the three-industry level of NACE Rev. 2 and used a two-year rolling window (changes between t and $t-2$) (EC 2008). Firms and sectors were weighted according to the employment weight in each activity and economy during the reference period. NACE = Statistical Classification of Economic Activities in the European Community.

To strengthen the forces of creation, governments and stakeholders in the MICs need to focus more attention on young businesses with high-growth potential. The business demography of these countries is characterized by an excess of incumbent small and medium enterprises (SMEs) and a scarcity of large firms. This phenomenon might be dubbed the "missing large" challenge. Start-ups in ECA countries enter the market at half the size of their peers in the United States, suggesting that barriers to entry are low in the region, but also that business opening may be driven more by necessity than by market opportunities. ECA firms grow less than US firms over the life cycle. In the United States, the average size of firms five years or older is six times that of new firms, while, in the ECA region, the size of the former is less than four times the size of the latter. Firms in the ECA region are small at entry and tend to grow less.

Traditional policies centered on supporting SMEs in general are often misguided because they lead to an excess of SMEs and do little to promote growth in jobs and output. Start-ups and young firms, rather than SMEs in general, drive job dynamism in the ECA region and around the world. In MICs and HICs in the ECA region, start-ups and young companies generate 25 percent of gross jobs each, even though, together, they account for less than 20 percent of total employment. Large companies account for a substantial share of overall employment, but they create a small share of the overall jobs.

Large incumbent companies, including SOEs, are often the main forces preserving the status quo. Ensuring that new entrants in the market for renewable energy obtain the permits necessary to build, operate, and connect to the grid, for example, will require government efforts to overcome these forces of preservation.

Governments in the MICs can help enterprises become more dynamic by focusing on foundational or horizontal policies to improve the business environment and on policies targeting firms. Chapter 2 specifies such policies in detail across the categories of ECA countries. The horizontal policies include the following:

- Ensure market contestability by strengthening and empowering competition agencies, reducing the presence of SOEs in competitive sectors, limiting red tape, and enforcing intellectual property rights.

- Make it easier for unproductive firms to close.

- Direct support toward young, dynamic enterprises, which account for the bulk of job creation.

- Deepen capital markets to expand access to long-term finance. Facilitate venture capital and other forms of risk capital to support innovative entrepreneurs.

- Develop a skilled workforce, together with quality management staff.

These horizontal policies need to be supplemented by policies directly targeting firms, as follows:

- Enhance technology adoption; incentivize private R&D investments, especially among younger firms; and foster collaboration between businesses and academia.

- Support firms in accessing global markets by reducing trade barriers and improving logistics and border procedures.

- Enhance management quality. Create incentives for businesses to invest in upskilling the workforce and in technical training programs anchored in market and business demand.

Talent and Social Mobility

The shortage and misallocation of talent are becoming an increasingly binding growth constraint in ECA countries. This limits the ability of firms to invest; to infuse technologies, capital, and expertise from abroad; and to innovate.

Social mobility—proxied in this report by educational mobility—is the most important measure of intergenerational improvement in welfare status, that is, whether children are doing better than the previous generation or whether their talents are being wasted. Social mobility has been declining among the younger generations in the ECA region. The probability that children are more well educated than their parents has been decreasing. The correlation between a child's education and the education of the child's parents has also increased, and household circumstances are playing a larger role in determining educational attainment among children. The only bright spot is the increasing probability that children will be able to attain higher education even if their parents were not able to do so.

The gains from equal access to education are limited if the quality of education is low or if job opportunities are few. Talent will flourish only if good education systems have been established. Basic primary and secondary education must provide foundational skills, and higher education institutions must produce innovators, thereby strengthening the forces of creation. However, the quality of primary and secondary education as measured by the scores of the Program for International Student Assessment (PISA) (15-year-olds) and the Progress in International Reading Literacy Study (9-year-olds) has been declining, a trend that preceded and was then aggravated by the COVID-19 pandemic. Over the past decade, PISA math scores across the region have plummeted by the equivalent of a full year of schooling.

One of the most pressing issues in the region is the effectiveness of vocational education and training (VET). Almost 45 percent of upper-secondary students in the region and as many as 80 percent in some countries are channeled early in their school careers into VET. While VET programs are frequently touted as a viable pathway to enhance employability, they often fail to equip students with the skills to thrive in a rapidly evolving job market. This disconnect raises concerns about the negative impact of such programs on the effort to nurture talent, foster upward mobility, and reduce inequality.

The situation is gloomier at universities. The quality of higher education is below the level that might be expected given the quality of basic education in the region (refer to figure O.6). Obtaining diplomas trumps receiving knowledge or skills. Because individuals with higher educational attainment are more likely to become innovators, the poor quality of university education poses an existential risk to the region's long-term growth prospects. In the Times Higher Education world university rankings, only one university in the region is ranked among the top 100, and only nine universities are ranked among the top 500.[3] Academic capture (whereby universities prioritize political or business interests over academic excellence), inadequate funding, outdated curricula, a lack of modern infrastructure, and the proliferation of tertiary institutions are among the leading causes of the poor quality of tertiary education.

FIGURE O.6 In Europe and Central Asia, higher education quality is low relative to basic education

Quality of higher education (university quality score)

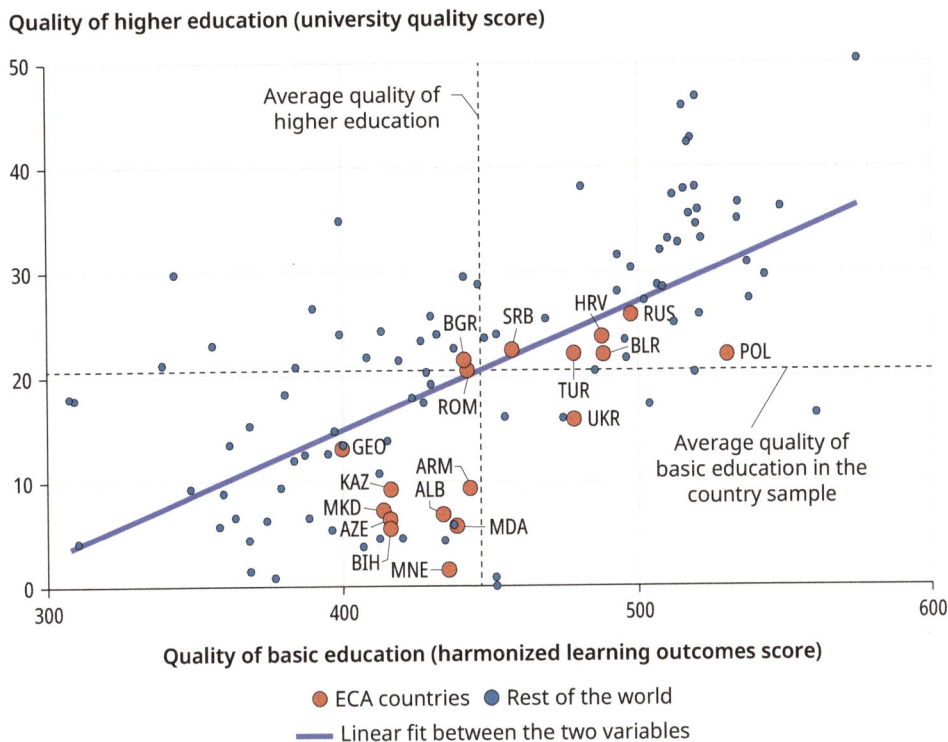

Quality of basic education (harmonized learning outcomes score)

● ECA countries ● Rest of the world
— Linear fit between the two variables

Sources: Demirgüç-Kunt and Torre 2022; HLO (Harmonized Learning Outcomes) Database, World Bank, Washington, DC, https://datacatalog.worldbank.org/search/dataset/0038001; Human Capital (Data Portal), World Bank, Washington, DC, https://humancapital.worldbank.org/en/home.

Note: The quality of basic education is proxied by the harmonized learning outcomes score by country (refer to the sources). The quality of higher education is proxied by the aggregate university quality score as calculated by Demirgüç-Kunt and Torre (2022). For country abbreviations, refer to International Organization for Standardization (ISO), https://www.iso.org /obp/ui/#search.

Talent is nurtured not only in the educational system. Societies in which talented individuals are not employed miss the opportunity to foster a productive population, especially among women, who are typically better educated than men in the ECA region, and among disadvantaged groups. Female labor force participation in the region is heterogeneous. A low participation rate may not be explained by differences in skills but by social norms. Without urgent action to boost social mobility; reverse the decline in educational quality, especially in higher education; and improve the allocation of workforce talent, the MICs in the region will not be able to reach high-income status in the next one or two generations.

The authorities are invited to consider the following policy options to address these challenges (discussed in chapter 3):

- Strengthen foundational skills to reverse the decline in the quality of secondary education.

- Thoroughly revamp VET systems, first, by raising the age of VET track selection and reinforcing the links with industry to ensure the delivery of relevant skills.

- Preserve equal access to higher education, but implement merit-based policies to promote successful graduation.

- Merge research centers with universities and strengthen university–industry links to foster innovation.

- Consolidate universities to make more effective use of resources, and improve the management of universities.

- Facilitate the broader participation of women in the labor market.

Energy

Reaching and sustaining high-income status in the ECA countries depend crucially on tackling energy inefficiencies and ensuring the transition to better energy security, lower energy intensity, and lower emissions. MICs in the region are on the verge of decoupling growth in emissions from growth in output, a feat accomplished mostly only by high-income economies. The ECA region is the most energy-intensive developing world region and maintains some of the world's highest energy subsidies. An average 1.5 times more energy is required to produce one unit of GDP in ECA countries than in East Asia and the Pacific and 2.5 times more than in the EU. Policy, market, and regulatory barriers and resistance from incumbent SOEs often hinder energy-efficiency-enhancing reforms and the rapid transition to cleaner energy sources.

The impact of lower-emission technology innovation on GDP growth and jobs is already visible in China, Europe, and the United States. It is also clear in the ECA countries in which the transition to a market economy has advanced the most, the pressure exerted by incumbents is better contained, and young and dynamic firms enjoy a level playing field. Among the ECA solar and wind frontrunners (Croatia, Poland, Romania, and Türkiye), the share of renewables in power generation has increased to 15 percent, in line with the global average, though it is below the 30 percent share of the global frontrunners, including Germany and the United Kingdom.

But lower emissions technology adoption and innovation may not occur without a push because of the general scarcity of frontier innovation activities across most of the region. Policy makers observing China, the EU, and the United States may be thinking that industrial policy offers an answer to the slow pace of technology adoption and innovation. However, expenditures of scarce public resources on such policy interventions should be carefully weighed against alternative resource policies and uses, including the critical need to raise dramatically the quality of education and improve the competitive environment.

Part of the reason the forces of creation have been inadequate in the region's energy sector is the dominance of powerful SOEs. In the ECA region, SOEs control 100 percent of transmission, more than 80 percent of fossil fuel power generators (double the global average), and more than 65 percent of electricity distributors. Besides the huge disincentives of fossil fuel subsidies on the transition to lower emissions and lower energy intensity, a crucial obstacle is the low profitability across energy SOEs in the region. Around 30 percent of these SOEs are unprofitable, double the share in other MICs.

ECA market participants believe that most electricity transmission companies do not have the capacity to facilitate any additional connections by independent renewable power producers. More than four in five private companies in the ECA region deem grid access a high or remarkably elevated risk. They expect most ECA countries to encounter issues in integrating the planned solar and wind volumes without substantial investment in transmission and distribution networks. Without adequate battery storage, a lot of the energy produced by the new entrants would be wasted, while average electricity prices remain high.

To facilitate creation, governments need to help cushion the impact of the forces of destruction. The transition to lower carbon emissions generates losses among consumers, workers, and businesses and thus encounters resistance. If energy is costlier, vulnerable households may ration energy consumption, energy-intensive firms may lose competitiveness, and pressures for government subsidies may grow. Affected groups will push back against well-intentioned reform.

Addressing these political economy concerns requires careful policy sequencing so that reforms impose no unbearable burdens on any group. Yet, focusing only on low-hanging fruit that is unlikely to create a backlash may not lead to the emergence of new firms and the destruction of inefficient practices and enterprises. Reductions in fossil fuel subsidies among vulnerable groups may be balanced by income support, while saving money because most fossil fuel subsidies apply to all population groups, including the most affluent. Because destruction also involves job losses, such as in coal mining, cushioning policies must reach beyond income transfers and support new opportunities for affected workers.

While the transition to lower energy intensity and lower emissions may promote the transition to high-income status, the link is not automatic and will require the following deliberate, well-sequenced steps (discussed in chapter 4):

- Enable prices to reflect the true economic and social cost, phase out fossil fuel subsidies, and introduce a carbon tax or an emission trading system. Fossil fuel subsidies represent the greatest market disincentives for reducing energy intensity and decarbonization. Explicit carbon pricing that reflects the negative externalities of emissions and pollution encourages efforts to reduce carbon emissions.

- Facilitate the tighter integration of enterprises into global markets by supporting structural transformation among enterprises that can accelerate the adoption of energy-efficient, lower-emission, and more highly productive technologies and strengthen the ability of firms to overcome the limits to potential growth associated with the small size of many economies in the region.

- Discipline incumbent energy SOEs to ensure that new competitors can enter the market and connect to the grid without hindrance.

- Introduce more stringent standards and regulatory policies for the decarbonization of housing, transport, and other economic sectors in which emissions are difficult to abate.

- Design and implement policies to bolster domestic and foreign investment in renewable energy generation, while ensuring economic merit–order dispatch (that is, the sources of electricity with the lowest marginal cost are dispatched first).

- Sustain macroeconomic stability, and ensure investor certainty.

Notes

1. The 10 countries that have attained high-income status since 1990 are Croatia, the Czech Republic, Estonia, Hungary, Latvia, Lithuania, Poland, Romania, the Slovak Republic, and Slovenia. The World Bank reclassified Bulgaria and the Russian Federation as having reached the high-income threshold in July 2024, but the 2024 data behind most of the statistics used in this report are not consistently available. As a result, in this report, these two countries are still considered middle-income countries.

2. In the ECA region, the footprint of the state is still large. Clearly, this is associated with the long history of central planning in many of the countries in the region (refer to World Bank 2023).

3. See THE (Times Higher Education) World University Rankings (dashboard), Times Higher Education, London, https://www.timeshighereducation.com/world-university-rankings.

References

Demirgüç-Kunt, Asli, and Iván Torre. 2022. "Measuring Human Capital in Middle Income Countries." *Journal of Comparative Economics* 50 (4): 1036–67.

EC (European Commission). 2008. *NACE Rev. 2: Statistical Classification of Economic Activities in the European Community*. Eurostat Methodologies and Working Papers Series. Luxembourg: Office for Official Publications of the European Communities.

Melitz, Marc J., and Sašo Polanec. 2015. "Dynamic Olley-Pakes Productivity Decomposition with Entry and Exit." *RAND Journal of Economics* 46 (2): 362–75.

Schumpeter, Joseph Alois. 1942. *Capitalism, Socialism, and Democracy*. New York: Harper and Brothers.

World Bank. 2023. *The Business of the State*. Washington, DC: World Bank.

World Bank. 2024. *World Development Report 2024: The Middle-Income Trap*. Washington, DC: World Bank.

Transitioning to High Income—or Not

Country Case in Brief: Poland

Poland is one of the world's most impressive successes in sustaining a high rate of economic growth over an extended period. Its per capita gross national income (GNI) is about $20,000, roughly 10 times more than in 1992. Rapid growth helped the country reach high income in 2009, only 20 years after the start of the transition from a planned to a market economy. This represented an income shift from 30 percent of the European Union (EU) average in 1992 to 80 percent in 2022. Throughout the period of rapid growth, income inequality did not widen in Poland. The country thus offers important lessons for other countries seeking a similar growth acceleration.

How did Poland's economy become one of the most rapidly growing in the world? After the big bang reforms of the transition from central planning, the government first got the edifice right, that is, the rule of law, property rights, democratic accountability, and the functioning of basic market institutions. It then used the EU accession process, including membership in 2004, to reinforce the effectiveness of the new institutional structures.

A widely shared vision of a socially responsible market economy helped provide policy consistency and continuity over several decades. Indeed, the medium-term direction of reform was sustained, even as 17 different governments came and went as part of Poland's multiparty democracy.

Similar to other rapidly growing developing economies, Poland became connected to regional and global markets, while opening up to foreign trade and foreign

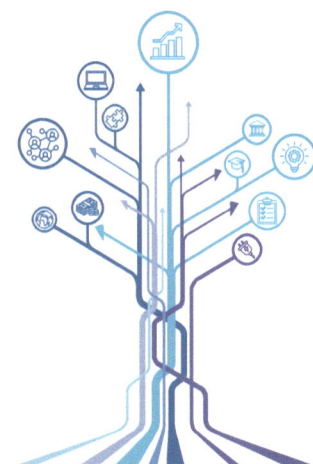

direct investment. EU accession was essential in this process. Large foreign investment flowed in from other EU member states, and trade with the European market boomed. Domestic market competition promoted appropriate pricing and facilitated effective resource allocation across sectors and firms, producing efficiency gains. Labor productivity rose quickly, and education reforms succeeded in raising quality standards equally quickly. Sound macroeconomic and financial policies provided a solid basis for private investment. Infrastructure investments, supported by generous EU structural funds, complemented these positive steps (Piatkowski 2018; World Bank 2017).

But the agenda is incomplete. Poland aspires not only to converge with the average EU income, but to surpass it. This will not be easy. It has to navigate a formidable energy transition amid overlapping shocks. As it moves closer to the development frontier through a shift to innovation-driven growth, deeper reforms will be needed to boost productivity, strengthen institutions, and improve skills. While past performance is no guarantee of future success, Poland's positive experience of the last three decades leaves the country well placed to continue successfully on its development journey toward high-income status.

Introduction

Economic development in Europe and Central Asia (ECA) has been dominated by the transition from a planned to a market economy that began in the early 1990s. The advance of broad and deep structural reforms, the emergence of private initiative as the main driver of growth, and the much-reduced role of the state have been key components on this development path. In less than three decades, 10 ECA countries have joined the EU. The successful transition of these countries to EU market integration with robust institutions and production structures has elevated them to high-income status. For another 20 countries in the region, however, the transition to high-income status is ongoing.

The pace of economic expansion in the ECA region peaked during the 2000s and has slowed substantially since the 2007–09 global financial crisis. Annual average economic growth weakened from 5.1 percent during 2000–09 to 3.1 percent during 2010–19 and to 2.7 percent during 2020–23 as the region was battered by the aftermath of the global financial crisis, the European debt crisis, the commodity price collapse of 2015, COVID-19, and the impact of the Russian invasion of Ukraine. While the pace of economic expansion also slowed in other developing regions and among advanced economies, economic growth in the ECA region, which had lower growth rates initially, lagged comparators, such as East Asia and the Pacific, which expanded by 4.1 percent a year, and the middle-income countries (MICs), which grew by an average of 3.2 percent a year in 2020–23.

Weaker growth in the ECA region resulted in a slowdown in income convergence with advanced economies and concerns that many countries in the region may be experiencing a middle-income trap. Real gross domestic product (GDP) per capita (in purchasing power parity prices) in the region rose from 22 percent of the US level in 1999 to more than 33 percent in 2009. Following the rapid convergence in 2000–09, the speed of convergence slowed by a factor of almost four in 2010–22. As a result, two decades after the global financial crisis, real GDP per capita in the ECA region reached only 38 percent of the US level in 2022. Although this slowdown mirrors global trends and the ratio to the US level was, on average, higher in the region than elsewhere, the slowdown in the region was much steeper. Indeed, from 2010 to 2022, real GDP per capita in the region grew only about 1 percentage point more quickly than the average growth rate of real GDP per capita in the United States.

Since the term "middle-income trap" was first coined 20 years ago, there has been concern because the shift from the policies needed to enable growth in a low-income country to the policies needed to enable strong growth in an MIC may not be easy (Gill and Kharas 2007). The transition to high-income status in the region will require foundational reform efforts to sustain the structural transformation in MICs (although at diminishing returns), while also pivoting to fresh transformative reform efforts to facilitate more complex economic structures and institutions and the creative destruction needed to propel the transition from a middle-income to high-income country (HIC).

World Development Report 2024 labels this shift as the 3*i* strategy, implying that MICs need to navigate two important and sequential development transitions to succeed at reaching the high-income threshold (World Bank 2024). The first transition is a shift from an investment-based growth strategy (investment = 1*i*) to a strategy that focuses on both investment and infusion (2*i*) and that requires welcoming ideas, practices, expertise, and technologies from abroad and diffusing them domestically. The transition from middle-income status to high-income status then requires a second transition that involves a shift toward greater emphasis on innovation (3*i*) by not only borrowing ideas from abroad, but also by expanding the technology frontier at home.

- *Investment, the first i.* Foundational reforms are necessary to maximize the fundamental drivers of economic growth, including investment in and maximizing the returns associated with scarce physical and human capital.[1] Foundational investments, policies, and institutions facilitate sustainable increases in public and private investment. They also unlock the full potential of human capital in quantity (to ensure full labor force participation) and in quality (education and skills formation). Equally important, they support the efficient allocation and productive use of scarce physical and human capital.

- *Infusion, the second i.* The structural reforms required to enable the transition from 1*i* to 2*i* involve the more complex institutional arrangements needed to sustain Schumpeterian creative destruction in a new and more challenging external environment (Schumpeter 1942). Infusion in its simplest form means that ECA countries must focus not only on sustaining strong investment, but also on facilitating crossborder trade and helping attract new private investment, particularly from abroad, to enable the entry and diffusion of ideas, practices, managerial expertise, and technologies. Across the countries that were or are part of the ECA region and have converged to high income, the bulk of the infusion has been driven by intense links between multinational companies and domestic firms and been greatly facilitated by accession to the EU.

- *Innovation, the third i.* Transformative reforms to enable the transition from 2*i* to 3*i* need to focus on managing the incumbency advantage associated with the behavior of existing elites and firms in the market, while supporting innovative new entrants with high-growth potential. Innovation can also arise from incumbents, and, indeed, in many advanced economies, incumbents provide a substantial share of innovation. Countries seeking to sustain growth beyond the HIC threshold need policies and institutions that allow for growth at the frontier, reducing the risk premium that firms face in investing in innovation.

The experience gained during past high-income transitions in the region points to the importance of higher ambitions and deeper commitments to reform among the current ECA middle-income economies. Based on growth trends, only a handful of ECA MICs can be expected to pass the HIC threshold in the next few years.

The 3*i* strategy is not only about helping countries achieve high-income status, it is helping them sustain this status. The high-income countries face a more demanding environment for growth in output, productivity, and jobs because their enterprises need to innovate regularly to remain relevant. While continuing to infuse foreign technologies, experience, and capital, the ECA HICs need to raise the level of their ambitions in improving the business environment for innovation, boosting the quality of education, especially higher education and postuniversity education, and effecting a dramatic change to more efficiently use energy.

Historical Income Convergence: The Region Has Experienced Both Success and Stagnation

The historical performance of the ECA countries in the high-income transition includes examples of both success and stagnation (refer to box 1.1). Of 26 countries that have transitioned from middle to high income since 1990, 13 are in Europe: 10 (Croatia, Czech Republic, Estonia, Hungary, Latvia, Lithuania, Poland, Romania, Slovak Republic, and Slovenia) emerged from centrally planned economies, while 3 (Greece, Malta, and Portugal) did not.[2] In both cases, they represent a laboratory of reform experience, potentially offering lessons for other countries in the region

BOX 1.1 **Growing to High Income Is Not Easy**

After three decades of transition from a planned to a market economy, the ECA region is solidly middle income, though the region is characterized by ambitions to escape the middle-income trap and converge to high income. Of current World Bank member economies in the region, 20 are middle-income countries (MICs) and three are high-income economies. An additional 7 countries—part of ECA in the 1990s and early 2000s—have become high-income economies. The 20 ECA MICs account for 75 percent of regional economic activity, 85 percent of the region's population, nearly 90 percent of the people living in poverty, and nearly 90 percent of carbon dioxide emissions.

Comparisons with other regions (East Asia and Latin America) and with the performance of countries that successfully transitioned from MIC to high-income country (HIC) status outside the ECA region are presented in spotlights 1.1 and 1.2.

Convergence to high-income status is not easy. It requires continuous, dramatic changes in policies and institutions. Globally, 27 countries have transitioned from middle- to high-income status since 1990. Of these, 13 are European Union (EU) member states, including 10 countries that were World Bank member economies in the 1990s. The EU convergence machine—through institutional change, trade, investment, and the flow of capital and managerial expertise from richer to poorer countries—has helped all EU members overcome the middle-income trap. The remaining countries include economies with substantial natural resource endowments, economies with a substantial reliance on tourism, and the economies of the Republic of Korea and Uruguay. Countries that do not have large natural resource endowments or that have not implemented significant structural reforms have exhibited a slower pace of convergence to high-income status.

The income per capita in the median ECA MIC is about a third of the income per capita in the United States. The corresponding income ratio of the average MIC worldwide is a fifth. The odds that these latter countries will transition to high-income status have deteriorated because of slower global growth and weaker growth potential, fragmented global value chains, increased geopolitical tensions, and rising populism. Even without these headwinds, MICs face long odds of becoming HICs and escaping the middle-income trap unless their institutions, policies, business environments, education systems, and levels of social mobility become more sophisticated. The need to achieve growth while ensuring climate change mitigation has added challenges to policy making in the MICs today that were much less daunting among the MICs that achieved high-income status in the more distant past.

(refer to figure 1.1). But the pace of convergence toward high income across the region appears to have slowed. Fewer countries have made the transition to HIC status in recent years. And a large gap remains between European countries that transitioned to HIC status in the last 30 years (here labeled "Convergers") and the legacy group of Europe high-income economies (refer to figure 1.2).[3] All 13 of the successful Convergers are members of the EU, raising questions about the growth path among countries that have not acceded to the EU because the process has stalled or has not become an option.

FIGURE 1.1 In Europe, 13 countries have transitioned from middle- to high-income status since 1990

Percent

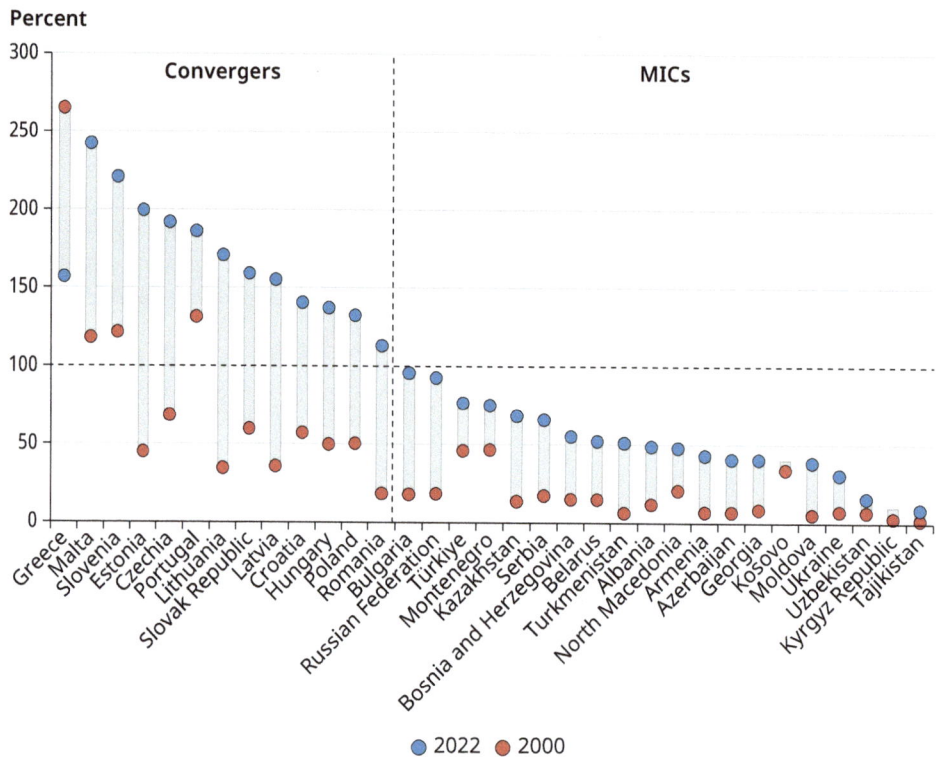

● 2022   ● 2000

Source: WDI (World Development Indicators) (dashboard), World Bank, Washington, DC, https://datatopics.worldbank.org/world-development-indicators/.

Note: Greece (2006, 2021), Kosovo (2010, 2021), Montenegro (2006, 2021), Turkmenistan (2000, 2019). Country groups do not overlap.

The ECA countries might be more accurately described as converging slowly or crawling toward high-income status, rather than converging quickly or sprinting relative to countries in the region that have previously transitioned to high income. Current growth trends—extrapolating average per capita GNI growth rates for the past 10 and 15 years—suggest that it is unlikely any of the 20 ECA MICs can be expected to pass the HIC threshold of $14,005 in the next few years (refer to table 1.1). First, growth rates have almost universally slowed across the ECA MICs. The average growth rate over the past 15 years is higher than the average growth rate over the past 10 years in every country except Kosovo. Growth in 2024–26 is projected at 2.7 percent a year compared with 4.1 percent in the 2000s. Second, even if the more optimistic 15-year average GNI per capita growth rate is extrapolated, only Montenegro and Serbia may be expected to pass the HIC threshold in the next decade. If the 10-year average GNI per capita growth rate is extrapolated, no countries would pass it in the next decade. Under the same 10-year scenario, it would take more than a hundred years for Azerbaijan, Tajikistan, and Uzbekistan to pass the threshold. Passing the threshold in these countries would take several decades under the 15-year scenario.[4]

Determinants of Growth and Convergence

Strong and durable growth in productivity and output are the foundation for sustainable social and economic development (Acemoglu 2009; Barro and Sala-i-Martin 2004). While economic growth alone may not be sufficient to achieve prosperity, create jobs, and reduce poverty, it is certainly a necessary condition. The Solow-Swan model of the 1950s was a cornerstone of the academic literature on economic growth and convergence, proposing that the long-run growth rate of economies is determined by changes in labor, capital, and technology (Solow 1956;

FIGURE 1.2 There is still a wide income gap between the successful Convergers and their high-income peers

Current US dollars, thousands

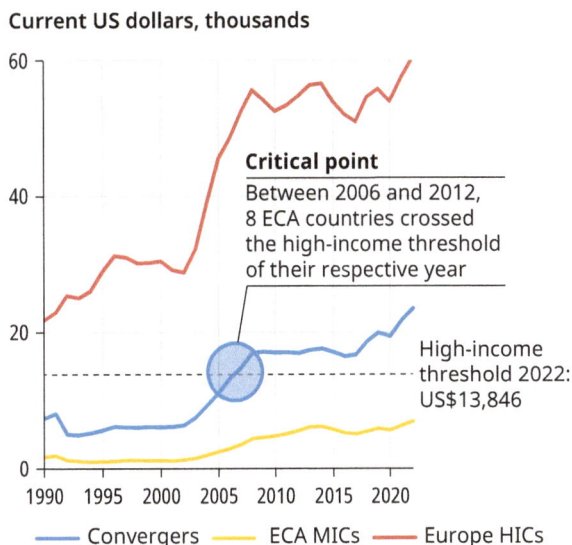

Critical point
Between 2006 and 2012, 8 ECA countries crossed the high-income threshold of their respective year

High-income threshold 2022: US$13,846

— Convergers   — ECA MICs   — Europe HICs

Source: WDI (World Development Indicators) (dashboard), World Bank, Washington, DC, https://datatopics.worldbank .org/world-development-indicators/.

TABLE 1.1 Passing the HIC threshold will be challenging

	GNI per capita[a]			Compound annual growth rates[b]		Years to threshold	
Country	2007	2012	2022	10-year	15-year	Based on 10-year average	Based on 15-year average
Albania	3,460	4,360	6,770	4.5%	4.6%	17	26
Armenia	2,690	3,840	5,960	4.5%	5.4%	19	24
Azerbaijan	2,730	4,820[c]	5,630	1.6%	4.9%	>100	22
Belarus	4,310	6,630	7,240	0.9%	3.5%	75	22
Bosnia and Herzegovina	3,680	4,900	7,660	4.6%	5.0%	14	21
Georgia	2,380	4,150	5,620	3.1%	5.9%	30	21
Kazakhstan	4,980	8,280[d]	9,470	1.4%	4.4%	29	12
Kosovo	3,150[e]	3,390	5,590	5.1%	3.9%	18	37
Kyrgyz Republic	610	1,040	1,410	3.1%	5.7%	75	47
Moldova	1,440	3,140	5,340	5.5%	9.1%	18	17

Continued

TABLE 1.1 Passing the HIC threshold will be challenging *(Continued)*

Country	GNI per capita[a]			Compound annual growth rates[b]		Years to threshold	
	2007	2012	2022	10-year	15-year	Based on 10-year average	Based on 15-year average
Montenegro	5,120	7,000	10,400	4.0%	4.8%	8	15
North Macedonia	3,620	4,770	6,640	3.4%	4.1%	23	27
Serbia	4,830	6,080	9,140	4.2%	4.3%	10	20
Tajikistan	570	1,140	1,210	0.6%	5.1%	>100	50
Türkiye	8,840	9,520[c]	10,590	1.1%	1.2%	26	32
Turkmenistan	2,250	5,370	6,970[f]	2.6%	7.8%	27	13
Ukraine	2,590	3,650	4,270	1.6%	3.4%	76	40
Uzbekistan	770	2,160	2,190	0.1%	7.2%	>100	27

Source: World Bank, World Development Indicators.

a. Atlas method (current US$).

b. Calculated between 2022 and 2012 or 2007 for 10-year and 15-year rates, respectively, unless otherwise noted.

c. 2009 values for Azerbaijan and Türkiye are used instead of 2012 because the respective 2012 values are lower than the latest values, resulting in a negative growth rate.

d. 2011 values are used for Kazakhstan because the respective 2012 values are lower than the latest value, resulting in a negative growth rate.

e. The 2010 value is used for Kosovo in 2007.

f. Due to lack of data, the 2019 value is used for Turkmenistan in 2022.

Swan 1956). In addition to the quantity of inputs, the method of allocation and the efficiency of the allocation also determine growth, especially over the longer term. The ability of an economy—often through a process of creative destruction—to foster firm-level innovation, the adoption of modern technologies, and firm upgrading, and to shift to the more efficient allocation of resources across firms and sectors is key. In the early days of modern efforts to analyze economic growth, economists considered technological progress and innovation as developments external to their models. Over time, countries with lower initial levels of capital also tend to experience higher rates of growth, leading to convergence with countries that initially had higher levels of capital.

Decades later, economists introduced technological progress and innovation into their models. This was the initial stage of the literature on endogenous economic growth. Economists recognized—as practitioners had known for a while—that new technologies emerge because of costly research and development efforts by individuals and companies (Grossman and Helpman 1991; Romer 1987, 1990).

And entrepreneurs undertake such efforts to be the first in an industry or a country to gain at least temporary monopoly power. These efforts and market motivations were missing from both the early economic growth models and the endogenous growth models (Akcigit and Van Reenen 2023).

Similarly, investments in human capital play a crucial role in driving economic growth; the positive relationship between educational attainment and economic growth is especially strong (Hanushek and Woessmann 2008). The quantity and quality of investment both matter. Efficiency improvements in public investment have a sizable effect on growth in low-income countries (Devadas and Pennings 2018; Loayza and Pennings 2022). Countries with strong political and economic institutions, efficient legal systems, low corruption, and political stability tend to attract more investment. They also foster entrepreneurship and create environments conducive to risk-taking, innovation, and long-term growth (Acemoglu, Johnson, and Robinson 2001, 2004; Rodrik, Subramanian, and Treddi 2004).

The next stage of evolution in the understanding of economic development involved the formalization of what is now known as Schumpeterian creative destruction, a process that is central to growth in both developed and developing economies (Schumpeter 1942). Earlier work on Schumpeterian creative destruction tended to focus on the importance of the availability of the right institutions, such as patent protection and competition policy (Aghion and Howitt 1992). Researchers tended to view the challenge of late development as primarily associated with catching up or growth through imitation and the adoption of technologies already in use elsewhere (Acemoglu 2009). Only subsequently would a shift to an innovation-based growth model become necessary. However, more recent work has highlighted the risks associated with such an approach. Countries that fail to make the leap to an innovation-based growth model earlier have tended to stop converging (Akcigit and Van Reenen 2023). Thus, policies and institutions need to evolve and incrementally adapt as countries climb the development ladder, and creative destruction processes need to be fostered along the way.

Decomposing the drivers of economic growth across ECA countries provides useful insights on the underlying determinants of growth and convergence. In broad terms, a decomposition of growth drivers shows key differences between the MICs in the ECA region and those countries that have transitioned to HIC status since 1990 (Convergers) as well as the Europe high-income economies that transitioned before 1990. While the pattern is unclear with respect to investment rates, Europe HICs show consistently higher rates of labor force participation, including among women (refer to figures 1.3 and 1.4). However, while there is also a substantial gap between MICs and Europe HICs in total factor productivity, a key measure of the efficiency with which capital and labor are utilized, the gap is being closed because of more rapid total factor productivity growth among MICs (refer to figure 1.5). Emissions intensity per capita has been declining among Europe HICs

FIGURE 1.3 Investment rates in ECA show no clear pattern across the country groupings

Percent of GDP

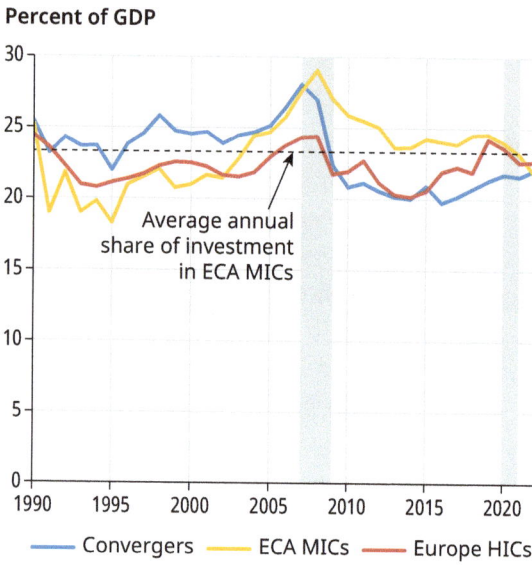

FIGURE 1.4 Labor force participation rates are higher among Convergers and Europe HICs

Percent of population

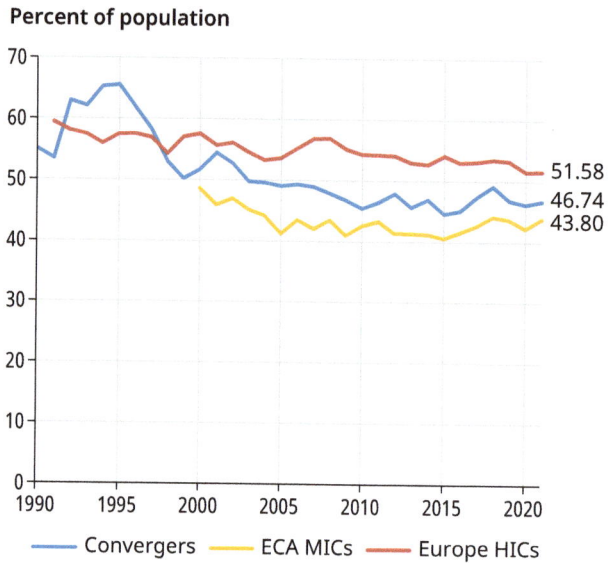

Source: WDI (World Development Indicators) (dashboard), World Bank, Washington, DC, https://datatopics.worldbank.org /world-development-indicators/.

Note: Country groups do not overlap. Figure 1.3: shaded areas indicate global recessions (2007–09 and 2020). The data are annual averages of growth over the entire reference period.

as countries look toward the green transition, but the pathway is more stable among MICs (refer to figure 1.6). Benefiting from external demand and market integration, Convergers and Europe HICs show much higher rates of trade openness relative to MICs, and their performance is better on measures of government effectiveness (refer to figures 1.7 and 1.8).

Differences in geography and natural resource endowments across the ECA region have implications for growth and convergence pathways. In broad terms, the countries in the region may be grouped into western and eastern segments based on physical location, proximity to large and developed markets, endowments, and growth characteristics. Developing economies in western ECA, including countries in Central Europe, Eastern Europe, and the Western Balkans, have fewer natural resources, but are more tightly integrated into advanced euro-centric manufacturing and services value chains. The ambition or aspiration to join the EU acts as a major incentive for reform and integration among countries in the EU periphery. In contrast, developing economies in the eastern ECA—Central Asia and the South Caucasus—are generally richer in natural resources, but less well integrated into global value chains and do not have such a strong regional integration pathway as that offered by the EU. Economic geography and natural resource endowments result in differing growth outcomes and trajectories in the ECA's west and east.

FIGURE 1.5 ECA MICs are closing the TFP gap with Europe HICs and Convergers

Year 2000 = 100, group averages

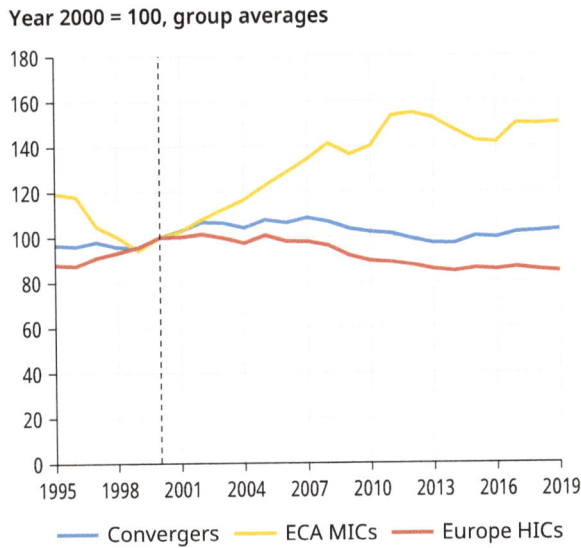

Convergers — ECA MICs — Europe HICs

FIGURE 1.6 Europe HICs and Convergers are reducing emissions intensity at a more rapid pace

Year 2000 = 100, group averages

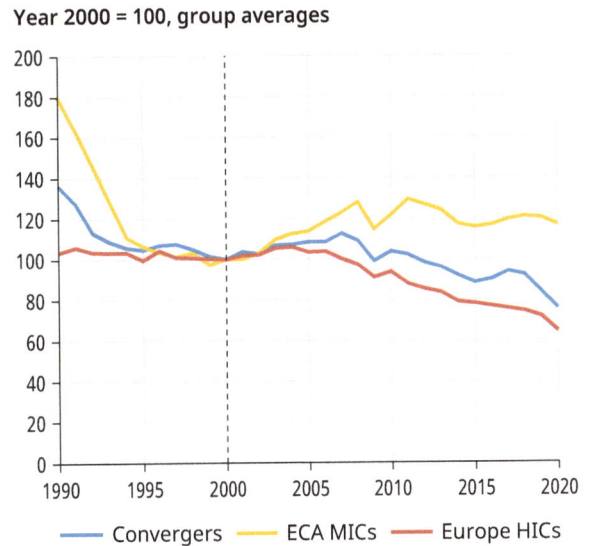

Convergers — ECA MICs — Europe HICs

Source: PWT (Penn World Table) (database version 10.1), Groningen Growth and Development Centre, Faculty of Economics and Business, University of Groningen, Groningen, the Netherlands, https://www.rug.nl/ggdc/productivity/pwt/.

Note: Country groups do not overlap. Rebasing is based on year 2000 values. TFP = total factor productivity.

FIGURE 1.7 Convergers and Europe HICs trade more intensely compared with ECA MICs

Percent of GDP

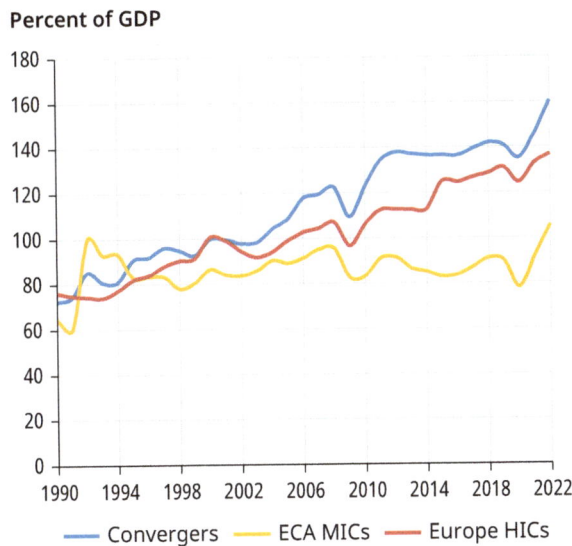

Convergers — ECA MICs — Europe HICs

FIGURE 1.8 Convergers and Europe HICs perform better on measures of governance and institutional quality

Range: −2.5 (bad) to 2.5 (good)

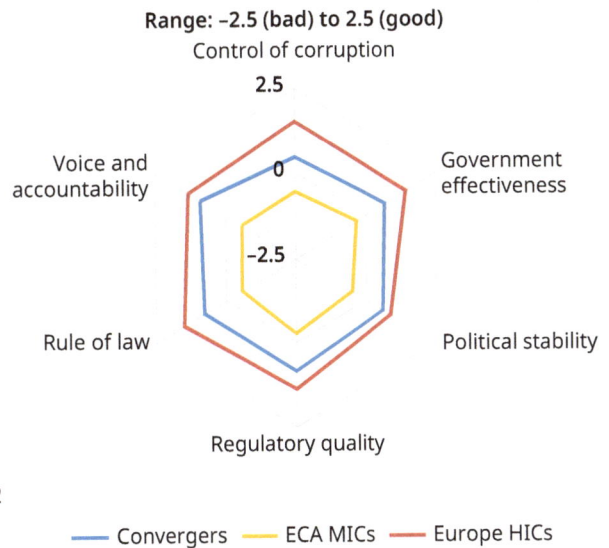

Convergers — ECA MICs — Europe HICs

Source: WGI (Worldwide Governance Indicators) (dashboard), World Bank, Washington, DC, http://info.worldbank.org/governance/wgi/#home.

Note: Country groups do not overlap.

ECA's west, centered around the EU and candidate countries, has embraced a common approach to economic and social progress (Gill and Raiser 2012). This consists of policies and institutions that govern trade and finance, enterprise and innovation, and labor and government. The integration of trade and financial flows in and around the EU single market has spurred an unprecedented convergence in living standards and is arguably the most successful element of the EU convergence machine. European private enterprises are more socially and environmentally responsible than companies in most other parts of the world. Some European enterprises are technological leaders, benefiting from a world-class ecosystem of public and private research, development, innovation, and tertiary education. Others, especially in southern Europe, are smaller, less productive, less innovative, and held back by cumbersome regulation. Labor is accorded relatively strong protection against employer abuse and enjoys income security after job loss and in old age. European governments are the most decentralized and the most representative of local interests, and Europe has developed effective institutions for regional coordination. For countries in ECA's west, it is easier to exploit markets to undertake infusion (trade and foreign direct investment) and to innovate.

ECA's east has developed by relying on its relatively more abundant endowment of natural resources. Greater integration in the world economy thanks to the surge in commodity prices since the 1990s has led to increasingly concentrated exports and other economic activity, and it has also generated enhanced development outcomes (Gill et al. 2014). Governments in the region need to worry less about the composition of exports and the profile of production and more about national asset portfolios, that is, the blend of natural resources, built capital, and economic institutions. The regional portfolio is heavy on tangible assets, such as natural resources and built capital. It is light in intangibles, such as institutions to manage volatile resource earnings, provide public services, and regulate enterprise. These should be the focus of policy going forward. Among countries in the east, infusion requires taking a step beyond raw material exports and building on comparative advantage. It also needs purposeful efforts to make economies more complex.

Lessons from Europe: The ECA Convergers Offer Insights

The 13 Convergers that have reached HIC status over the last 30 years offer key lessons for the ECA MICs. Among the Convergers, four in Western Europe transitioned to high income in the 1990s, while the remaining nine, in Eastern Europe, transitioned after 2000 (refer to table 1.2). The most rapid period of convergence was in the 2000s when eight European economies became high income (refer to figure 1.9).

All 13 Convergers are members of the EU, and their convergence to high-income status was strongly associated with their accession to and membership in the EU. Negotiations to join the EU and subsequent EU membership provide a mix of external drivers of institutional reform to meet the accession criteria, as well as significant capital flows in public resource transfers and private capital inflows associated with

TABLE 1.2 ECA Convergers offer lessons for ECA MICs that look to their own HIC transition

No.	Country	Year when they became high income
1	Croatia	2008
2	Czech Republic	2006
3	Estonia	2006
4	Greece	1996
5	Hungary	2007
6	Latvia	2009
7	Lithuania	2012
8	Malta	1998
9	Poland	2009
10	Portugal	1994
11	Romania	2019
12	Slovak Republic	2007
13	Slovenia	1997

Source: WDI (World Development Indicators) (dashboard), World Bank, Washington, DC, https://datatopics.worldbank.org/world-development-indicators/.

Note: The ECA MIC group excludes countries that have already converged to high-income status, including Bulgaria and the Russian Federation, both of which passed the high-income threshold in July 2024.

anticipated or actual access to the single market. Access to EU structural funds after joining also played a role in supporting high rates of public investment in economic infrastructure. This suggests that the EU remains a convergence machine. Nonetheless, after passing the HIC threshold, some Convergers continued to grow rapidly, while others exhibited a marked growth deceleration (refer to box 1.2).

It is unclear whether the EU convergence machine will continue to work for the next generation of prospective EU members. The pace of accession has slowed significantly among EU candidate countries in the Western Balkans over the last two decades. It is not certain that EU members are willing to accommodate further enlargement, though geopolitical tensions have catalyzed a possible acceleration in at least some countries. The EU's New Growth Plan for the Western Balkans also provides resources and new opportunities for early access to selected aspects of the EU single market. After decades of negotiation, Türkiye became an EU candidate in 1999, but has achieved only limited progress toward accession since then. Among the ECA MICs that are more distant from the EU, there is an open question about what determines international integration with China, Europe, the Russian Federation, or global markets more generally. There is also a question whether the same drivers of institutional reform can sustain growth after the EU accession process is complete. Portugal offers an example of a country experiencing a significant growth slowdown following accession.

FIGURE 1.9 **The most rapid convergence was in the late 2000s, when 8 MICs passed the HIC threshold**

Current US dollars, thousands

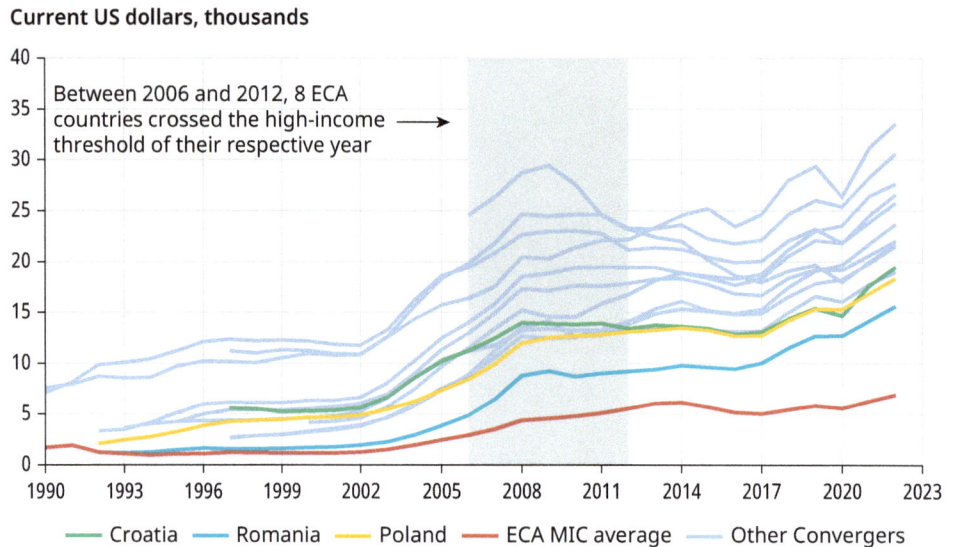

Between 2006 and 2012, 8 ECA countries crossed the high-income threshold of their respective year →

Legend: Croatia — Romania — Poland — ECA MIC average — Other Convergers

Source: WDI (World Development Indicators) (dashboard), World Bank, Washington, DC, https://datatopics.worldbank.org/world-development-indicators/.

BOX 1.2 **Income Convergence with Advanced Economies**

For ECA middle-income countries (MICs) to converge with the high-income country (HIC) threshold, they must reach a gross national income per capita of $14,005 (2024 data). But development does not stop once a country is reclassified from middle-income to high-income status based solely on the threshold. While the HIC threshold has increased incrementally at the pace of the gross domestic product deflators in Special Drawing Rights, it is essentially a static threshold. However, economic convergence is defined in the literature in dynamic terms, usually with respect to a country's per capita income as a share of the income in advanced economies, such as the European Union or the United States.

By this metric, progress among the ECA MICs has been limited. Between 1990 and 2021, most ECA countries remained at a similar per capita income relative to the United States (refer to figure B1.2.1).

Continued

BOX 1.2 Income Convergence with Advanced Economies *(Continued)*

FIGURE B1.2.1 Few ECA MICs have achieved relative convergence with the US

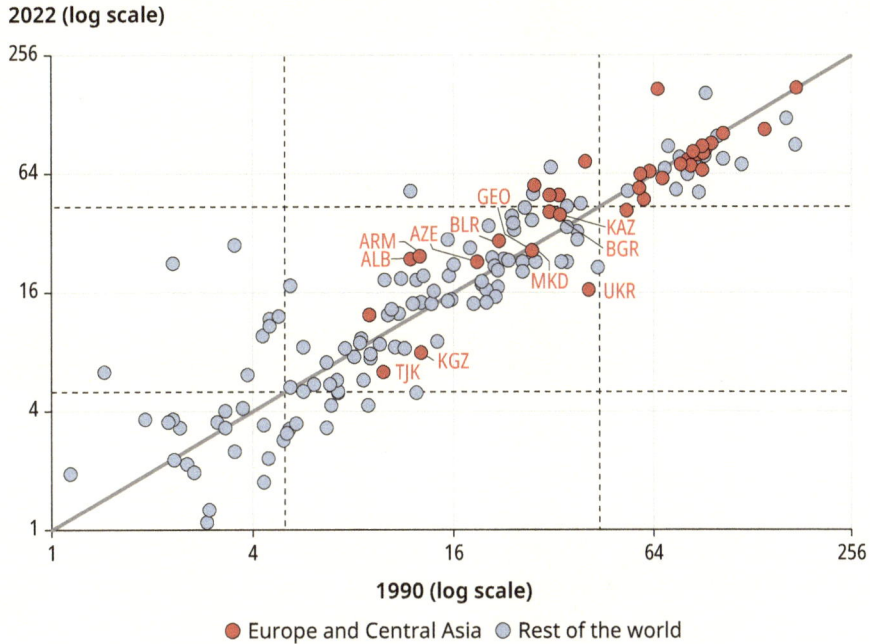

2022 (log scale)

1990 (log scale)

● Europe and Central Asia ○ Rest of the world

Source: WDI (World Development Indicators) (dashboard), World Bank, Washington, DC, https://datatopics.worldbank.org/world-development-indicators/.

Note: Dashed lines indicate the 5 percent and 44 percent thresholds relative to US per capita GDP: low-income countries < 5 percent of US per capita GDP; MICs = 5 percent to 44 percent; HICs > 44 percent.

Lessons from Europe: Assessing Convergence Through a Schumpeterian Lens

A key feature of *World Development Report 2024* on the middle-income trap is the adoption of a Schumpeterian lens on development and an emphasis on the extent to which institutions encourage (or discourage) creative destruction (World Bank 2024). Modern Schumpeterian growth theory has generated useful insights on the role of creative destruction in driving economic growth (Aghion, Akcigit, and Howitt 2013). A principal stylized fact of this theory is that technological progress must be maintained through innovation. But innovation does not take place in a vacuum. Individuals and firms incur costs and take risks to innovate.

FIGURE 1.10 **MICs have to balance creation, preservation, and destruction**

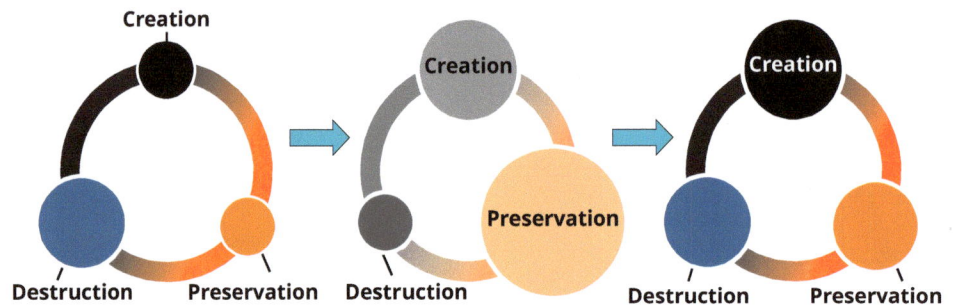

Source: Adapted from World Bank 2024.

To understand fully the underlying drivers of economic development, it is therefore necessary to connect the macroeconomic structure of growth with microeconomic determinants, such as the incentives, policies, and organizations that interact with the growth process, including how winners, losers, and rents associated with innovation are allocated and awarded (Akcigit and Van Reenen 2023).

The Schumpeterian process of creative destruction can be viewed through three overlapping dimensions, as follows (refer to figure 1.10):

• *Creation.* The key issue here is the extent to which governments facilitate or blunt the natural force of creation involved in the entry of new businesses, innovations, and innovative ideas at home and from abroad.

• *Preservation.* The issue is the extent to which governments allow the preservation of existing players to function as a blocking force either by protecting incumbents or by allowing incumbents to impede market competition.

• *Destruction.* This is the necessary process that allows scarce resources to be reallocated to the most efficient uses. It often takes place the most frequently during economic crises. Yet, for myriad reasons, governments often limit the extent to which they allow the process of destruction to actually occur.

Empirical work on the economics of creative destruction has highlighted the economy-wide risks associated with a lack of institutions that support the Schumpeterian process of creative destruction. The risks include increased market concentration, higher markups and profit margins, lower labor shares in output, a large productivity gap between industry leaders and other competitors, declining firm entry rates, the weak survival of young firms, low innovation and technology adoption, and weakening job reallocation and churning (Akcigit and Ates 2021). This risk critique seems particularly relevant for ECA MICs that appear to be stagnant in economic performance or exhibit slowing convergence. Hence, the fear arises of a middle-income trap in the ECA region amid a struggle to make the leap effectively to an innovation-based growth model (Akcigit and Van Reenen 2023).

FIGURE 1.11 Europe HICs spend much more on R&D

Percent of GDP

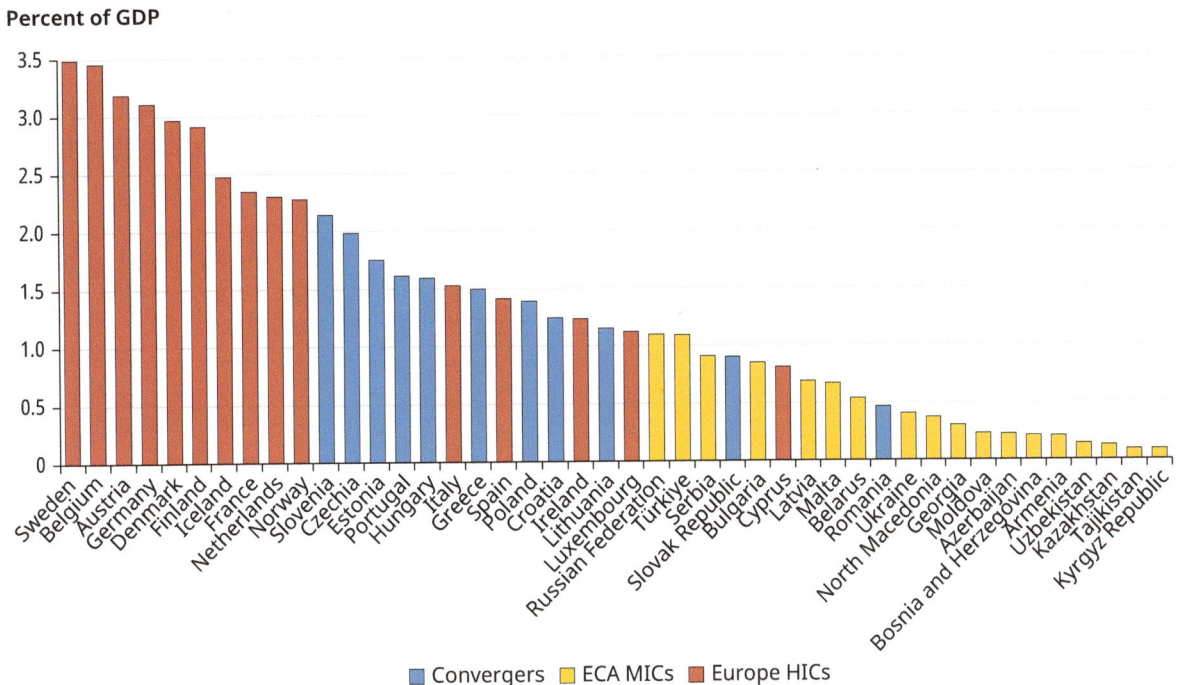

Source: GERD (Gross Domestic Expenditure on Research and Development), Institute for Statistics, United Nations Educational, Scientific and Cultural Organization, Montreal, https://data.uis.unesco.org/index.aspx?queryid=74.

Note: Country groups do not overlap.

Comparative analysis of the 20 ECA MICs with the 13 ECA Convergers and the 26 Europe HICs shows differences in the extent to which Schumpeterian forces can occur. For example, at the macrolevel, gross spending on research and development is significantly higher among the latter than among the MICs (refer to figures 1.11 and 1.12).

Other indicators associated with the creation phase of Schumpeterian growth across the three types of economies in the region show a more mixed pattern. The differences between Europe HICs, MICs, and Convergers are relatively small on indicators, such as the adoption of modern management practices and the use of international quality certifications (refer to figure 1.13). For the number of patents granted per unit of population, the gap between Europe HICs and Convergers and MICs is wide, though beginning to narrow (refer to figure 1.14).

FIGURE 1.12 R&D spending: flat among ECA MICs, but rising steadily among Europe HICs and Convergers

Percent of GDP

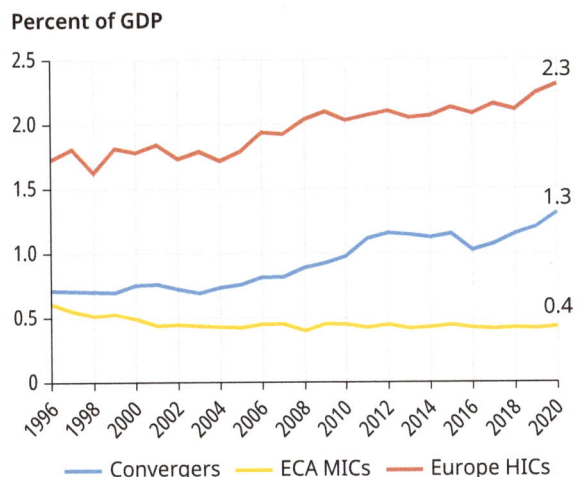

Source: GERD (Gross Domestic Expenditure on Research and Development), Institute for Statistics, United Nations Educational, Scientific and Cultural Organization, Montreal, https://data.uis.unesco.org/index.aspx?queryid=74.

Note: Country groups do not overlap.

FIGURE 1.13 Differences in technology licensing and management practices are relatively small

Indicator

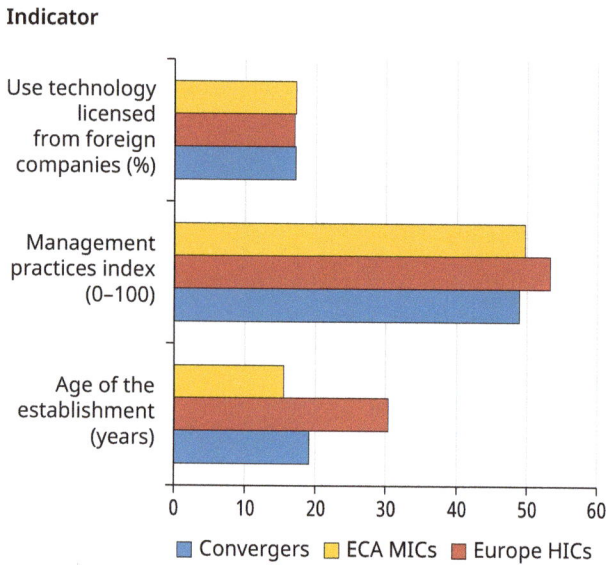

Source: WBES (World Bank Enterprise Surveys) (dashboard), World Bank, Washington, DC, https://www.enterprisesurveys.org/en/enterprisesurveys.

Note: Country groups do not overlap. Latest survey results for each country.

FIGURE 1.14 A sizable gap in patent applications remains between Europe HICs versus Convergers and ECA MICs

Patent grants per million population (log 10 scale)

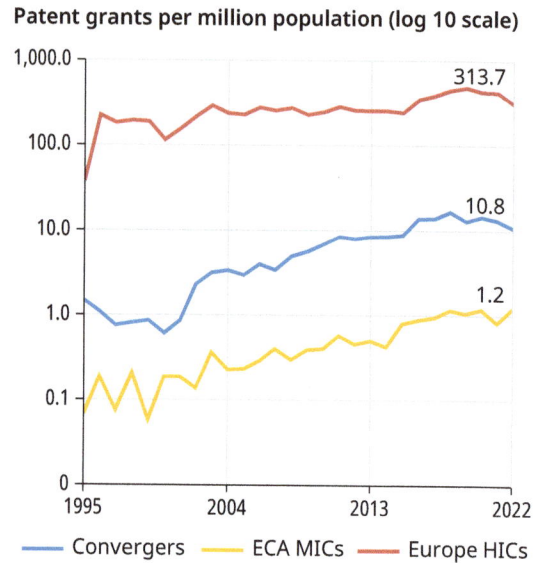

Source: IP Statistics (Intellectual Property Statistics) (dashboard), WIPO IP Statistics Data Center, World Intellectual Property Organization, Geneva, https://www.wipo.int/en/web/ip-statistics.

Note: Country groups do not overlap.

The enduring presence of state-owned enterprises (SOEs) dulls the impact of market competition on creative destruction in the ECA region. If a broader definition of businesses of the state is used (that is, counting businesses with at least a 10 percent government ownership share rather than the usual 50 percent), the presence of the state is revealed to be significantly larger than the results based on a traditional definition of a state-owned enterprise (refer to figure 1.15). If the SOEs are more prominent, the economy-wide impacts are broader in terms of reduced business entry and exit, investment, and job creation and destruction. There is a clear correlation in ECA countries in which product market regulations are more conducive to competition and higher levels of economic complexity in the export basket (refer to figure 1.16).

Measures of the extent to which product market regulations impede market competition show a clear gap favoring more competitive markets in Europe HICs and Convergers relative to markets in ECA MICs. Data on product market regulation suggest that the barriers to business entry are greater among ECA MICs (refer to figure 1.17). Patterns are similar at the sectoral level, although the extent to which regulations impede competition are greater in network sectors (such as energy and telecommunications) than in service sectors (such as professional services and retail trade) (refer to figure 1.18).

FIGURE 1.15 **The state plays a significant role in business in ECA MICs**

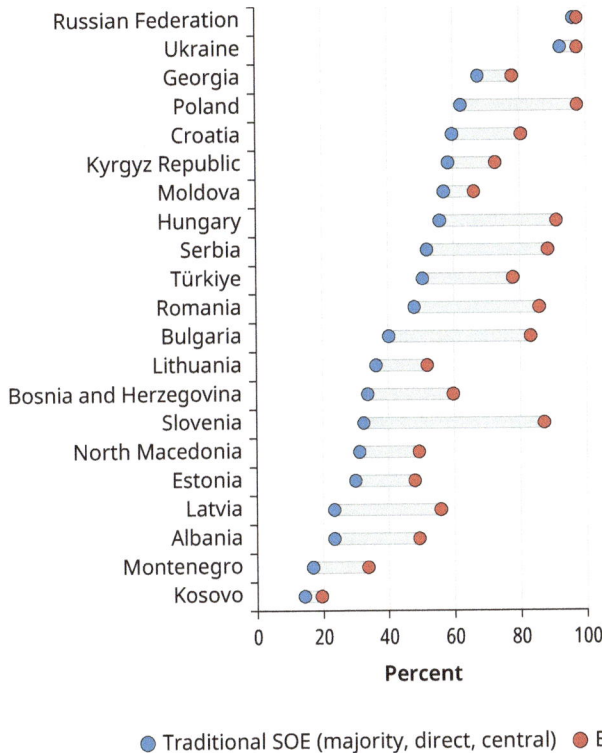

FIGURE 1.16 **Fewer regulatory barriers are correlated with greater economic complexity**

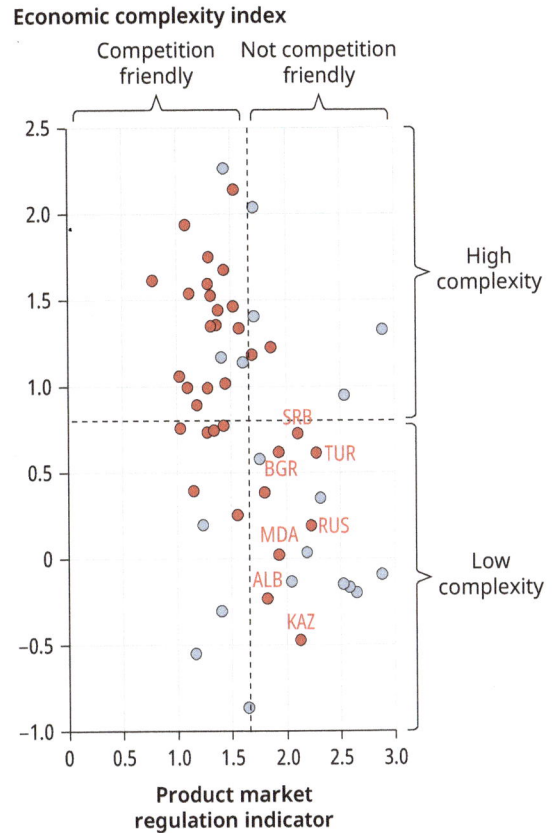

Sources: Atlas of Economic Complexity (dashboard), Growth Lab, Center for International Development, Harvard University, Cambridge, MA, https://atlas.hks.harvard.edu/; Global BOS database (Global Businesses of the State database) (internal database), World Bank, Washington, DC; PMR Database (OECD-WBG Product Market Regulation Database) (dashboard), World Bank, Washington, DC, https://prosperitydata360.worldbank.org/en/dataset/OECDWBG+PMR.

Note: ECA countries are in red. The threshold for a country classifiction as competition friendly is based on the average of the indicators of product market regulation across the relevant countries. Countries scoring less than the average are classified as low regulation. Countries socring above the average are classified as high regulation. The same approach is applied in the case of economic complexity. For more on the Global BOS database, refer to Dall'Olio et al. (2022); Licetti, Sánchez Navarro, and Patiño Peña (2023). BOS = businesses of the state; SOE = state-owned enterprises.

Broader indicators measuring the competitiveness of the investment climate and the environment for innovation show a sustained gap between ECA MICs and Europe HICs, while Convergers generally fall between the two. The business environment gap is widest in institutional quality, business dynamism, and technology adoption (refer to figure 1.19). The pattern is similar for measures that drive social mobility, such as relative mobility in education across generations (refer to figure 1.20). Measures associated with greater innovation capacity, such as business and market sophistication, creative outputs, and human capital for research,

FIGURE 1.17 ECA MICs exercise greater restrictions on product and market competition

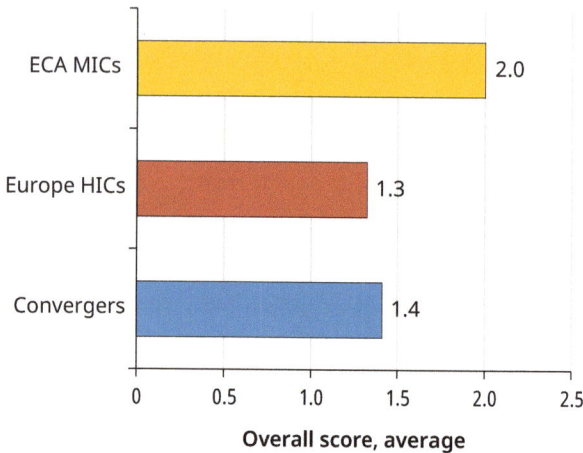

Overall score, average

FIGURE 1.18 Barriers in ECA MICs are higher in network sectors than in service sectors

Score by economic sector, average

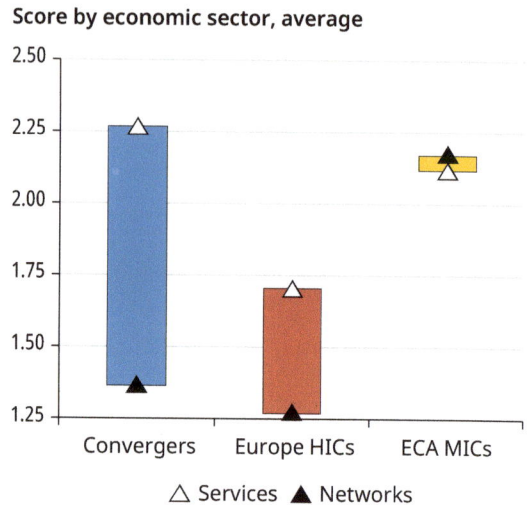

△ Services ▲ Networks

Source: PMR Database (OECD-WBG Product Market Regulation Database) (dashboard), World Bank, Washington, DC, https://prosperitydata360.worldbank.org/en/dataset/OECDWBG+PMR.

Note: Product market regulation indicators are numerical scores ranging from 0 to 6, where 0 means that a country is close to regulatory international best practice and 6 that it is quite far. Country groups do not overlap. The latest survey results are shown for each country group. Networks: transport, energy, e-communications. Services: professional services, retail.

FIGURE 1.19 There is a persistent gap in business environment indicators between Europe HICs and ECA MICs

Indicator

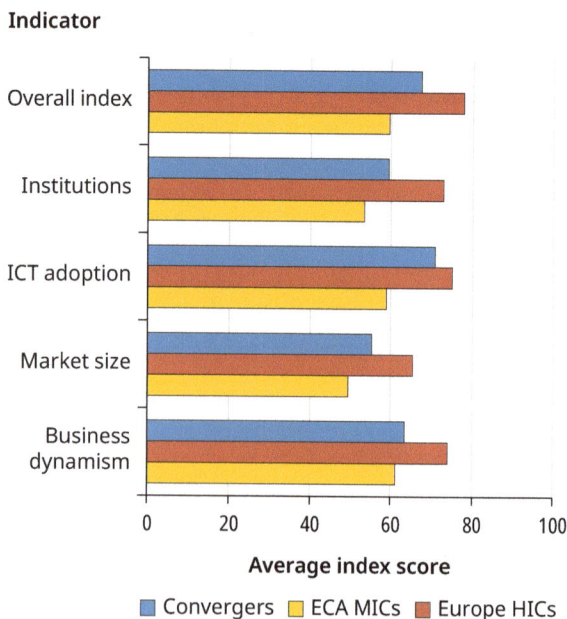

Average index score

■ Convergers ■ ECA MICs ■ Europe HICs

Source: Schwab 2019.

Note: The index ranges from 0 (low) to 100 (high). ICT = information and communication technology.

FIGURE 1.20 Europe HICs clearly lead Convergers and ECA MICs on measures of social mobility

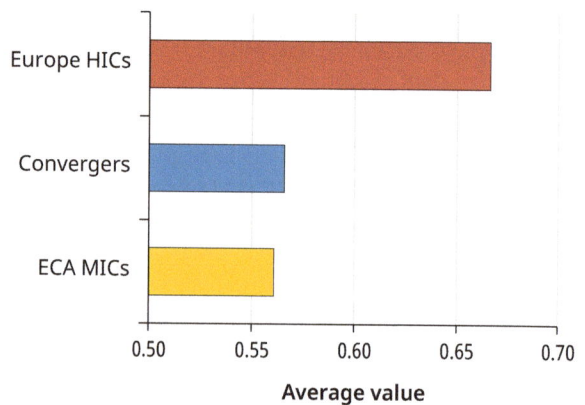

Average value

Source: GDIM (Global Database on Intergenerational Mobility) (dashboard), Data Catalog, World Bank, Washington, DC, https://datacatalog.worldbank.org/search /dataset/0050771/global-database-on-intergenerational -mobility.

Note: Country groups do not overlap. Relative mobility is measured as 1.0, minus the correlation coefficient between the years of schooling of children and of their mothers. A higher value indicates greater mobility.

show a similar pattern (refer to figure 1.21). There is a clear cross-country correlation between such composite measures of the forces underpinning innovation and the levels of per capita income (refer to figure 1.22).

Establishing institutions to support creative destruction and convergence to high income is more daunting in today's context of changing climate. Energy intensity has been declining over the last 20 years (refer to figure 1.23). However, there is still a large gap between ECA MICs and Europe HICs and significant dispersion across the MIC grouping. For the most part, countries with higher incomes tend to exhibit lower energy intensity per unit of output, though there are several outliers (refer to figure 1.24).

An analysis of ECA countries based on income per capita and emissions reveals that MICs experience the highest greenhouse gas emissions, followed closely by Europe HICs, while Convergers emit much less (refer to table 1.3). Though Europe HICs have high emissions overall, most countries are low emitters (eight countries), collectively emitting less than the MICs in the same emissions bracket (two countries). Meanwhile, most high emitters are MICs (seven countries), suggesting there is potential for a reduction in emissions as these countries progress to high income.

FIGURE 1.21 Innovation indicators show a consistent gap between ECA MICs and Europe HICs

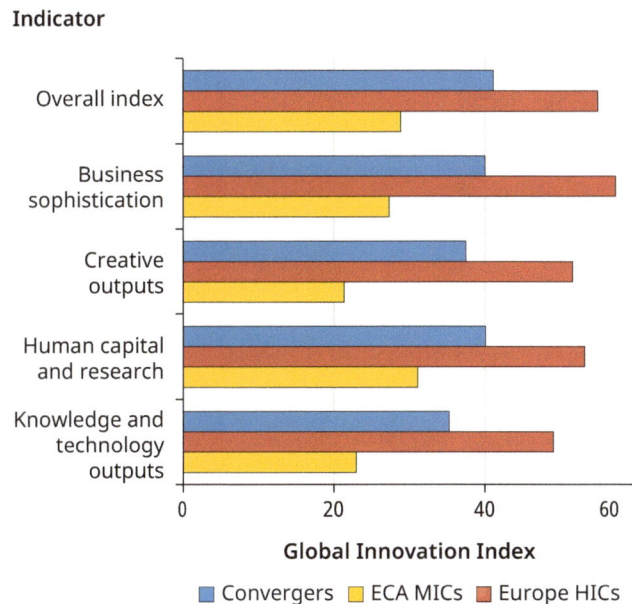

FIGURE 1.22 There is a strong correlation between innovation and GNI per capita

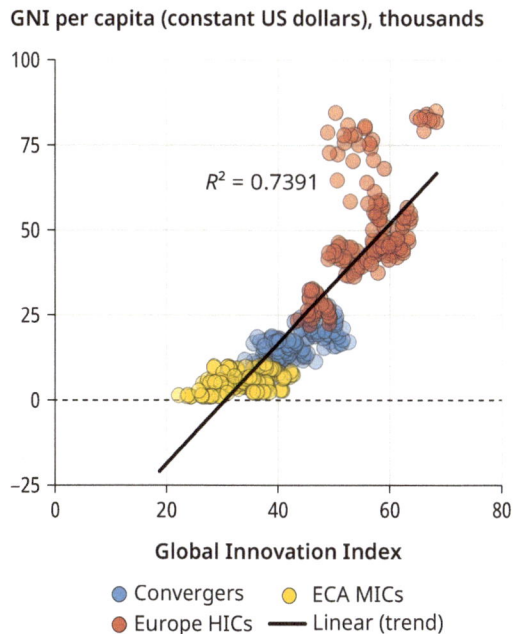

Indicator

GNI per capita (constant US dollars), thousands

$R^2 = 0.7391$

Sources: WDI (World Development Indicators) (dashboard), World Bank, Washington, DC, https://datatopics.worldbank.org/world-development-indicators/; World Intellectual Property Organization.

Note: Country groups do not overlap. The index ranges from 0 (low) to 100 (high). GNI = gross national income.

FIGURE 1.23 Energy intensity among ECA MICs has fallen in recent years

Year 2009 = 100, group averages

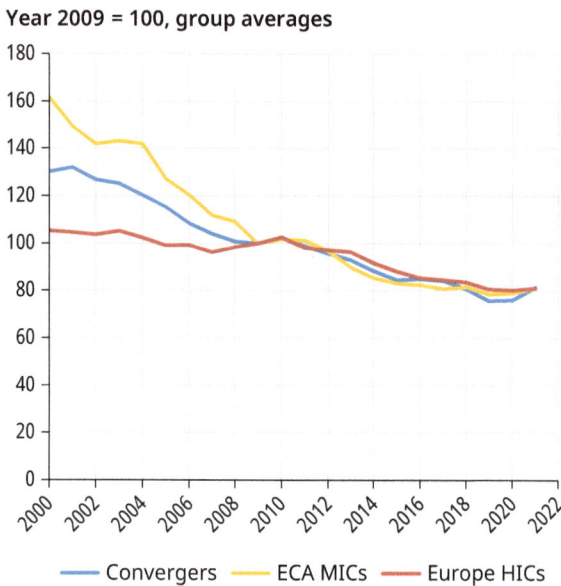

— Convergers — ECA MICs — Europe HICs

FIGURE 1.24 Europe HICs exhibit lower energy intensity than ECA MICs

GNI per capita, Atlas method (constant US dollars), thousands

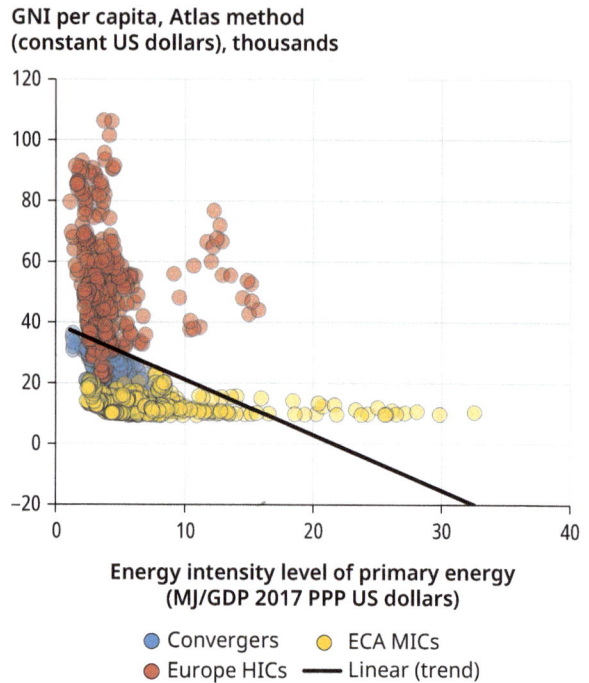

Energy intensity level of primary energy (MJ/GDP 2017 PPP US dollars)

● Convergers   ● ECA MICs
● Europe HICs   — Linear (trend)

Source: WDI (World Development Indicators) (dashboard), World Bank, Washington, DC, https://datatopics.worldbank.org/world-development-indicators/.

Note: Country groups do not overlap. GNI = gross national income; MJ = megajoules (10^6 joules); PPP = purchasing power parity.

TABLE 1.3 Classifying emission intensity, ECA countries, 2021

Emissions group	ECA MICs[a]	Convergers	Europe HICs	Total emissions
Low emission countries[b]	3.04 (2 countries)	0.40 (1 country)	0.53 (8 countries)	3.97
Medium emission countries[c]	0.09 (10 countries)	0.002 (10 countries)	0.04 (7 countries)	0.13
High emission countries[d]	1.24 (7 countries)	0.49 (2 countries)	2.40 (4 countries)	4.13
Total emissions per capita[e]	*4.37*	*0.89*	*2.97*	*8.23*

Sources: Calculations based on data from CO_2 and Greenhouse Gas Emissions (dashboard), Our World in Data, Global Change Data Lab and Oxford Martin Program on Global Development, University of Oxford, Oxford, UK, https://ourworldindata.org/co2-and-greenhouse-gas-emissions#explore-data-on-co2-and-greenhouse-gas-emissions; GCP (Global Carbon Project), Future Earth, Montreal, https://www.globalcarbonproject.org/.

Note: There is no overlap within the country or emissions groups. Colors refer to the total amount emitted by each emitter group, ranging from low (light blue) to high (dark blue).

a. The ECA MIC group excludes countries that have already converged to high-income status.
b. Countries emitting less than 5 tons.
c. Countries emitting between 5 tons and 10 tons.
d. Countries emitting more than 10 tons.
e. Average emissions, multiplied by the number of countries in the group.

Conclusions and Introduction to the Rest of the Report

Cross-country evidence presented in this chapter suggests that ECA MICs will need to sustain both foundational and transformative reforms to enable them to transition to high-income status. Foundational reforms that boost investment should evolve into efforts to support the impact and diffusion of knowledge (progressing from a 1*i* strategy to a 2*i* strategy) and then blossom into a strategy that helps firms advance to frontier innovation (a 3*i* strategy). Reform efforts to enable ECA MICs to escape the middle-income trap and thrive beyond the HIC threshold would have to support investment, infusion, and innovation. According to this classification:

- The countries of Central Asia are MICs generally at the initial stages of transition to high income. They should focus primarily on a 1*i* strategy and accelerate private investment in physical and human capital. Their efforts would also have to focus on reducing the role of the state in the economy and helping to create or complete markets.

- As MICs approaching the HIC threshold, EU candidate countries, including countries in the South Caucasus and the Western Balkans and Moldova, Türkiye, and Ukraine should focus on a 2*i* strategy that combines policies to boost investment with policies to facilitate greater openness to foreign trade and investment. This would enable the infusion of foreign capital, modern technologies, practices, expertise, and ideas. Stepped-up efforts are also needed to improve secondary and tertiary education quality to nurture talent and reduce the misallocation of talent.

- As HICs looking to sustain growth beyond the transition, EU members need to focus on a 3*i* strategy to manage the incumbency advantage and enable frontier innovation, support high growth companies and new entrants, and ensure dramatically higher quality in university and postuniversity education.

Notes

1. Economic growth is ultimately driven by the accumulation of physical and human capital and by improvements in productivity. This accumulation and improvements are recognized as fundamental drivers of growth.

2. Among the 13 success stories, Malta was the only economy in the ECA region highlighted by the Commission on Growth and Development in their 2008 report (refer to Commission on Growth and Development 2008).

3. Although Bulgaria and the Russian Federation have surpassed the high-income threshold, they are excluded from the Convergers in this analysis. Their recent transition to high-income status suggests a positive trajectory toward convergence, similar to other countries in the ECA region, but it may be too early to be more confident about the future of this trajectory.

4. GNI per capita is measured using the Atlas method, current US dollars. The growth rates in these two countries have been volatile, resulting in starkly different averages depending on the period of reference. While steady growth was observed in 2007–12, the trend has narrowed sharply in more recent years. As a result, the differences between the 15-year and 10-year compound averages are large in these countries. See World Bank Atlas Method: Detailed Methodology (Data Help Desk), Data, World Bank, Washington, DC, https://datahelpdesk.worldbank.org/knowledgebase/articles/378832-what-is-the-world-bank-atlas-method.

References

Acemoglu, Daron. 2009. *Introduction to Modern Economic Growth*. Princeton, NJ: Princeton University Press.

Acemoglu, Daron, Simon Johnson, and James A. Robinson. 2001. "The Colonial Origins of Comparative Development: An Empirical Investigation." *American Economic Review* 91 (5): 1369–1401.

Acemoglu, Daron, Simon Johnson, and James A. Robinson. 2004. "Institutions as the Fundamental Cause of Long-Run Growth." NBER Working Paper 10481 (May), National Bureau of Economic Research, Cambridge, MA.

Aghion, Philippe, Ufuk Akcigit, and Peter Howitt. 2013. "What Do We Learn from Schumpeterian Growth Theory?" NBER Working Paper 18824 (February), National Bureau of Economic Research, Cambridge, MA.

Aghion, Philippe, and Peter Howitt. 1992. "A Model of Growth Through Creative Destruction." *Econometrica* 60 (2): 323–51.

Akcigit, Ufuk, and Sina T. Ates. 2021 "Ten Facts on Declining Business Dynamism and Lessons from Endogenous Growth Theory." *American Economic Journal: Macroeconomics* 13 (1): 257–98.

Akcigit, Ufuk, and John Michael Van Reenen. 2023. *The Economics of Creative Destruction: New Research on Themes from Aghion and Howitt*. Cambridge, MA: Harvard University Press.

Barro, Robert J., and Xavier Sala-i-Martin. 2004. *Economic Growth*, 2nd ed. Cambridge, MA: MIT Press.

Commission on Growth and Development. 2008. *The Growth Report: Strategies for Sustained Growth and Inclusive Development*. Washington, DC: World Bank. https://openknowledge.worldbank.org/handle/10986/6507.

Dall'Olio, Andrea Mario, Tanja K. Goodwin, Martha Martínez Licetti, Jan Orlowski, Fausto Andres Patiño Peña, Francis Ralambotsiferana Ratsimbazafy, and Dennis Sanchez-Navarro. 2022. "Using ORBIS to Build a Global Database of Firms with State Participation." Policy Research Working Paper 10261, World Bank, Washington, DC.

Devadas, Sharmila, and Steven Michael Pennings. 2018. "Assessing the Effect of Public Capital on Growth: An Extension of the World Bank Long-Term Growth Model." Policy Research Working Paper 8604, World Bank, Washington, DC.

Gill, Indermit Singh, Ivailo Izvorski, Willem van Eeghen, and Donato De Rosa. 2014. *Diversified Development: Making the Most of Natural Resources in Eurasia*. With Mariana Iootty De Paiva Dias, Naoko Kojo, Kazi M. Matin, Vilas Pathikonda, and Naotaka Sugawara. Washington, DC: World Bank.

Gill, Indermit Singh, and Homi Kharas. 2007. *An East Asian Renaissance: Ideas for Economic Growth*. With Deepak Bhattasali, Milan Brahmbhatt, Gaurav Datt, Mona Haddad, Edward Mountfield, Radu Tatucu, and Ekaterina Vostroknutova. Washington, DC: World Bank.

Gill, Indermit Singh, and Martin Raiser. 2012. *Golden Growth: Restoring the Lustre of the European Economic Model*. With Andrea Mario Dall'Olio, Truman Packard, Kaspar Richter, Naotaka Sugawara, Reinhilde Veugelers, and Juan Zalduendo. Washington, DC: World Bank.

Grossman, Gene M., and Elhanan Helpman. 1991. "Quality Ladders in the Theory of Growth." *Review of Economic Studies* 58 (1): 43–61.

Hanushek, Eric Alan, and Ludger Woessmann. 2008. "The Role of Cognitive Skills in Economic Development." *Journal of Economic Literature* 46 (3): 607–68.

Licetti, Martha Martínez, Dennis Sánchez Navarro, and Fausto Andres Patiño Peña. 2023. "Unveiling the True Extent of the Businesses of the State (BOS) in the Economy." *Let's Talk Development* (blog), November 28, 2023. https://blogs.worldbank.org/en/developmenttalk/unveiling-true-extent-businesses-state-bos-economy.

Loayza, Norman V., and Steven Michael Pennings, eds. 2022. *The Long Term Growth Model: Fundamentals, Extensions, and Applications*. Washington, DC: World Bank.

Piatkowski, Marcin. 2018. *Europe's Growth Champion: Insights from the Economic Rise of Poland*. New York: Oxford University Press.

Rodrik, Dani, Arvind Subramanian, and Francesco Treddi. 2004. "Institutions Rule: The Primacy of Institutions over Geography and Integration in Economic Development." *Journal of Economic Growth* 9 (2): 131–65.

Romer, Paul Michael. 1987. "Growth Based on Increasing Returns Due to Specialization." *American Economic Review* 77 (2): 56–62.

Romer, Paul Michael. 1990. "Endogenous Technological Change." *Journal of Political Economy* 98 (5, Part 2): S71–S102.

Schumpeter, Joseph Alois. 1942. *Capitalism, Socialism, and Democracy*. New York: Harper and Brothers.

Schwab, Klaus, ed. 2019. *Insight Report: The Global Competitiveness Report 2019*. Geneva: World Economic Forum. http://www3.weforum.org/docs/WEF_TheGlobalCompetitivenessReport2019.pdf.

Solow, Robert M. 1956. "A Contribution to the Theory of Economic Growth." *Quarterly Journal of Economics* 70 (1): 65–94.

Swan, Trevor W. 1956. "Economic Growth and Capital Accumulation." *Economic Record* 32 (2): 334–61.

World Bank. 2017. *Lessons from Poland, Insights for Poland: A Sustainable and Inclusive Transition to High-Income Status*. Washington, DC: World Bank.

World Bank. 2024. *World Development Report 2024: The Middle-Income Trap*. Washington, DC: World Bank.

The Lessons of High-Income Transitions in East Asia and in Latin America

East Asia and the Pacific has been the world's most rapidly growing region over the last five decades. Economic growth has averaged 4.8 percent annually since 1980, compared with 1.9 percent among ECA countries over the same period. Such impressive growth has occurred despite (or perhaps because of) the limited natural resources of East Asia and the Pacific.

The region has experienced several waves of development. The first four Asian tigers—Hong Kong SAR, China; the Republic of Korea; Singapore; and Taiwan, China—passed the HIC threshold during the 1980s, and Korea a second time in the 1990s.[a] Following quickly on that success was the next set of tiger economies, Indonesia, Malaysia, the Philippines, and Thailand, which enjoyed high rates of growth through the 1990s. The southeast Asian economies of Cambodia, the Lao People's Democratic Republic, and Viet Nam experienced similar accelerations in the 2000s. Once home to half the world's population living in poverty, these countries today have barely 1 percent of the population in the region living below the international poverty line.

However, the region's growth pathway has not been free of challenges. The Asian financial crisis of 1997–98 dented confidence. Critics suggested that East Asian growth was driven more by perspiration than innovation and that countries were caught up in crony capitalism. While growth has remained strong, trend rates since the 1997–98 crisis have weakened, as productivity growth faltered. Despite impressive progress, no country in East Asia and the Pacific has passed the high-income country (HIC) threshold since Korea's transition more than 20 years ago, although China ($12,850) and Malaysia ($11,780) are on the cusp of passing the HIC per capita threshold.

Broadbased evidence points to the following key success factors in East Asia's growth trajectory:

• The maintenance of macroeconomic stability, particularly low inflation, and steady (often undervalued) exchange rates, together with high rates of savings and investment.

• Foundational investments in human capital, coupled with favorable demographics, which have allowed for rapid structural transformation from agriculture into manufacturing.

• Openness to foreign trade and investment, especially in manufacturing, at a time when globalization was at an apex.

Gaps in addressing broader standards of governance have begun to weigh on growth, however. The evidence is mixed on the role of the state in this outcome. There are examples of industrial policy interventions that support growth and others that sap growth. Similarly, not all countries have been successful in developing advanced human capital or in shifting to the next stage of innovation-led development. East Asia's demographic changes are starting to shift from supporting growth to weighing down growth. The region must face the major decarbonization challenge in the years ahead.

Latin America and the Caribbean has been lagging other regions for decades. Its economic growth has averaged only 2.4 percent annually since 1980. As a result, the region is unable to converge toward high income. Average per capita gross domestic product (GDP) has been stuck at around one-third of the US level for more than a century. In the last two decades, most Latin American countries have been successful at macroeconomic stabilization and have made progress with structural reforms in factor and product markets. Yet, these efforts remain insufficient to propel the region to high-income status.

Investment in physical and human capital substantially lags high-income countries, but also other, more successful regions. Gross fixed capital formation has averaged 20 percent of GDP, compared with 22 percent in the ECA and 32 percent in East Asia and the Pacific. The level of human capital, measured by the human capital index, also lags, reaching 0.56 in Latin America and the Caribbean compared with 0.70 in ECA and 0.61 in East Asia and the Pacific.[b] Economic efficiency (total factor productivity [TFP]) remains stubbornly low because of limited innovation, widespread barriers to competition, and a turbulent social context that renders reform consensus difficult.

On the upside, firms in the region are relatively more innovative. According to the World Bank Enterprise Surveys, an average of 53.0 percent of firms in the region have introduced new or improved products, compared with 36.6 percent in the ECA and 27.2 percent in East Asia and the Pacific.[c] However, the quality of technology is part of the reason Latin America has largely failed to integrate into global value chains. The exception is Mexico, with its clusters in automobiles, car parts, and machinery. Countries in Latin America and the Caribbean display widespread barriers to competition, as measured, for instance, by indicators on product market regulation and a regulatory environment that stifles creative destruction and reduces productivity.

Only two countries in Latin America and the Caribbean have been successful in the transition to high income. Chile, with an income per capita of $14,358, crossed the high-income threshold in 2012. Its success rests on sound institutions that foster social consensus, macroeconomic stability, and the ability to take advantage of its natural resource wealth. (Chile is the world's largest producer of copper.) Uruguay, with an income per capita of $18,215, also became a high-income country in 2012. It stands out in Latin America because its society is viewed as egalitarian. The share of the middle class in the population, at more than 60 percent, is the largest in the Americas. Sound macroeconomic management and favorable external conditions have supported an economic expansion that has lasted two decades. However, to maintain their high-income status, both Chile and Uruguay will need to implement second-generation reforms supporting innovation.

a. Korea initially transitioned to HIC status in 1995. However, the impact of the 1997–98 Asian financial crisis pushed the country back into MIC status. Korea passed the HIC threshold for the second time in 2001.

b. HCI (Human Capital Index) (dashboard), World Bank, Washington, DC, https://datacatalog .worldbank.org/search/dataset/0038030.

c. WBES (World Bank Enterprise Surveys) (dashboard), World Bank, Washington, DC, https://www .enterprisesurveys.org/en/enterprisesurveys.

SPOTLIGHT 1.2
Assessing ECA MICs Relative to Global Convergers

Throughout this chapter, the performance of ECA MICs is benchmarked against the 13 ECA Convergers, countries that have successfully transitioned from MIC to HIC status in the past 30 years. ECA MICs are benchmarked here against the larger group of 31 Global Convergers (excluding Bulgaria, Palau, and the Russian Federation).

There is no significant difference in investment rates between ECA MICs and Global Convergers (refer to figure S1.2.1). However, there is a noticeable gap in labor utilization, where ECA MICs appear to lag (refer to figure S1.2.2).

FIGURE S1.2.1 In investment, ECA MICs and Global Convergers perform at a similar level

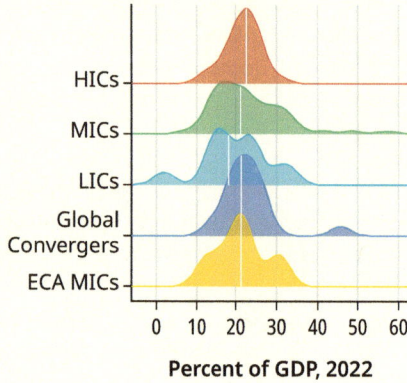

Percent of GDP, 2022

Source: 2023 data from WDI (World Development Indicators) (dashboard), World Bank, Washington, DC, https://datatopics.worldbank.org/world-development-indicators/.

Note: Country groups do not overlap. Shaded areas are density plots. The lines represent medians.

FIGURE S1.2.2 ECA MICs lag Global Convergers, notably in labor utilization

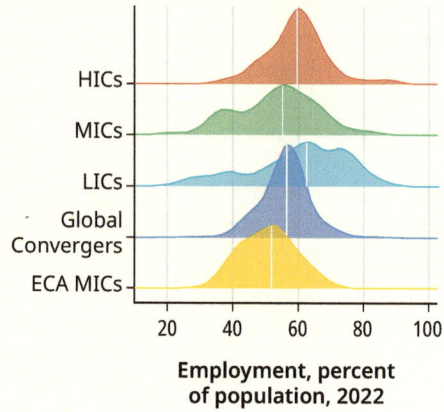

Employment, percent of population, 2022

Source: International Labor Organization, ILOSTAT, 2023.

Note: Country groups do not overlap. Shaded areas are density plots. The lines represent medians.

FIGURE S1.2.3 ECA MICs lag Global Convergers in productivity

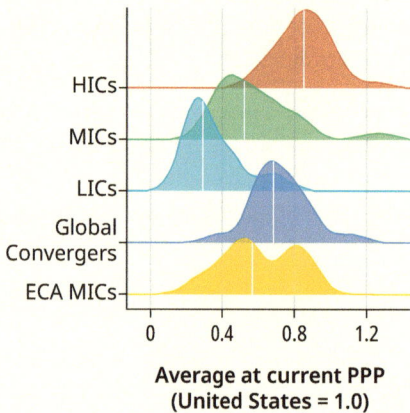

Average at current PPP (United States = 1.0)

Source: PWT (Penn World Table) (database version 10.1), Groningen Growth and Development Centre, Faculty of Economics and Business, University of Groningen, Groningen, the Netherlands, https://www.rug.nl/ggdc/productivity/pwt/.

Note: Country groups do not overlap. Shaded areas are density plots. The lines represent medians. PPP = purchasing power parity.

FIGURE S1.2.4 ECA MICs lag Global Convergers in trade openness

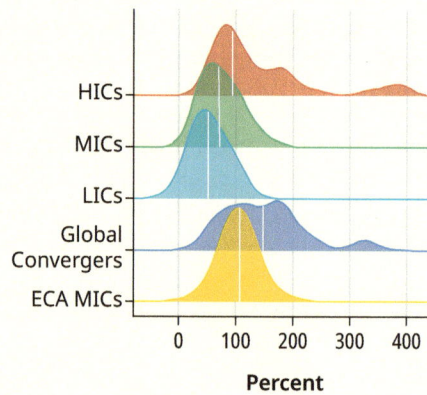

Percent

Source: 2023 data from WDI (World Development Indicators) (dashboard), World Bank, Washington, DC, https://datatopics.worldbank.org/world-development-indicators/.

Note: Country groups do not overlap. Shaded areas are density plots. The lines represent medians.

FIGURE S1.2.5 Institutional performance indicators are better in Global Convergers than in ECA MICs

Range: −2.5 (bad) to 2.5 (good)

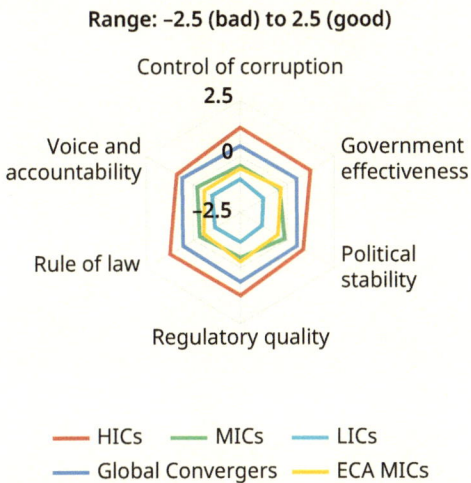

Source: 2023 data from WDI (World Development Indicators) (dashboard), World Bank, Washington, DC, https://datatopics.worldbank.org/world-development-indicators/.

Note: Country groups do not overlap.

FIGURE S1.2.6 The gap in R&D spending between Global Convergers and ECA MICs is widening

Percent of GDP

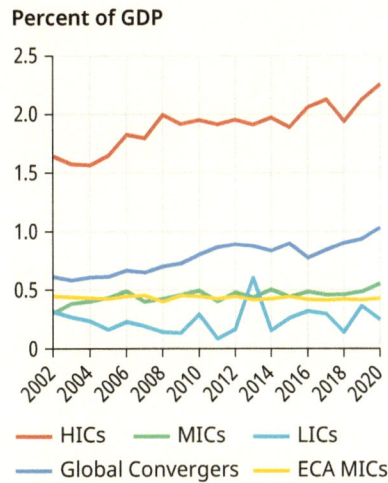

Source: GERD (Gross Domestic Expenditure on Research and Development), Institute for Statistics, United Nations Educational, Scientific and Cultural Organization, Montreal, https://data.uis.unesco.org/index.aspx?queryid=74.

Note: Country groups do not overlap.

Similarly, performance gaps are evident in measures of total factor productivity and openness to trade, where ECA MICs lag Global Convergers (refer to figures S1.2.3 and S1.2.4).

The most significant performance gaps between ECA MICs and Global Convergers occurs in institutional performance and research and development expenditures, suggesting that, in these two areas, policy reforms will be needed to accelerate growth and convergence in ECA MICs (refer to figures S1.2.5 and S1.2.6).

Enterprises and Productivity

Country Case in Brief: Estonia

Kristo Käärmann and Taavet Hinrikus wanted to transfer money between the United Kingdom and Estonia, but the two Estonians were frustrated with expensive bank fees. So, in 2011, they came up with a solution. They would put money into each other's bank accounts. Kristo, based in the United Kingdom, put money into Taavet's UK account, and Taavet, based in Estonia, put money into Kristo's account in Estonia. Because the money transfers did not cross borders, no high fees had to be paid, and the money was exchanged readily. This is how TransferWise, now known as Wise, was born. Fast forward a decade. Wise's revenues were $1.2 billion in 2023. During these 12 years, the innovative start-up traveled from ingenious idea to global fintech leader, mirroring Estonia's bolder, broader economic policies and innovation-driven growth.

The company's expansion was rapid. It scaled up to serve millions of customers worldwide. The growth was supported by Estonia's policy environment, which encouraged entrepreneurial ventures and innovation. The country's digital-first approach, with initiatives such as e-governance and e-residency, created a seamless business environment. The government cultivated innovation and research and development (R&D) by offering incentives, funding R&D activities, and promoting collaboration between universities and businesses. These steps were coupled with world-class information technology infrastructure, one of the highest rates of internet penetration worldwide, and widespread access to high-speed broadband. Estonia's regulatory framework—transparent and efficient—allowed Wise to operate easily with little bureaucratic hindrance. This supportive foundation was instrumental in enabling Wise to focus on innovation and global expansion.

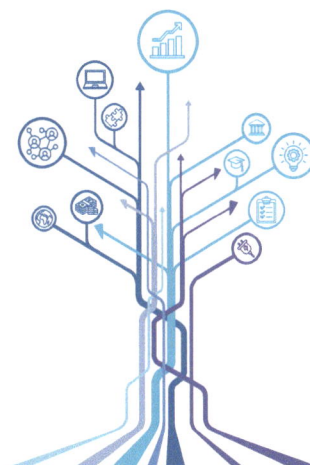

The success of Wise reflects Estonia's broader economic strategy. The government—focused on creating a competitive market with low barriers to entry and a strong push for digital innovation—set the stage for start-ups such as Wise to flourish. Estonia's integration with the global economy, particularly its accession to the European Union (EU), provided Wise with access to a vastly larger market and a more diverse customer base. Non-Estonians were free to set up and run businesses in Estonia remotely, in an open economy with a trade-to-gross domestic product (GDP) ratio close to 160 percent, alongside limited state presence in the economy and healthy levels of competition.[1]

A skilled workforce, fostered by the government's emphasis on education and digital literacy, provided Wise with the talent it needed to innovate and grow. Estonia has one of the best education systems in the world, producing a skilled workforce that meets the country's needs in modern technology and generates a steady supply of tech-savvy professionals to support its growing tech sector.

These policies have made Estonia one of Europe's most thriving start-up hubs with more than 1,000 start-ups among a population of only 1.3 million. Estonia stands out for the number of start-ups, but also for the capacity of the start-ups to grow to scale, given that the country has produced several unicorns—start-ups that reach a valuation of more than $1 billion—besides Wise, including Bolt, Pipedrive, Playtech, and Skype.

Estonian companies have a global outlook and rely on global markets for growth. A digital-first strategy has vastly reduced administrative barriers and costs among both start-ups and established businesses. The Estonian Development Fund complements EU-funded programs and offers financial support and mentorship to early-stage companies (the stage at which uncertainty is greater) and has attracted venture capital and a vibrant financial ecosystem that supports start-ups. The government has promoted four strategic areas that have been crucial to the emergence of such a vibrant entrepreneurial ecosystem: concentrating on innovation and technology, targeting the value added created by businesses (rather than a focus on size), focusing on top-tier and frontier businesses, and supporting market contestability and global market integration.

Introduction

The example of Estonia shows how middle-income countries (MICs) in the Europe and Central Asia (ECA) region could spur economic development through a similar four-strategy approach. Each government needs to identify the appropriate development path. The principles embodied in these strategic areas represent a model for other MICs, particularly the emphasis on an innovation-driven growth model and the capacity to generate a thriving entrepreneurial ecosystem with significant dynamism at the top of the entrepreneurial distribution. The most successful companies should be able to compete in global markets and drive growth.

This chapter focuses on three main questions, as follows:

First, have ECA MICs followed Estonia's example and supported the forces of creative destruction to spur economic dynamism and growth? In short—no. Productivity growth has stemmed primarily from structural shifts out of agriculture into manufacturing and services and from shifts in resource reallocation from less efficient firms to more efficient ones. Among ECA high-income countries (HICs), by contrast, innovation is more important in driving productivity growth. As ECA MICs aspire to high-income status, these middle-income economies—previously dependent on resource reallocation—now need to prioritize innovation and technological upgrading strategically to facilitate this critical transition.

Second, is targeting small and medium enterprises (SMEs) for business support producing the desired results? This chapter finds that governments need to focus on start-ups and young businesses and not, as often happens now, on SMEs in general, because mature SMEs often contribute little to job creation, which is driven primarily by start-ups and young firms. Productive development policies therefore need to deemphasize size as a criterion for policy support and targeting, because a size-dependent policy approach has not been productive and may be counterproductive in that policies targeting SMEs focus more on preservation (Garicano, Lelarge, and Van Reenen 2016). Policies supporting firms should promote business dynamism and creative destruction.

Third, which factors produce economic vibrancy and dynamism? Restricted competition invariably stifles entrepreneurial dynamism, job creation, and productivity. State-owned enterprises (SOEs), especially in key sectors, such as energy generation and distribution and even in transmission, are critical to future growth and to the transition to a lower-emission future. In many cases, however, the prices SOEs charge are below cost recovery, limiting profitability and making innovation and support for the energy transition difficult for the SOEs. Moreover, SOEs tend to dampen entrepreneurial dynamism and act as a force of preservation, limiting the creative destruction shifts associated with entrepreneurial dynamism. The negative impacts of SOEs differ across countries, depending on governance structures and the effective separation of ownership and management control. Less international competition and suboptimal public procurement practices hinder the forces of creative destruction and entrepreneurial dynamism.

Supporting Creation: The Drivers of Productivity Growth in the Region

Productivity growth is driven by various forces in the ECA MICs and HICs (Syverson 2011). In the MICs, productivity performance depends mostly on the between-firm reallocation of resources within sectors and the change in the composition of the economy (structural transformation), while, in the HICs, it is largely driven by within-firm productivity growth because of innovation and technological upgrading. As countries become richer, the importance of innovation and technology adoption becomes more important, especially in the transition from MICs to HICs.

Structural Transformation Shows Limits in Boosting Productivity Growth

The pace of labor productivity growth varies across the ECA region. The increase in the pace has been considerable in most HICs, but only in a few MICs. Productivity growth measured as firm revenue per worker grew in most countries by 1 percent to 5 percent a year over the last 15 years.[2] Labor productivity growth in the ECA MICs underperformed relative to the ECA HICs. For example, sales per worker rose by more than 3 percent a year in firms in Poland and Romania. ECA MICs—Georgia, Kazakhstan, Kosovo, North Macedonia, and Serbia—grew less than 2 percent a year, while sales per worker contracted in Bulgaria and Montenegro.

At an aggregate level, the role of structural transformation appears less important among the HICs. This is because the increase in average sectoral productivity growth matters much more as countries become richer. Over the last few decades, many ECA countries have undergone profound transformations in economic structure and made significant productivity gains in certain sectors. Structural transformation—that is, changes in overall productivity because of sector structural shifts—has been the primary source of productivity growth in most ECA MICs, but, in the ECA HICs, the effect of structural transformation has been negligible or even negative. As income grows, countries rely more on their capacity to lift within-sector productivity rather than on structural change.

Besides structural transformation, sector-level productivity growth may be driven by market efficiency, within-firm growth, and market selection. Aggregate productivity changes may be decomposed into three components. The first, the reallocation component (or between-firm growth), measures the productivity growth derived from improving market efficiency, that is, how resources flow between firms at varying levels of productivity within sectors (from low- to high-productivity firms). The second, the within-firm component, captures the contribution of growing productivity among surviving firms. The third component refers to market selection, which gauges the contribution of firm entry and exit. If entering firms exhibit greater productivity relative to incumbents and exiting firms are less productive than the firms that survive, business selection will lead to a rise in the overall productivity of the economy.

Within-Firm Productivity Growth Is Inadequate in Many ECA MICs

The ECA MICs are struggling to boost within-firm productivity, unlike the ECA HICs. Figure 2.1 illustrates the decomposition of productivity growth—measured

FIGURE 2.1 Within-firm productivity growth does not drive overall ECA MIC productivity growth

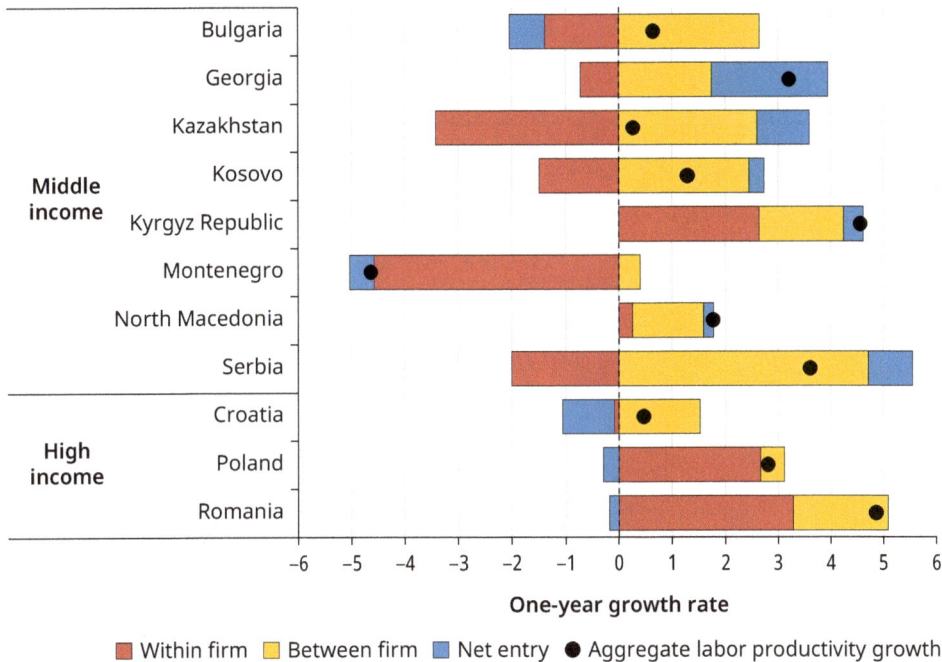

Sources: World Bank elaboration based on data of national statistical institutes; Melitz and Polanec 2015; Orbis (portal), Moody's, New York, https://www.moodys.com/web/en/us/capabilities /company-reference-data/orbis.html.

Note: The data reported are one-year arithmetic averages. A dynamic Olley-Pakes decomposition was performed at the three-industry level of NACE Rev. 2 and used a two-year rolling window (changes between *t* and *t* −2) (EC 2008). Firms and sectors were weighted according to the employment weight in each activity and economy during the reference period. NACE = Statistical Classification of Economic Activities in the European Community.

as sales per worker—into within-firm, between-firm, and market selection (entry and exit) components. The ECA MICs and ECA HICs differ systematically in the relative importance of the within-firm productivity component, which measures the changes in the productivity of incumbents over time. This component has been systematically negative in ECA MICs except in the Kyrgyz Republic and North Macedonia. Meanwhile, within-firm productivity growth has been the main driver of aggregate productivity growth in the ECA HICs. In Poland and Romania, which experienced large productivity increases in the last 15 years, within-firm productivity gains accounted for at least two-thirds of overall productivity growth.

The average productivity among incumbent businesses declined and suggests there were gaps in innovation, new products, the skilled labor force, management capacities, and technology adoption (OECD 2018b). These factors are associated with efficiency upgrading and improved within-firm performance.[3] The lack of improvements within firms may also be explained by an enabling business environment that is not conducive to firm investments in innovation and technology adoption because of the quality or enforcement of regulations, the lack of competition, and underdeveloped credit markets. These drawbacks generate constraints to growth among high-potential entrepreneurs.

Creative destruction requires market selection through the exit of less efficient businesses and their replacement by new, more productive firms. Firm selection, the exit of lower-productivity businesses, and the entry of higher-productivity start-ups that introduce new products or new processes are the last channel through which productivity can grow. If the productivity of new businesses outperforms that of incumbents, or exiting businesses are less efficient than those that manage to survive, aggregate productivity grows through this market selection process. With few exceptions, this channel has played a minor role in the ECA region, indicating that current entrepreneurial ecosystems should become more dynamic to generate a robust stream of higher-productivity start-ups and that market selection mechanisms should be strengthened to lead to the exit of less efficient firms.[4] On average, surviving firms display higher productivity than exiting firms, but there is still a large overlap between both distributions, suggesting that unproductive incumbents often survive, while similarly productive or more productive businesses tend to close operations.

Business innovation and experimentation lead to higher levels of productivity. As Cusolito and Maloney (2018) point out, firms that introduce new products or production methods or that adopt new technologies face great uncertainty over risks and returns. They need to learn to assess these risks and make decisions through a process of entrepreneurial discovery. If successful, their productivity would rise, and innovation would be reflected in an increase in the within-firm term of the dynamic Olley-Pakes decomposition. Most ECA countries lag high-income EU countries in innovation and experimentation. As suggested by the Schumpeterian framework, economic growth is driven by innovation in the long run (Schumpeter 1942). This is ultimately grounded in investment in R&D, training, digitalization, and improvements in management and organization (Griffith, Redding, and Van Reenen 2024). Among firms and entrepreneurs operating in competitive sectors, innovation offers the opportunity to escape competition (the escape competition effect).

ECA countries, especially the MICs, lag Europe HICs and the United States on global innovation and the number of patents per capita (refer to figure 2.2).[5] The share of firms introducing products new to the market rises with income, as does the number of patents per capita. In the latter case, European peers, such as Hungary, Latvia, Lithuania, Slovakia, and Slovenia, display a higher degree of patent innovation even compared with ECA HICs.

Less innovation in most countries in the region reflects the fact that the ECA MICs are still focusing on the 2i strategy of infusion and have not yet shifted to a 3i strategy, which includes innovation and is associated with within-firm productivity gains. The current number of patents per capita in the region differs greatly between

FIGURE 2.2 **ECA MICs lag Europe HICs on innovation**

Innovation Index

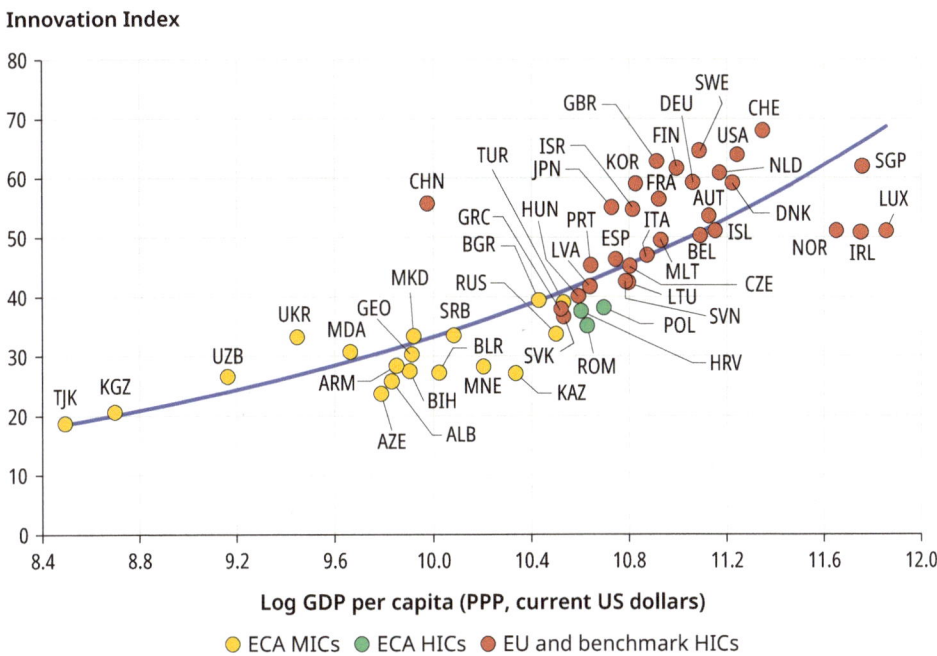

Sources: World Bank data and elaboration based on Dutta et al. 2023; GII (Global Innovation Index) (dashboard), World Intellectual Property Organization, Geneva, https://www.wipo.int/global _innovation_index/en/.

Note: GDP per capita (in log, current US dollars adjusted by purchasing power parity) as of 2022. For country abbreviations, refer to International Organization for Standardization (ISO), https://www.iso.org/obp/ui/#search. PPP = purchasing power parity.

the MICs and HICs, and the innovation gap is substantial. In 2003, the ECA MICs produced 0.15 patents per million inhabitants, while the share in the ECA HICs was 0.4 patents per million inhabitants. The innovation gap between the ECA HICs and MICs widened considerably until 2013 (refer to figure 2.3). Although the patent gap between the ECA MICs and HICs narrowed subsequently, the ECA HICs still had more than twice the patent innovations per million population in the ECA MICs: 0.88 versus 0.38. A similar pattern may be observed

FIGURE 2.3 **The innovation gap between ECA MICs and ECA HICs has not narrowed**

Three-year moving average

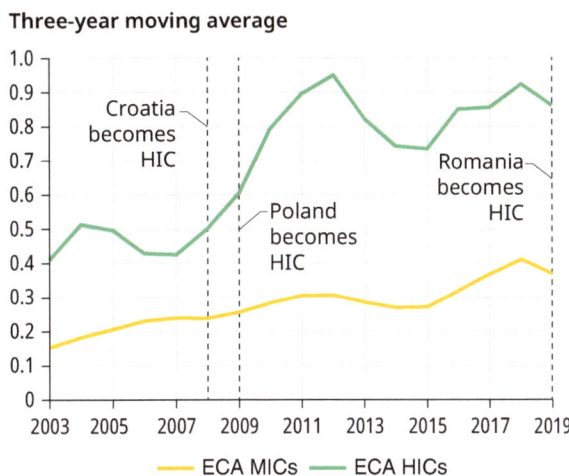

Sources: World Bank calculations; data of PATSTAT (Patent Statistical Database), European Patent Office, Munich, https://www.epo.org/en/searching-for-patents/business/patstat#:~:text=PATSTAT%20contains%20bibliographical%20and%20legal,or%20can%20be%20consulted%20online.

across other areas of innovation (patents related to the environment, renewable energy, and sustainable technologies).[6]

Innovation is a prerequisite, not a result in achieving and maintaining high-income status. Within-firm innovation and experimentation require talented managers and workers, the availability of funds, access to technology and knowledge, incentives to invest, and integration with global markets that offer growth opportunities. The HICs do not outperform the MICs on innovation solely because these complementary factors are more abundant in high-income economies. Examining the three ECA countries that have transitioned to high-income status, one may see that the number of patents per capita was already rising before these countries reached the HIC threshold and continued to increase thereafter.[7]

Economies and firms require key complementary factors to boost innovation. Improving the quality of management, deepening capital markets, investing in human capital, and creating a more dynamic, enabling business environment are crucial in spurring innovation, and these areas allow substantial room for improvement among ECA countries, especially MICs. Moreover, a broad spectrum of public interventions has been shown to crowd in private R&D investments and enhance innovation outcomes among firms, but these require that beneficiary firms have the required capabilities to perform innovative activities.[8]

Financial Market Development and Access to Finance

The ECA countries underperform on investment relative to the MICs globally. Gross fixed capital formation as a share of GDP in the ECA is consistently below that of countries at similar incomes, and the gap has widened since the global financial crisis in 2007–09. Among firms, lower investment leads to lower capital intensity. Modern capital and machinery are important because they represent embedded knowledge, and paltry investment means that firms must rely on older technologies that are not at the industry frontier (Keller 2000).

ECA credit markets are less well developed relative to European peers, and this hinders investment in innovation and technology adoption. The ECA countries rank below the median in credit access distribution, and most are at the bottom of the scale (refer to figure 2.4). Among the small number of firms that do have access to long-term debt financing, the share of debt financing capital (the long-term debt-to-assets ratio) is small, indicating the need to develop long-term credit markets. Absent any long-term financing, firms must rely on their own funds and short-term commercial bank credit for investment. This usually finances working capital rather than the acquisition of tangible and nontangible assets. Additionally, efficient capital markets that allocate resources to high-potential entrepreneurs and businesses require an institutional context that provides appropriate incentives, such as profits, long-term stability, and access to markets (Nanda and Rhodes-Kropf 2016).

FIGURE 2.4 Relatively few ECA firms access long-term financing

Share of firms (%) / ratio

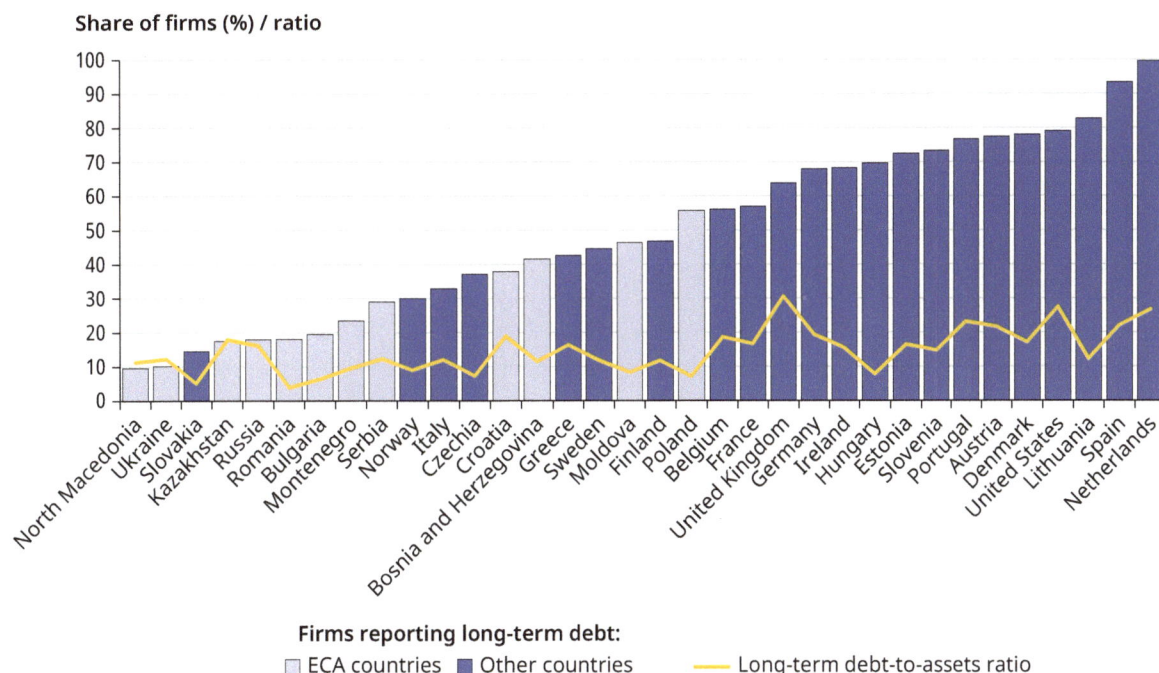

Firms reporting long-term debt:
☐ ECA countries ■ Other countries ── Long-term debt-to-assets ratio

Source: World Bank elaboration based on data of Orbis (portal), Moody's, New York, https://www.moodys.com/web/en/us
/capabilities/company-reference-data/orbis.html.

Note: Average 2010–19. Countries with at least 1,000 firms per year are considered.

The ECA countries need to boost the role of venture capital to foster the emergence of innovative entrepreneurs (Didier and Cusolito 2024). Venture capitalists typically focus on investments in start-ups, innovative businesses, and early-stage growth firms that they believe have long-term growth potential in that they are developing cutting-edge technology and creating innovative business models. Because these entrepreneurs and firms usually struggle to gain access to commercial bank loans, venture capital is crucial if they are to expand quickly. Per capita venture capital funding rates in the ECA region, especially among the MICs, are extremely low in absolute and relative terms, demonstrating that venture capital funding is underdeveloped (refer to figure 2.5).

Besides the depth of the financial sector, the efficiency of credit allocation is critical in realizing productivity gains. Productivity and innovation require credit to be channeled to firms with better growth prospects and higher productivity. Yet, more productive firms do not always have access to credit. Evidence from World Bank Enterprise Surveys shows that, even though companies that accessed credit were, on average, more productive than those that applied for it but were rejected, a considerable share of credit-constrained firms, that is, those unable to access

FIGURE 2.5 Venture capital is underdeveloped in the ECA region

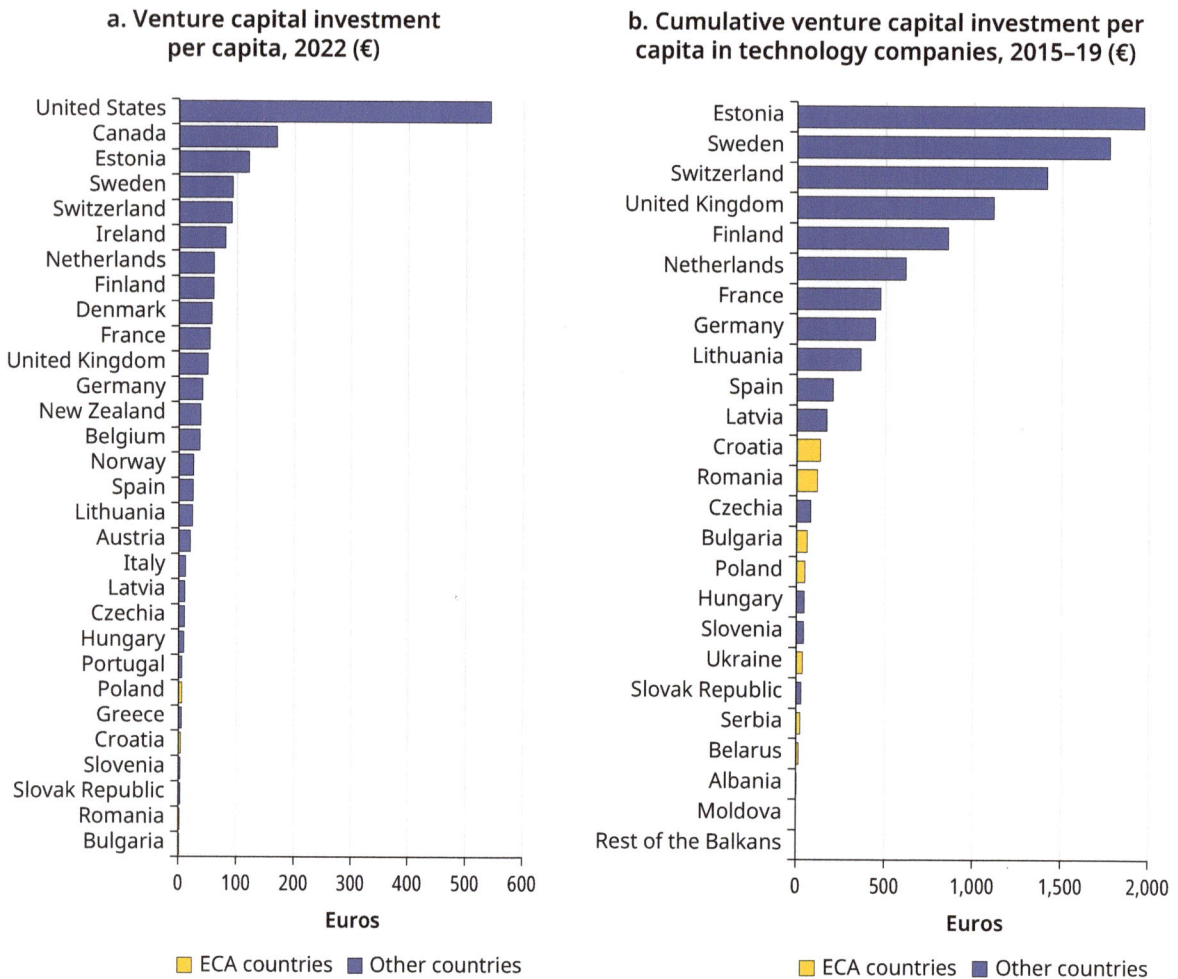

a. Venture capital investment per capita, 2022 (€)

b. Cumulative venture capital investment per capita in technology companies, 2015–19 (€)

ECA countries   Other countries

Sources: World Bank elaboration based on 2021 data of Dealroom, https://dealroom.net/; 2022 data of Organisation for Economic Co-operation and Development.

credit, exhibit similar or even higher productivity relative to those with access.[9] This conclusion was formally assessed through an econometric analysis, which found that, while, on average, more productive firms are more likely to obtain credit in ECA countries, this is driven by efficient credit allocation among relatively inefficient firms, defined as those below the median. Meanwhile, firms with productivity above the median are associated with lower access to credit.

Banks seem good at screening out bad projects, but often fail to identify good ones. This task becomes more challenging as economic complexity increases and projects come to involve more risk, but also potentially more innovation and reward. Reversing misallocation may be crucial in boosting the transition from middle- to high-income status in the region. Cusolito et al. (2024) find that hypothetical productivity gains from the efficient allocation of finance is 20 percent to 80 percent in most European countries, with the highest gains in ECA MICs and HICs.[10]

Management Capacities

Management capacity and business organization account for a large share of the productivity differences between firms and countries. Enhancing these elements should lead to more productive and innovative firms (Cirera and Maloney 2017). The role of management within firms has been extensively investigated. The results suggest that management practices account for nearly 30 percent of the productivity differences across countries and 20 percent of the productivity differences within countries (Bloom, Sadun, and Van Reenen 2016; Bloom and Van Reenen 2010). In Croatia, an increase among firms in management quality from the 10th to the 90th percentile is associated with a 36 percent rise in labor productivity and a 32 percent gain in profit margins (Grover, Iacovone, and Chakraborty 2019).

Management practices are a technology whereby the quality of management is an element of intangible capital that increases output (Bloom, Sadun, and Van Reenen 2016). Improved management capacity and business capabilities help firms undertake more investment in modern technology and become more innovative. The capacity of firms to adopt and exploit technologies depends greatly on management and organization (Cirera, Comin, and Cruz 2022; Cirera and Maloney 2017). Management decisions, such as adopting performance-based rewards systems, influence the motivation and behavior of employees, which translates into firm-level innovation outcomes (de Jong and den Hartog 2007; Ederer and Manso 2013; Leiblein and Madsen 2009). Similarly, firms with better management and organization are more likely to adopt more sophisticated technology and to innovate (Grover, Iacovone, and Chakraborty 2019).

In the ECA, too, well-managed firms are more likely to innovate and to experiment with and adopt technology from foreign firms, and management quality is positively associated with the innovative behavior of the firms. Evidence from the World Bank Enterprise Surveys on selected ECA countries shows that the share of firms investing in R&D and of firms using technologies licensed by a foreign-owned company increases with management quality, even after accounting for industry and country effects and for the size and age of the firms.[11] Firms at the bottom of the management quality distribution are half as likely to invest in R&D as firms at the top of the distribution, even if they operate in the same country and industry and are similar in size and age.

Market Competition

Market competition is crucial for business dynamism, boosting firm and sector performance. When firms compete neck and neck, they escape competition through innovation and upgrading (Iacovone, Pereira López, and Schiffbauer 2023). By developing new products or increasing the quality of existing ones, enterprises can charge higher prices or reduce costs relative to noninnovating firms. In this Schumpeterian framework, in which innovation stems from entrepreneurial investment and replaces old technologies, entrants (1) put additional pressure on incumbent firms to lower prices and innovate and (2) benefit consumers with lower product prices and higher quality, and the business environment with higher productivity and innovation (Aghion 2017). Incumbents, however, respond by delaying the entry of potential competitors. This is the reason why new firms and talented entrepreneurs are vital for innovation and economic growth and why economic policy and institutions should bolster business dynamism (Akcifit, Pearce, and Prato 2020; Murphy, Shleifer, and Vishny 1991). The rest of this subsection assesses the influence of various measures of competition on employment and productivity dynamics in ECA countries.

Pro-competition policy is positively correlated with income per capita. The market organization criterion score in the Transformation Atlas measures the fundamentals of market-based competition and the stability of competition rules (refer to figure 2.6, panel a). The Organisation for Economic Co-operation and Development's product market regulation indicators measure the regulatory obstacles that discourage the entry of firms and competition (refer to figure 2.6, panel b). Product market regulation scores are lower among the HICs, indicating that firms in these countries face lower barriers to entry and expansion. In the ECA region, the HICs outperform the MICs both on the market organization criterion score and the product market regulation indicators. Thus, the ECA HICs have improved the competition environment, which is consistent with their greater firm dynamism and better innovation intensity outcomes.

FIGURE 2.6 **MICs tend to have worse product market regulation and therefore less competition**

a. Market organization score

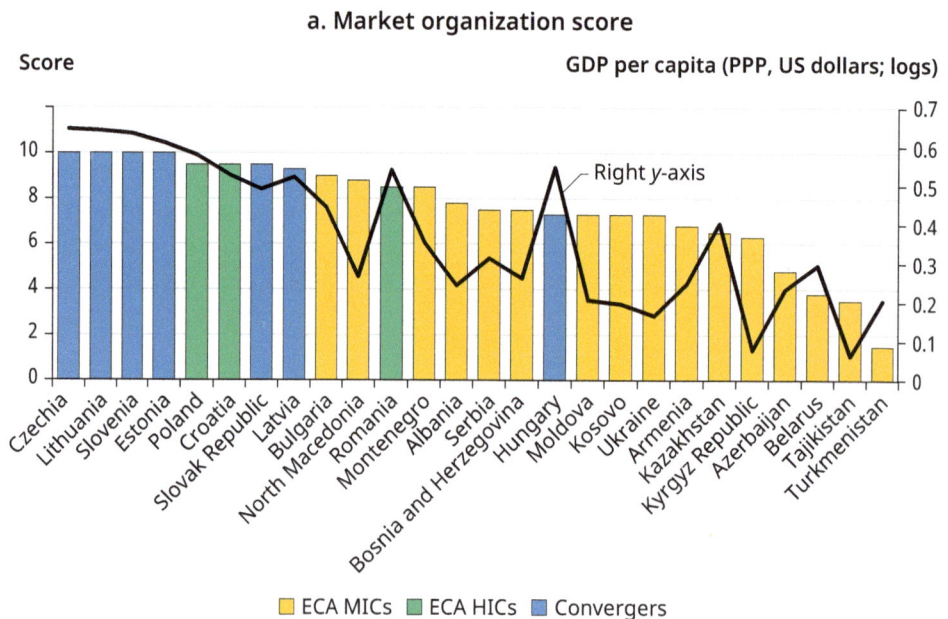

Continued

FIGURE 2.6 **MICs tend to have worse product market regulation and therefore less competition** *(Continued)*

b. Production market regulation

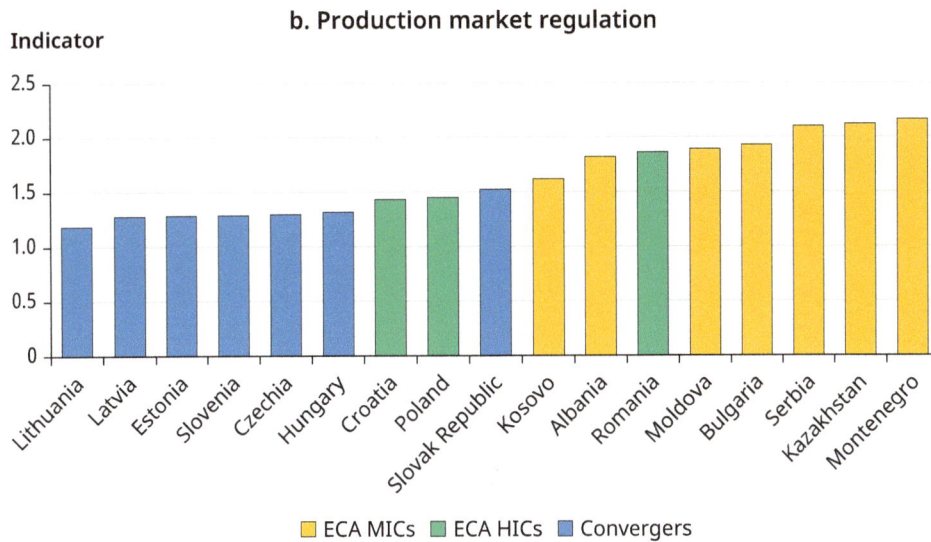

Sources: World Bank elaboration based on data of BTI (Bertelsmann Stiftung) Transformation Atlas (dashboard, Bertelsmann Stiftung, Gütersloh, Germany, https://bti-project.org/en/atlas; PMR (Product Market Regulation) (dashboard), Organisation for Economic Co-operation and Development, Paris, https://www.oecd.org/en/topics/product-market-regulation.html.

Note: PPP = purchasing power parity.

Market concentration is lower in the ECA HICs than in the ECA MICs, which is consistent with the presence of more efficient markets among the former. The Herfindahl-Hirschman index gauges the competition environment by measuring the distribution of market shares across firms (Herfindahl 1950; Hirschman 1964).[12] ECA HICs, Bulgaria, and Georgia rank at the bottom of the index score relative to the MICs, suggesting that enterprises in these countries operate in less concentrated markets, which typically allow for a higher degree of contestability and greater incentives to compete and innovate (refer to figure 2.7).

Trade openness is a vital element in enhancing competition among firms, especially firms producing tradable goods (Autor, Dorn, and Hanson 2013, 2016; Iacovone, Rauch, and Winters 2013). The logistics performance index measures the quality of trade- and transport-related infrastructure, the efficiency of customs and border management clearance, and the overall quality of logistics services.[13] ECA countries, both MICs and HICs, underperform on logistics relative to EU countries. Even within the region, there are notable differences between MICs and HICs. The HICs show better performance. In the last 15 years, the region has made progress on logistics competitiveness, but the gap between MICs and HICs persists, even slightly widening. Tariffs are notably higher in the MICs than in the HICs. The tariffs

FIGURE 2.7 ECA MICs tend to exhibit greater market concentration

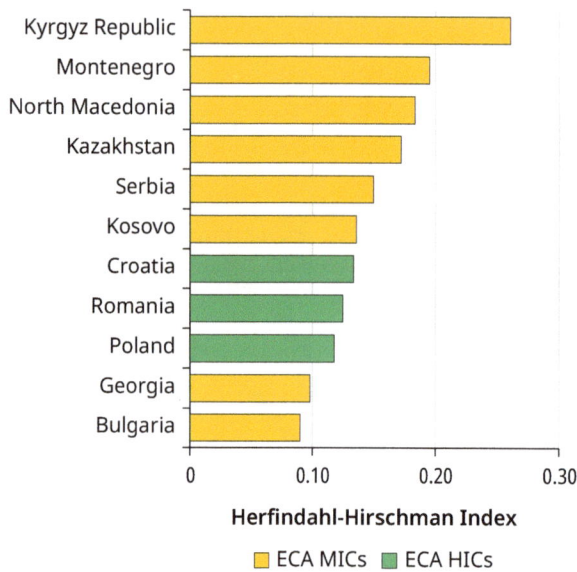

Herfindahl-Hirschman Index

■ ECA MICs ■ ECA HICs

Sources: World Bank elaboration based on data of national statistical institutes; Orbis (portal), Moody's, New York, https://www.moodys.com/web/en/us/capabilities/company-reference-data/orbis.html.

in the HICs are in line with the average in EU countries, the United Kingdom, and the United States even though the ECA MICs have lowered tariffs substantially in the last 15 years.[14]

The Forces of Preservation: Small Firms and Incumbent SOEs

ECA countries do not lack businesses, but have too many small, low-productivity firms, often a result of regulatory policies, governance issues, or limited capabilities. Most ECA countries also lack very large companies. There are legacy SOEs, some of them large, and large, newly established enterprises, such as retailers, banks, and others. There are typically no very large firms, however. This is the reason for the emphasis here on the need for comprehensive policies that also focus on top companies and help them realize productivity growth and innovation.

The Business Ecosystem in ECA: Too Many Small, Low-Productivity Firms

In ECA countries, there is a substantial number of businesses per capita, but active enterprises generate less employment than might be expected based on their income and even less compared with HICs. The ECA countries have an average of nearly 30 enterprises per 1,000 inhabitants, more than comparable upper-middle-income countries, such as Brazil and Costa Rica (14 and 13 firms per 1,000 inhabitants, respectively), more than Germany (29 per 1,000 inhabitants), and much more than the United States (16 per 1,000 inhabitants). Despite the similar or greater firm density relative to Germany and the United States, ECA firms generate far less employment, a pattern especially marked across the ECA MICs. Employment density in the MICs is lower than in countries with similar business density (refer to figure 2.8). This is because MICs businesses do not expand sufficiently.

FIGURE 2.8 ECA MICs: employment density is low because firms do not expand sufficiently

Employment density (employees per 1,000 population)

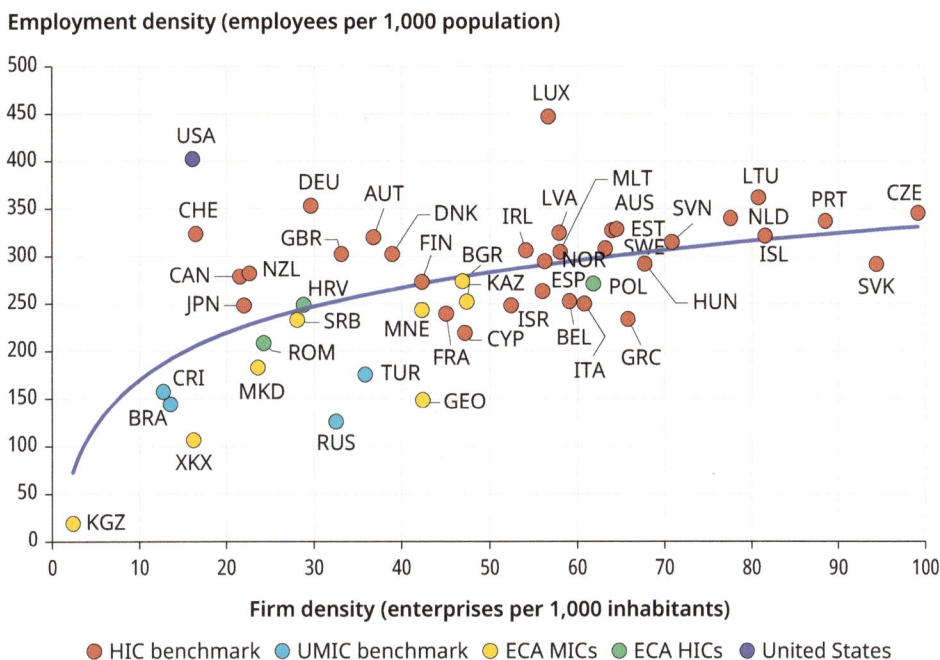

Firm density (enterprises per 1,000 inhabitants)

● HIC benchmark ○ UMIC benchmark ○ ECA MICs ● ECA HICs ● United States

Sources: World Bank elaboration based on data of national statistical institutes; OECD; Orbis (portal), Moody's, New York, https://www.moodys.com/web/en/us/capabilities/company-reference-data/orbis.html.

Note: The HIC benchmark involves selected high-income OECD and EU member countries. UMICs = selected upper-middle-income countries based on data availability. Firm counts and employment are cross-checked with published data on the web portals of national statistical institutes. For country abbreviations, refer to International Organization for Standardization (ISO), https://www.iso.org/obp/ui/#search. NACE = Statistical Classification of Economic Activities in the European Community.

Firms generate more employment in the ECA HICs. Adjusted by firm density, employment density is higher in ECA HICs Croatia and Poland, though it is as high as expected in ECA HIC Romania. This contrasts with the ECA MICs, such as Georgia, Kosovo, Kyrgyz Republic, Montenegro, and North Macedonia, where the number of jobs per capita generated by firms is significantly below the expected employment density. This finding suggests that firms in the ECA HICs face lower barriers to growth. According to a neo-Schumpeterian framework, as firms realize their productivity potential through innovation and technology adoption, their growth leads to the displacement of low-productivity firms that eventually exit the market. In the presence of market distortions and barriers to firm growth, however, firms enter the market and do not grow (Acemoglu and Restrepo 2018; Aghion, 2017; Baumol 1990).

SMEs exhibit lower labor productivity in the ECA region than in the EU, underscoring the importance of enhancing the capabilities of the ECA SMEs for income transition. Across all size classes of enterprises, ECA businesses show significantly lower labor productivity relative to businesses in selected HICs, such as Denmark, France, Italy, and the United Kingdom (refer to figure 2.9). For instance, a worker in an ECA microfirm generates half the value added of a worker in an enterprise of similar size in Germany and even less than counterparts among microfirms in France or the United Kingdom. Workers in small ECA companies (10–49 employees) produce 30 percent to 80 percent of the value added of equivalent workers in small German firms. This productivity gap persists at similar magnitude across midsize firms, indicating pervasive productivity disparities between ECA and EU businesses. Inefficient firms are less competitive in international markets, impeding their integration in global value chains, and are less likely to access financial resources to upgrade technology and equipment. To become more productive, ECA firms need to invest in their productive capacities.[15] A healthy business environment is crucial for rewarding such investments.

FIGURE 2.9 **MIC micro-, small, and medium enterprises are less productive**

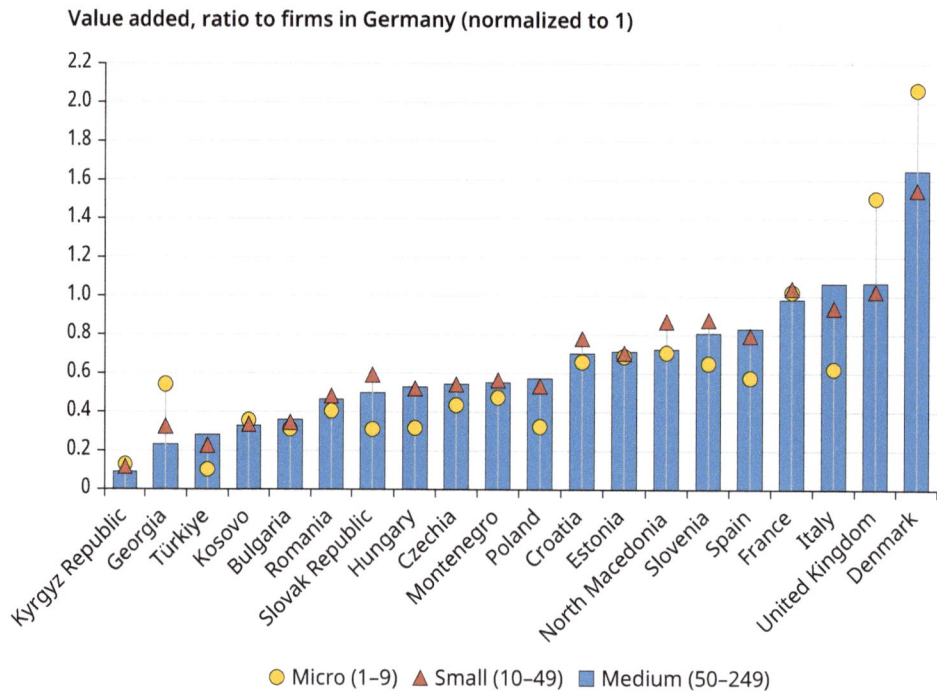

Value added, ratio to firms in Germany (normalized to 1)

● Micro (1–9)   ▲ Small (10–49)   ■ Medium (50–249)

Sources: World Bank elaboration based on data of national statistical institutes; EC 2008; NAICS (North American Industry Classification System) (database), US Census Bureau, Suitland, MD, https://www.census.gov/naics/.

Note: ECA country data are cross-checked with official data published by national statistical agencies. The original values are expressed in euros using the latest information for comparability.

The ECA Lacks Very Large Companies

Medium and large firms—that is, firms with at least 50 employees—are less relevant in employment in the ECA region than among the HICs. Although such firms usually represent a small share of enterprises, they account for a large segment of employment. In the region, their more limited relevance derives either because they are fewer in number or because they are smaller, with lower average employment among firms with at least 50 employees.

In most ECA countries, the labor share of medium and large firms is in the range of 40 percent to 50 percent. This is smaller than the share in EU countries, such as Denmark, France, Germany, and the Netherlands, and the share in the United Kingdom and the United States, where three jobs in four are in such firms. Compared with the United States especially, the labor share of large companies is low (this is also the case relative to what might be expected in a typical Pareto distribution). Firms with fewer than five employees account for 20 percent of employment in the ECA MICs and 15 percent in the ECA HICs, but around 5 percent in the United States. These variations are not evident only in microfirms, but also in larger companies. For instance, firms with fewer than 500 employees account for 80 percent of employment in the ECA MICs and 73 percent in the ECA HICs, but only 47 percent in the United States.[16]

The ECA problem arises because of the lack of large firms and of medium firms that grow into large ones rather than to a putative missing middle, that is, a lack of midsize firms (Abreha et al. 2023). The missing middle hypothesis is often associated with evidence of distortions introduced by business regulations, tax thresholds (higher taxes that kick in if a specified size threshold is reached), and policy support programs that create incentives for small firms to remain small, while favoring large incumbent businesses. The analysis reported here formally explored this hypothesis following a methodology proposed by Teal (2023) and Tybout (2014) that compares the observed employment shares across firms of varying size and the shares predicted by a Pareto distribution.[17] The analysis found that, in most ECA countries, there is an excess labor share accounted for by SMEs and a shortage of very large firms (here defined, respectively, as firms with 1–249 employees and at least 500 employees; refer to figure 2.10). These observed differences become more visible at lower country income levels, suggesting that the problem of missing large firms is more accentuated among the ECA MICs.[18]

These findings should not be interpreted as a call to promote national champions and subsidize large businesses. On the contrary, the evidence suggests that it is crucial for governments to focus on addressing the constraints to growth faced by companies with high-growth potential through the set of policies recommended in this report, such as expanding access to global markets, attracting foreign direct investment, deepening financial markets, and developing robust equity markets.

FIGURE 2.10 ECA countries have too little employment in large firms—the missing large problem

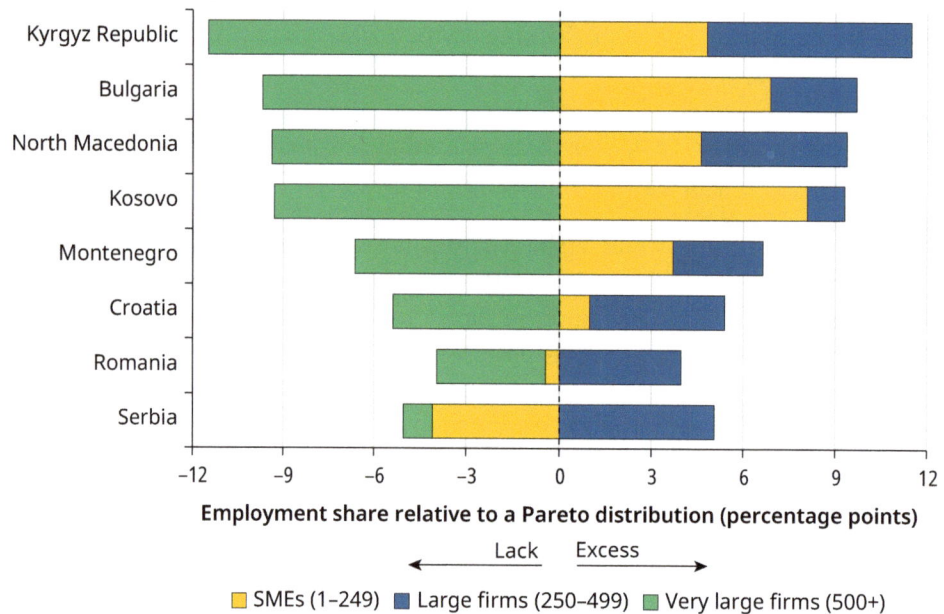

Employment share relative to a Pareto distribution (percentage points)

Lack   Excess

☐ SMEs (1–249) ■ Large firms (250–499) ■ Very large firms (500+)

Sources: World Bank calculations based on national statistical institutes; EC 2008; Orbis (portal), Moody's, New York, https://www.moodys.com/web/en/us/capabilities/company-reference-data /orbis.html.

Note: Shown is the share of employment in each size bin relative to the employment share predicted by a Pareto distribution. Positive bars suggest an excess of employment in the size bin, while negative bars indicate a lack of employment in the size bin compared with a Pareto distribution prediction.

It is likewise essential to take account of the need for better market functioning and for eliminating the preferential treatment provided to SOEs or connected businesses.

Trouble at the Top: Zooming in on Large ECA Companies

The presence of highly productive large firms in an economy indicates a dynamic environment in which innovation is occurring and small and large firms coexist symbiotically (World Bank 2024). Large firms typically invest more in management capacities and innovation, hire highly skilled workers in greater numbers, and learn continuously about new production technologies and goods by participating in global markets. However, in economies characterized by limited growth opportunities and by distortions in market functioning, such as limited competition, large firms may seek to exploit their market power and buttress the privileged position they enjoy thanks to access to finance or to procurement contracts rather than promoting innovation and productivity growth (De Loecker, Eeckhout, and Unger 2020). In such contexts, large firms do not show exceptional performance and do not drive growth. Instead, they may display productivity on a par with SMEs. In contrast, in competitive, dynamic business environments, larger firms innovate, become more productive, and grow to escape competition and raise profitability.

In the ECA region, however, larger size is not necessarily associated with greater productivity. This is especially true in the ECA MICs. Although sales per worker tend to rise with firm size in the region, the relation between labor productivity and employment is negative among the ECA MICs beyond a certain size threshold (refer to figure 2.11). Sales per worker increase with employment up to a certain point in firms with fewer than 50 employees, but remain flat or even decline in firms with more than 50 employees. For example, a worker in a firm with around 350–400 employees in the ECA MICs produces as much in sales as a worker in a firm with 20–30 employees. By contrast, across the ECA HICs, the association between productivity and size is always positive.

In the MICs, the labor productivity premium among larger firms is driven by capital intensity rather than by superior overall efficiency. This suggests that these firms have easier access to credit, but do not use resources more efficiently than smaller firms. In both MICs and HICs, capital intensity (assets per worker) is positively correlated with firm size in line with previous results on labor productivity.[19]

FIGURE 2.11 Larger firms are not always more productive in the ECA MICs

Sales per worker residuals

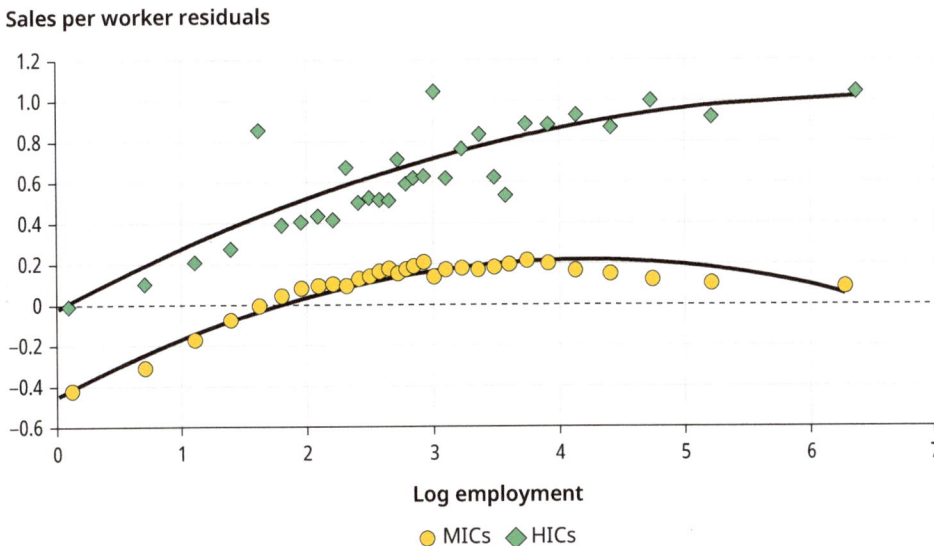

Log employment

○ MICs ◆ HICs

Sources: World Bank elaboration based on data of national statistical institutes; Orbis (portal), Moody's, New York, https://www.moodys.com/web/en/us/capabilities/company-reference-data /orbis.html.

Note: Binscatter of sales per worker and firm employment level (both in logs). The number of bins is set to 100. The data show sales per worker residuals from regressing the log of sales per worker on capital per worker (in logs) and 3-digit sector fixed effects, year effects, and ownership controls.

In the MICs, however, total factor productivity (TFP) declines with size among firms with more than 20 employees. This contrasts with the HICs, which show a positive association. Thus, while in the HICs, larger companies are more capital intensive and use production factors more efficiently, higher sales per worker among larger firms in the MICs are explained by the stock of assets per worker rather than overall efficiency. Examining country-specific patterns confirms that large firms in the region exhibit higher labor productivity, scale (intermediate consumption per worker), and capital intensity than SMEs, but that they are not necessarily more efficient in using factors of production.

Large firms in the region are far from the global frontier, indicating that policy should also focus on helping these firms catch up through innovation and upgraded capabilities (Brown et al. 2016). The labor productivity gap between ECA and European HIC businesses is considerable. It is even wider among the ECA MICs (refer to figure 2.12). For example, one worker in Bulgaria, Georgia, Kosovo, the Kyrgyz Republic, Montenegro, or Türkiye produces roughly only 10 percent to 40 percent of the value added produced by a worker in the average large

FIGURE 2.12 **The labor productivity gap with Germany is considerable**

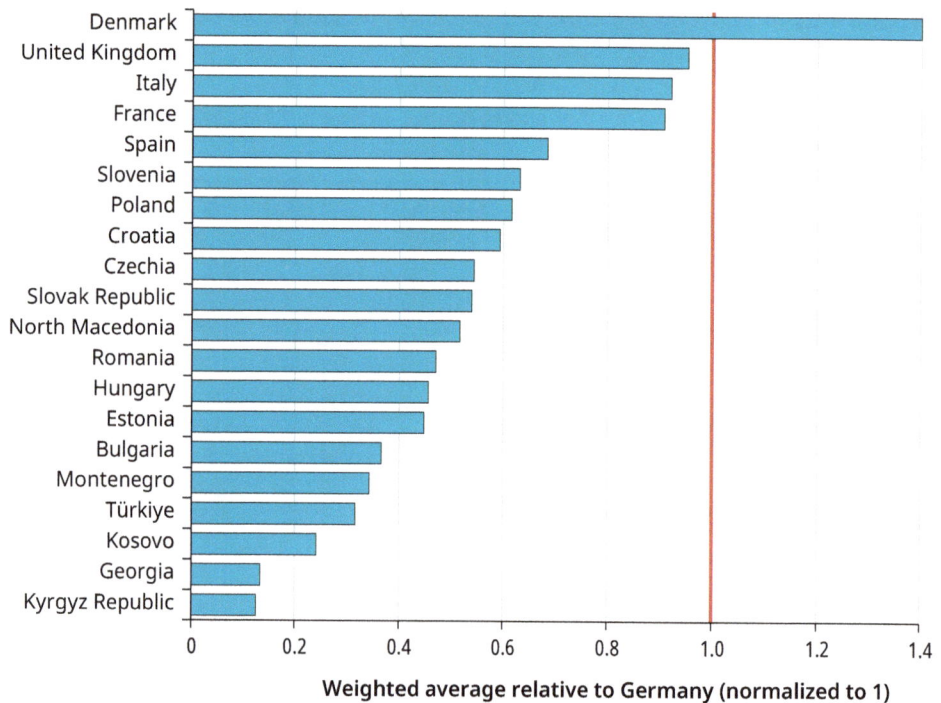

Weighted average relative to Germany (normalized to 1)

Sources: World Bank elaboration based on data of national statistical institutes; EC 2008; Orbis (portal), Moody's, New York, https://www.moodys.com/web/en/us/capabilities/company -reference-data/orbis.html.

Note: Firms with at least 250 employees are considered. For comparability purposes, labor productivity is defined as value added per worker (sales net of intermediate consumption). Countries are selected according to information availability.

firm in Germany. Among the ECA HICs, these differences are still relevant, albeit much smaller. The average worker in a large Croatian or Polish firm produces nearly 60 percent of the value added produced by the average worker in a British, German, French, or Italian firm. The labor productivity gap between the ECA and high-income European countries is likely to be driven by both more limited access to capital and lower firm efficiency, explained by factors correlated with productivity, such as innovation, management capacities, and technology-absorption capabilities. Policy should therefore not focus only on smaller firms, but should also consider interventions that help larger businesses become more innovative and compete in global markets.

The top and the largest ECA firms underperform. Policy therefore needs to focus not only on the left tail of the firm distribution (the presence of many unproductive SMEs), but also on the right tail (the lack of dynamism and innovation). Relying on Orbis data, this subsection examines the performance of the top 100 companies by sales in ECA, several other European countries, and the United States.[20] The analysis reveals that the top 100 firms in the ECA MICs and HICs are not global innovators and perform less well than the top 100 firms in Europe and the United States.

The top 100 companies in each ECA country are far less productive and exhibit lower capital intensity relative to the top EU and US firms. For instance, one worker in the average top ECA firm produces half the value added generated by the same worker in the average top EU firm and two-fifths of the value added produced in a top US firm (refer to figure 2.13). Part of these differences are likely to be driven by tangible and intangible capital intensity, even though the labor productivity disparities are greater than the disparities in tangible assets per worker. Indeed, the value of tangible assets per worker in the average top firm in the ECA MICs and HICs is around two-thirds the corresponding value in the EU and the United States.

The top ECA firms in the MICs and HICs are not global innovators. Businesses move the technological frontier as they experiment, invest in R&D, and innovate. With improved capabilities, better access to finance, and stronger market positions, top firms can invest more resources in R&D and typically drive private innovation. Yet, the innovation behavior of top ECA MIC and HIC firms contrasts with that observed in the EU and the United States. Differences in the amount of intangible assets per worker are striking. Specifically, the endowment of intangible assets per employee among the average top 100 firms in the ECA MICs is only 4 percent of the corresponding value in top US firms and 7 percent of the value in top EU firms.[21] Although slightly smaller, the gap is still considerable between the top ECA HIC firms and the top firms in the EU or the United States. Intangible assets per worker in the top ECA HIC firm are one-fifth the level in the top US firm and two-fifths the level in the top EU firm.

FIGURE 2.13 Performance of the top 100 firms in the ECA, the EU, and the United States, 2019

US dollars, thousands

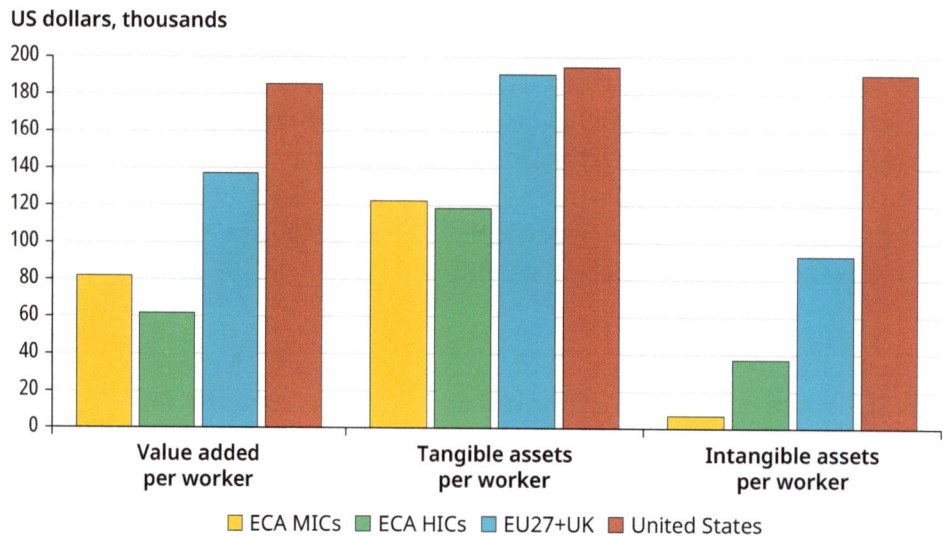

Source: World Bank elaboration based on data of Orbis (portal), Moody's, New York, https://www.moodys.com/web/en/us/capabilities/company-reference-data/orbis.html.

SOEs Dampen Firm, Job, and Productivity Dynamism

SOEs often possess policy mandates that do not correspond to efficiency needs or the profit motive. SOE operations may reflect specific mandates, such as providing the population with essential goods at below-market prices, controlling prices in highly concentrated markets, or providing certain goods or services that would not otherwise be provided under current market conditions. To achieve these mandates, SOEs require special support from governments through subsidies, regulatory benefits, or preferential market conditions, which may discourage incentives favoring efficiency and productivity improvements and create market distortions in the competition between SOEs and private firms. SOEs may therefore affect the functioning of markets and influence private employment and productivity (Cirera, Brolhato, and Martins-Neto 2023; Dall'Olio et al. 2022; Ferro and Patiño Peña 2023; World Bank 2023).

To gauge the presence of SOEs, the analysis involved the computation of the share of firms and the share of SOEs in a market (3-digit sector and Nomenclature of Territorial Units for Statistics, level 3 combinations).[22] It is regressed on indicators of firm, job, and productivity dynamics on the presence of SOEs.[23] It determined that a greater presence of SOEs dampens firm entry, especially in more competitive sectors, which ultimately means lower experimentation and fewer entrepreneurs.[24]

SOEs may affect entrepreneurial behavior and start-up rates because firms may base entry decisions on future expected profits, and a greater presence of SOEs may reduce profits. The analysis results show that firm dynamism is negatively associated with SOE presence.[25] A greater presence of SOEs is associated with significantly lower entry rates in competitive sectors and in sectors characterized by a lower degree of competition (natural monopolies or partly contestable markets). A 10 percentage point increase in the share of SOEs is associated with a nearly 1.5 percentage point lower entry rate in competitive and noncompetitive markets. If the labor share of SOEs is used, the magnitude of the results is slightly smaller; entry rates are lower by 0.4 percentage points. Competitive markets seem to be affected by SOEs regardless of how SOE presence is measured, by the share of firms, labor, or market share. A higher share of SOEs in the market also reduces exit, affecting overall business dynamism and market selection. Exit rates in the ECA region tend to decline if markets include a larger proportion of SOEs.

Because of lower entry and exit rates, the presence of SOEs is negatively associated with lower net entry (entry rates, minus exit rates) in competitive sectors, meaning that, in naturally competitive industries, SOEs prevent entry and distort market-selection mechanisms. In the same vein, the presence of SOEs is negatively associated with firm churning, which is usually a proxy for entrepreneurial dynamism and is correlated with lower business turnover rates.[26] The estimated effects of SOEs across the region are similar between ECA MICs and HICs, suggesting that SOEs affect firm dynamism in a similar manner across these economies, irrespective of country income.

SOE presence in the region also dampens job dynamism, especially in competitive industries. Job-rich growth is crucial to reducing poverty and increasing welfare in the region. Empirical analysis suggests that greater exposure to SOEs is associated with lower gross and net job creation, as well as lower job churning (job creation, plus job destruction) in competitive sectors. For instance, a 10 percentage point greater presence of SOEs in competitive sectors is correlated with a 0.4 percentage point lower gross job creation rate and 1.2–2.2 percentage points lower job churning rates, while, in natural monopoly industries or partly contestable sectors, these effects tend to be negative, but not statistically significant.

SOEs are also associated with slower productivity growth in competitive sectors. To assess this aspect, the analysis examined the impact of SOE presence on various measures of productivity at the market level, that is, sales per worker, value added per worker, and TFP. Each specification controls for market fixed effects. The result should therefore be interpreted in terms of changes in the productivity growth rate. SOE presence systematically slows productivity growth in competitive industries, but does not affect natural monopoly or partly contestable sectors. Negative effects on competitive sectors become larger in absolute terms if exposure is measured using the labor or market share of SOEs instead of the firm share, which suggests that the market influence of SOEs rather than the relative number of SOEs sways productivity growth.

SOE presence in ECA markets significantly affects firm, job, and productivity dynamism, especially in competitive industries. A top priority of ECA governments should therefore be to assess carefully the rationale for promoting SOEs, especially in contestable sectors, and consider that the presence of SOEs may be accompanied by significant costs in economic dynamism and business growth.

Understanding Firm Dynamism and Job Creation

Business dynamism is critical to growth. Transitioning to high-income status requires creative destruction, a shift from a 1*i* strategy to a 2*i* strategy and then to a 3*i* strategy of innovation-led growth supported by entrepreneurial dynamism and productivity catch-up. Creative destruction occurs as unproductive and unprofitable firms exit, while more productive and higher potential businesses enter and grow (Aghion 2017; Akcigit and Ates 2021; Akcigit and Kerr 2018; Caballero and Hammour 1994; Schumpeter 1942).

This section analyzes how business size and age drive employment dynamics. The main findings are as follows: (1) ECA firms show stunted job growth and rarely upscale; (2) start-ups and young SMEs are the main contributors to net job creation in the region; (3) mature SMEs destroy more jobs than they create; and (4) SOEs dampen dynamism. These findings suggest that, instead of focusing on increasing the number of businesses, policy should focus on alleviating business growth constraints, particularly among start-ups and young firms, if their growth potential is higher and they face specific constraints, such as access to finance. Policy should also support an environment that promotes selection, in addition to experimentation, through efficient bankruptcy procedures.

Business Size at Entry and Growth Postentry

New businesses entering the market are small. So, improving the business environment by reducing distortive regulations, enhancing credit access, lowering trade barriers, and upgrading firm capabilities may encourage the entry of larger, more capital-intensive, and riskier innovative projects. Start-ups in ECA countries enter the market at half the size of their peers in the United States, suggesting that ECA barriers to entry are low, but also that business openings may be driven more by necessity than by market opportunities. Indeed, new businesses average almost six employees in the United States and between three and five in ECA countries and between three and four in most ECA HICs (refer to figure 2.14).

The size gap between start-ups and companies older than four years is significantly smaller in ECA countries than in the United States, implying that ECA firms grow less than US firms over the life cycle. In the United States, the average size of firms older than four years is six times that of new firms, which indicates the growth

FIGURE 2.14 ECA firms show stunted job growth

Number of employees

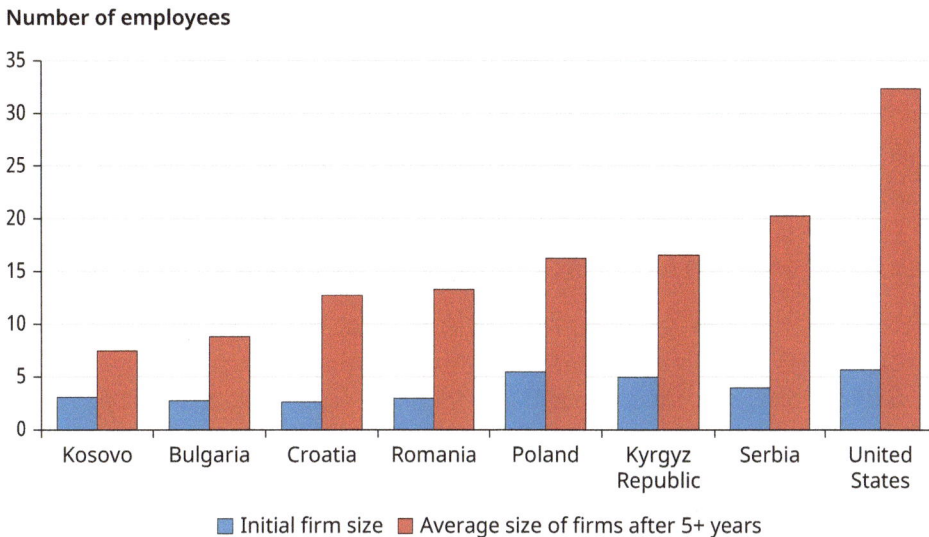

Sources: World Bank elaboration based on data of national statistical institutes; Orbis (portal), Moody's, New York, https://www.moodys.com/web/en/us/capabilities/company-reference-data /orbis.html.

Note: Although the average size of entrants is above five in Poland, filing business registries is not mandatory among microfirms, which increases the average size of the observed sample of firms. The minimum size threshold in Poland may therefore be considered as five employees.

potential of survivors. In the ECA countries, the size differences are far narrower, averaging less than four employees.[27] In short, not only do US firms enter the market at a larger size, but also grow considerably more than ECA firms. The US business environment (the quality of regulations, red tape and bureaucracy, and incentive programs), plus access to capital (even among risky projects), market access, and finding appropriate skilled workers all determine the growth potential of US firms and endogenously lead to the emergence of new businesses that are not driven by necessity, but by opportunity.

Postentry employment growth is stunted in ECA countries, indicating the existence of constraints to business expansion. Firms make entry decisions based on expected profits and market conditions, but, if they enter, they face uncertainty about market demand and their own level of efficiency (Hopenhayn 1992). Supported by efficient market-selection mechanisms, more productive start-ups may survive and expand, while unproductive start-ups shrink and exit. In the ECA region, limited job growth, coupled with the small size of firms at market entry, means that businesses rarely create jobs in volume. At the same time, growth volatility decreases only slightly among older cohorts.[28] Besides sluggish employment expansion, such volatility remains high among older cohorts, suggesting that market selection may not be operating efficiently. If markets are functioning efficiently, growth dispersion tends to be higher among younger cohorts, but, as firms mature and learn about their relative efficiency and market conditions, firms with higher growth opportunities should expand, while others should contract and exit. As firms become older, this discovery process typically slows, and growth volatility declines, but, apparently, this is not happening in ECA countries.

ECA Firms Only Rarely Transition to Larger Size Classifications

Only a few ECA firms scale up their operations substantially, confirming the presence of obstacles to expansion. In well-functioning competitive markets, incumbent firms that survive over long periods are likely to grow as they become more productive. The focus of the analysis here is on transition between different-size groups—scaling-up—among ECA firms that survive at least five years.[29] Only a small share of ECA firms transition to higher bins, especially among smaller firms.[30] Only firms with 20–29 employees tend to reach a 25 percent probability of climbing to a higher class. The probability falls by half among firms with more than 100 employees.

ECA HIC firms are more likely to scale up than ECA MIC firms, suggesting that the latter face more obstacles. After assessing the probability of such a transition and considering the sectoral composition of economies and age differences among firms, the analysis finds that the probability of transitioning in the HICs is consistently higher than in the MICs across all employment bins, although the differences are more considerable among the larger size classes. The negative relationship between firm age and employment growth is consistent with the results in transition. Older firms are significantly less likely to transition than start-ups, emphasizing once again the importance of focusing support on start-ups and young businesses to dismantle the barriers to growth.

Jobs

Start-ups and young firms are the main source of net job creation in the region. It is widely recognized that young firms contribute to job creation globally (Criscuolo, Gal, and Menon 2014; Decker et al. 2020; Haltiwanger, Jarmin, and Miranda 2013). Although most employment is in mature and large firms, young businesses disproportionally contribute to job creation (refer to figure 2.15). Start-ups and young SMEs only account for 14 percent of total employment, but they contribute to almost 40 percent of gross job creation. Large businesses also contribute substantially to net job creation. By contrast, mature small and medium businesses destroy more jobs than they create. Among mature micro- and small firms, gross job destruction is disproportionally greater than gross job creation.

FIGURE 2.15 Young firms and start-ups account for nearly half the gross job creation in the economy

Total job creation/total job destruction, %

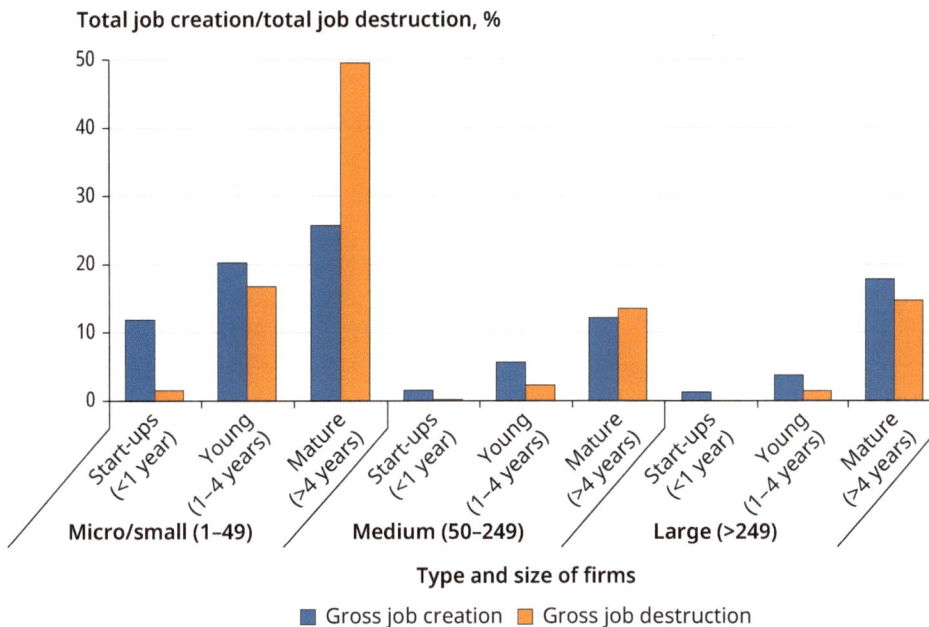

Type and size of firms

■ Gross job creation   ■ Gross job destruction

Sources: World Bank elaboration based on data of national statistical institutes; Orbis (portal), Moody's, New York, https://www.moodys.com/web/en/us/capabilities/company-reference-data /orbis.html.

Note: Share of gross job creation based on the reporting age of firms.

Because start-ups and young firms, rather than SMEs, generally drive ECA job dynamism, current policies and strategies for promoting SMEs should shift toward the start-ups and young firms. This is often difficult because of political economy considerations. But governments must consider ways to support the enterprises that create more jobs and generate more business dynamism. Such a policy shift requires the identification of different targeting criteria and deemphasizing the size criterion as the central parameter of policy design in supporting private firms. The value created, the infusion of foreign technology and capital, and the potential for innovation appear to be better criteria for anchoring policy support and access to finance (Artola and Genre 2011; Beck, Demirgüç-Kunt, and Maksimovic 2005; Beck, Demirgüç-Kunt, and Martínez Pería 2011; Ferrando and Griesshaber 2011; Foster, Haltiwanger, and Syverson 2016).

Conclusions and Policy Recommendations

The ECA MICs have made substantial progress in integrating in global markets and opening up to international trade. The progress in ECA EU member states is more advanced. In these countries, the continued policy emphasis needs to be on the

3i strategy, that is, on spurring innovation, while adopting foreign technology, expertise, and capital to bolster within-firm productivity growth. For the ECA EU candidates, notably, Türkiye and the Western Balkans, the analysis concludes that these countries must continue to stress the infusion of global technology, expertise, and capital, that is, the 2i strategy. Kazakhstan and some countries in the South Caucasus should also focus on the 2i strategy. The resource-rich countries in the region should focus on the fundamentals by promoting the creation of markets, allowing prices to send signals about the value of goods and services, and establishing the conditions for more substantial private sector investment and more private sector dynamism.

Start-ups and young firms face unique challenges. They need targeted support because of the role they play and their potential in job creation. Policy makers should therefore shift their focus away from firm size as a criterion for government support or from increasing the number of businesses to fostering an environment that welcomes the entry of more dynamic and innovative firms and facilitates the growth of such firms. A comprehensive policy package of reforms might center on four pillars: (1) providing incentives through an appropriate competition and regulatory framework; (2) supporting and incentivizing internationalization and integration with the global economy; (3) nurturing innovation and R&D investment among high-productivity firms and the adoption of technology among firms lagging behind the technological frontier; and (4) de-risking entrepreneurial experimentation and learning by easing firm exit procedures and expanding access to risk capital.

Strengthening incentives and the capacities of top-tier and frontier enterprises is crucial. Beyond the discussion on the excessive number of small businesses in the region, which this report confirms, the analysis has uncovered two notable stylized facts. First, the region lacks large, superstar firms, that is, exceptionally large and innovative companies at the global productivity frontier. Second, leading businesses exhibit significant weaknesses. Thus, they do not generate many jobs, and they are not particularly productive and innovative relative to businesses in richer countries, such as the United States. Policy makers must address the quantity, quality, and performance of these top-tier enterprises. The objective is not merely to promote large businesses or national champions. Rather, the objective is to promote innovation and value added growth, as indicated in the first three pillars outlined above.

The ECA countries have relied extensively on structural transformation and the reallocation of market shares within sectors. Now, they need to prioritize infusion (technology upgrading) through a 2i strategy and begin to shift to an innovation-led growth model through a 3i strategy. This chapter proposes two types of policy recommendations: policies to improve the business environment and policies targeting firms.

Policies to Improve the Business Environment

Competition Framework

- Provide a competition framework that ensures market contestability. The business competition environment in the region needs to incentivize the entry of productive, innovative firms, the reallocation of resources toward more productive firms, and the exit of low-productivity firms.

- Promote internationalization and integration with the global economy to expand markets and provide discipline to domestic companies. Lowering trade barriers and expanding integration with the regional and global economy are two key goals associated with the effort to encourage growth, given the knowledge that is embedded in imported goods and technologies and the incentives to innovate and upgrade that accompany the endeavor to supply larger markets.

- Attract knowledge-intensive foreign direct investment to create a more vibrant business ecosystem. Foreign direct investment is a positive input to local development through employment creation, economic growth, and higher wages. It also generates positive spillover effects among local suppliers as they transfer knowledge and technology to domestic firms and require them to upgrade to comply with foreign standards (Bloom, Schankerman, and Van Reenen 2013).

Human Capital, Management Capacities, and Workforce Skills

- Improve capacities and skills through training and business-support initiatives. Innovation in many small firms often involves incremental changes in capability upgrading, including shifts in management capacities. As firms progressively build on their accumulated capabilities, they can gradually undertake more sophisticated investment and innovation activities.

- Improve the environment to attract and retain the talent of highly skilled workers and entrepreneurs (Bernstein et al. 2022; Hunt 2011; Kerr and Pekkala Kerr 2020; Venturini, Montobbio, and Fassi 2012).

- Ensure high-quality education to develop a skilled technology-savvy workforce beginning in early childhood. Chapter 3 presents in more detail recommendations on ways to unleash the talent and abilities of people by improving education systems, from primary school to universities and beyond (Akcigit, Pearce, and Prato 2020; Bianchi and Giorcelli 2019; Toivanen and Väänänen 2016).

Finance

- Deepen capital markets to expand the access of businesses to long-term financing. Robust capital markets are essential to addressing the maturity mismatch between short-term deposits and long-term financing needs. The development of capital markets could help banks raise long-term financing, which could then be extended to firms to support investment. Specific reforms include (1) developing an efficient government securities market; (2) developing a robust regulatory framework in capital markets; (3) strengthening the institutional capacity of capital market regulators and participants; (4) bolstering the regulatory framework to promote the development of new markets and instruments (for instance, the establishment of stock exchanges focused on listing SMEs) and developing new financial instruments, such as venture capital trusts and innovation bonds; and (5) fostering a culture of savings and investment (for example, through financial literacy programs).

- Expand venture capital, which is critical to nurturing innovation, particularly among early-stage companies. Private equity funds and venture capital play a major role in supporting start-ups, young businesses, and high-growth businesses because they transfer financing in combination with expertise and market knowledge that often help commercialize innovative ideas. Specific recommendations to promote the growth of private equity and venture capital include temporary tax incentives for venture capital funds. This has been a feature of successful start-up hubs globally (for instance, in Estonia and Israel). Another area of reform is the debt-equity bias reduction allowance currently under discussion in the EU.

- Address credit misallocation, especially in the case of highly productive firms. Specific policy measures to improve credit allocation efficiency include (1) promoting the development of alternative credit scoring models, (2) enhancing the capacity of financial institutions to assess the growth potential of innovative businesses, and (3) addressing information asymmetries through more effective credit registry systems to secure higher investment in technology upgrading and firm growth.

- Provide guarantees rather than lines of credit. For innovation-related investments by firms, debt financing will be needed along with other types of financing. Especially in contexts in which banks are quite liquid (such as is often the case in ECA countries), credit guarantees can be a more impactful and more market friendly tool to enable lending for innovation-related investments.

Policies Targeting Firms

Innovation

- Provide larger, but more well-targeted R&D incentives to boost private investment in innovation and technology adoption. ECA countries should implement wide innovation policy support, including tax incentives for R&D, tax credits, grants, loans, and subsidies. Among young or smaller firms, support might target specific activities and planned outcomes, while providing additional support through technical advice and collaboration with academics to crowd in private investment (What Works Centre for Local Economic Growth 2015).

- Facilitate de-risk entrepreneurial learning and experimentation to reduce costs by enabling financing for innovative entrepreneurship and reducing downside risks. Access to finance is critical to undertaking risky investments and helping innovative entrepreneurs develop and realize their ideas.

- Shift the traditional policy focus from sustaining incumbents to improving the business environment for start-ups and high-growth businesses. Beyond enabling greater access to financing, policy makers should improve civil justice efficiency, reduce bureaucracy, simplify taxes and make them fairer, and help ensure the movement of talent between firms and countries.

Technology

- Oversee and ensure technology-oriented initiatives, R&D investment, digitalization, and internationalization. Accessing cutting-edge technology, ensuring the appropriability of innovations, and promoting collaboration between universities and firms will foster innovation. Internationalization will exert positive effects because, in competing with world-leading firms, ECA top-tier companies will have to learn how to upgrade their capacities (Cirera et al. 2020).

- Promote technology adoption and digitalization among early adopters and in the presence of uncertainty and information asymmetries. Subsidies delivered through vouchers and grants for information and communications technology could have an impact if they generate positive externalities. These technologies complement management quality and help firms plan production and management systems. If technologies require a critical mass of adopters, subsidizing early adopters could be an optimal approach to increasing public knowledge and facilitating coordination.

- Minimize restrictions on foreign technology licensing and on hiring foreign managers and specialized workers. These reforms would facilitate technology adoption and the access to external knowledge, which could be a key contributor to innovation.

The appropriate mix of policy recommendations depends on the context of a country. For this purpose, the analysis identified four groups of countries: (1) EU members states (Bulgaria, Croatia, Poland, Romania); (2) EU candidates (Georgia, Moldova, Ukraine, Western Balkans); (3) Türkiye; (4) Central Asia and South Caucasus (Armenia, Azerbaijan, Kazakhstan, Kyrgyz Republic, Tajikistan, Turkmenistan, Uzbekistan).

- Among the EU members, the priority areas involve promoting foreign direct investment (especially in knowledge-intensive sectors) and attracting global talent, together with deepening the financial sector (particularly the venture capital industry), creating incentives to foster private R&D, and reducing the focus on SMEs, while increasing the focus on start-ups and high-growth firms.

- For the EU candidates, the key priority areas are facilitating private investments and integration with global markets, together with strengthening competition and disciplining incumbents to provide space for new entries and start-ups. Other high priorities include improving management and the governance of firms and deepening financial markets.

- For Türkiye, the key priority areas are promoting technology adoption and digitalization, together with increasing the incentives for private R&D.

- For the countries of Central Asia and the South Caucasus, the key priorities are facilitating private investment, reducing the footprint of the state, and disciplining incumbents, together with strengthening competition policy and improving management and the governance of firms. Improving access and the allocation of credits, together with promoting technology adoption and digitalization, are also priorities in supporting firm-level productivity.

Table 2.1 provides the relative priorities for each set of countries. Detailed recommendations follow.

TABLE 2.1 Enterprises and productivity: summary of recommendations

Recommendation	EU members	EU candidates	Türkiye	Central Asia and South Caucasus
Facilitate private investment	Low	High	Medium	High
Reduce regulatory burden and digitalize administrative procedures	Medium	Medium	Medium	Medium
Reduce the state footprint	Medium	Medium	Low	High
Strengthen competition policy and discipline incumbents	Medium	High	Medium	High
Support integration with global markets	Medium	High	Medium	High
Promote foreign direct investment, especially in knowledge-intensive business areas	High	Medium	High	Medium
Make it easier to attract global talent	High	Medium	High	Medium
Improve management and firm governance	Medium	High	Medium	High
Deepen capital markets and long-term finance	High	High	Medium	Medium
Facilitate venture capital investment	High	Medium	High	Medium
Improve access to credit and credit allocation	Medium	Medium	Low	High
Reduce focus on small and medium enterprises and increase focus on start-ups/high-growth potential businesses	High	Medium	Medium	Medium
Promote technology adoption and digitalization	Medium	Medium	High	High
Create incentives for private R&D investments	High	Medium	High	Low
Eliminate restrictions on foreign tech licensing and foreign managers	Low	Low	Low	Medium

Source: World Bank.

Annex 2.1: Main Dataset and Methodological Definitions

Chapter 2 relies on a novel firm-level longitudinal database with more than 20 million registries, of which more than 16 million refer to enterprises operating in the business economy. The business economy category follows the Statistical Classification of Economic Activities in the European Community (EC 2008), which groups these firms according to activities, ranging from mining and quarrying (B) to administrative and support service activities (N), and excluding the activities of holding companies (K64.2), public sector organizations, and nonmarket activities (O–U). The main data sources are national statistical institutes, tax and financial agencies, and Orbis, and they cover the period 2007–21, although the exact time span varies by country.[31] Table A2.1.1 reports key country-level statistics on firms operating in the ECA region.

TABLE A2.1.1 Firm characteristics, by country

Income class	Country	Firm counts	Firms (employee counts) (%)				Employment	
			Micro (1-9)	Small (10-49)	Medium (50-249)	Large (>249)	Median	Mean
Middle income	Bulgaria	2,513,036	86.6	8.1	1.5	0.2	2.00	7.09
	Georgia	111,366	50.6	35.2	11.9	2.2	9.00	36.33
	Kazakhstan	306,532	59.3	24.9	12.2	3.1	5.00	43.43
	Kosovo	167,913	83.9	6.8	1.0	0.2	2.00	6.11
	Kyrgyz Republic	101,266	78.8	16.7	3.8	0.7	3.00	13.16
	Montenegro	150,232	91.9	6.4	1.4	0.2	1.00	6.04
	North Macedonia	456,020	87.2	8.5	1.6	0.3	2.00	7.47
	Serbia	866,717	81.2	14.2	3.5	0.8	3.00	15.84
High income	Croatia	1,097,181	86.6	10.8	2.1	0.5	2.00	10.02
	Poland	6,529,603	87.8	7.3	1.5	0.3	5.00	11.55
	Romania	4,003,928	80.0	10.0	2.0	0.4	2.00	10.31
MICs and HICs	*Total*	*16,303,794*	*84.4*	*9.3*	*2.0*	*0.4*	*5.00*	*11.28*

Sources: World Bank elaboration based on data of national statistical institutes; Orbis (portal), Moody's, New York, https://www.moodys.com/web/en/us/capabilities/company-reference-data/orbis.html.

Note: Raw data based on business activities B–N, except K, of NACE Rev. 2. NACE = Statistical Classification of Economic Activities in the European Community.

Annex 2.2: Estimating Firm-Level Labor Productivity and Defining the Frontiers

Labor productivity is the output produced per worker. Because measuring firm-level output requires detailed information on the sales and product prices of each good and service produced by the firms, this report uses the deflated sales per worker, calculated as in equation A2.2.1:

$$\gamma_{ijrct} = ln\left(\frac{Sales_{ijrct}}{employment_{ijrct}}\right) \qquad (A2.2.1)$$

where subscript i denotes the unit of analysis (firm), j the sector, r and c the region and country of location, and t the time unit (year).

Chapter 2 also examines the existence and magnitude of spatial and sectoral spillovers from more to less productive firms. It assesses two questions. First, it examines whether the productivity frontier at the local, sector, and regional levels (the average productivity of the top 25 percent of firms) affects the productivity of lower-productivity businesses. Second, it assesses if changes in the productivity frontier (changes in the productivity level of high-productivity firms) affect productivity growth among less-productive enterprises. These factors are related to the transfer of technology and knowledge (spillovers), considering that they may vary across regions, industries, and markets (sector-by-region) because technology, capital access, expertise, and proximity to innovation hubs may greatly vary across regions and among regions across countries. Equation A2.2.2 refers to the calculation of the local frontier, defined as the average productivity of the top 25 percent of the most productive firms (in terms of sales per worker) within the sector and region where the business operates.

$$\underline{\gamma}_{jrt} = \frac{1}{\underline{n}_{jrt}} \times \sum_{i \in \underline{i}_{jrt}} \gamma_{ijrt}, \qquad (A2.2.2)$$

Similarly, equations A2.2.3 and A2.2.4 define the sectoral and regional frontiers, respectively.

$$\underline{\gamma}_{jt,-r} = \frac{1}{\underline{n}_{jt,-r}} \times \sum_{i \in \underline{i}_{jt,-r}} \gamma_{ijt,-r}, \qquad (A2.2.3)$$

$$\underline{\gamma}_{rt,-s} = \frac{1}{\underline{n}_{rt,-j}} \times \sum_{i \in \underline{i}_{rt,-j}} \gamma_{irt,-j}, \qquad (A2.2.4)$$

where the subscripts $-r$ and $-j$ denote that firms within the same region (equation A.2.2.3) or sector (equation A2.2.4) of the firm are excluded from the calculation of each indicator.

Annex 2.3: Dataset Characteristics

Table A2.3.1 presents the characteristics of each dataset used in chapter 2. Most databases are associated with census registries, although, in some cases, such as Bulgaria and Poland, commercial information sources are used as well. In Poland, because of limitations in the commercial dataset, the registries are complemented by administrative sources. Given the data-access policies, however, it was not possible to work with the dataset outside the facilities of Statistics Poland, which limits the capacity to pool datasets. Each use of the Polish datasets is therefore explicitly indicated.

All datasets cover all industries considered in this analysis (business activities B–N, except K, of NACE Rev. 2), but may rely on different classification nomenclatures (EC 2008). The sector taxonomies were harmonized to NACE Rev. 2 because most countries use this classification, and this therefore minimizes information losses that typically result from mapping sectors across classification systems.

TABLE A2.3.1 Information sources, industry coverage, and country dataset characteristics

Country	Source	Type	Time span	Minimum size	Industry coverage	Sample size (*M*)
Bulgaria	Orbis	Commercial	2011–18	≥1 emp	NACE R2	2.560
Croatia	Financial agency (FINA)	Census	2008–20	≥0 emp	NACE R2	1.288
Georgia	National Statistics Office of Georgia (GEOSTAT)	Census/survey	2007–21	≥1 emp	NACE R1	0.114
Kazakhstan	Bureau of National Statistics	Census	2009–18	≥0 emp	ISIC R3	0.313
Kosovo	Tax registry	Census	2011–18	≥0 emp	NACE R2	0.221
Kyrgyz Republic	National Statistical Committee	Census	2010–21	≥0 emp	NACE R2	0.103
Montenegro	Statistical Office of Montenegro (MONSTAT)	Census	2011–19	≥0 emp	NACE R2	0.152
North Macedonia	Statistical Institute of MKD	Census	2011–20	≥0 emp	NACE R2	0.530
Poland	Orbis Statistics Poland	Commercial/survey	2009–20	≥5 emp	NACE R2	6.591 0.911
Romania	Ministry of Public Finance	Census	2011–20	≥0 emp	NACE R2	4.350
Serbia	Statistical Office of Serbia	Census	2006–19	≥0 emp	NACE R2	0.885

Sources: World Bank elaboration based on data of national statistical institutes; EC 2008; Orbis (portal), Moody's, New York, https://www.moodys.com/web/en/us/capabilities/company-reference-data/orbis.html.

Note: Raw data based on business activities B–N, except K, of NACE Rev. 2. emp = employees; ISIC = International Standard Industrial Classification; NACE = Statistical Classification of Economic Activities in the European Community; R = Revision.

Time spans differ across countries. While most countries report firm-level registries for 2011–19, there are differences in the time periods covered, which are considered in this analysis.

Table A2.3.2 presents information on the data availability of selected performance variables. It reports the share of firms with nonmissing values of employment, sales, value added, and estimated total factor productivity (TFP) based on previously defined time periods and business sectors. Nearly all firms report employment and sales, but, because of missing intermediate consumption and fixed asset values, value added is available for around 50 percent to 85 percent of firms, while TFP is available for around 35 percent to 75 percent of firms. The share of missing value added and TFP is considerable in certain countries, such as Kazakhstan, Kosovo, and Poland. In Poland, this is strictly driven by firm reporting because only firms with at least five employees are obliged to report performance variables. Because the Orbis dataset contains information about all Polish firms, missing values mostly correspond to businesses with fewer than five workers.

TABLE A2.3.2 **Data availability, by country**

Selected performance variables; share of firms (%)

Income class	Country	Share of firms with nonmissing data			
		Employment	Sales	Value added	TFP
Middle income	Bulgaria	96.4	91.6	49.9	37.4
	Georgia	100.0	100.0	86.4	62.7
	Kazakhstan	99.5	78.3	68.4	15.4
	Kosovo	91.9	90.5	9.4	8.5
	Kyrgyz Republic	99.9	90.1	59.0	34.2
	Montenegro	99.9	74.8	64.7	50.4
	North Macedonia	97.6	95.8	73.2	73.2
	Serbia	99.7	93.8	83.4	72.4
High income	Croatia	99.9	96.3	85.1	69.3
	Poland	96.9	8.9	5.3	4.9
	Romania	92.4	82.3	57.8	57.7

Sources: World Bank calculations based on data of national statistical institutes; Melitz and Polanec 2015; Orbis (portal), Moody's, New York, https://www.moodys.com/web/en/us/capabilities/company-reference-data/orbis.html.

Note: Raw data based on business activities B–N, except K, of NACE Rev. 2. NACE = Statistical Classification of Economic Activities in the European Community; TFP = total factor productivity.

Notes

1. Estonia's product market competition score is higher than the average in the Organisation for Economic Co-operation and Development (OECD 2018a).

2. If value added is used as the measure instead of firm revenue per worker, labor productivity growth would have been much more modest. This would, however, imply losing one-third of the observations because, while information on sales and workers is available for most firms, intermediate consumption, which is necessary to calculate value added, is missing in some cases. The firm revenue measure used here is based on firm-level registries rather than on macronational accounts. As a robustness check, the correlation between micro- and macrodata labor productivity growth rates was assessed. This revealed that they are positively and statistically correlated (at the 1 percent significance level). Nonetheless, in specific years, there may be discrepancies in productivity growth rates because of differences in statistical sources. The measure used here is based on revenues and employment reports of enterprises operating in business activities B to N (except K) of the Statistical Classification of Economic Activities in the European Community (NACE), Rev. 2 (EC 2008), while the macrodata are based on national account methodologies. Refer to annexes 2.1 to 2.3.

3. The results do not change qualitatively if value added per worker is used as the labor productivity measure. In most ECA MICs (except Kosovo and the Kyrgyz Republic), the contribution of the within-firm component is still negligible, while the effect of the between-firm component is much more modest.

4. There is a caveat. Entry or exit in the sample may sometimes be the result of misreporting rather than a purely economic event, especially in countries such as Georgia, where the firm survey involved minimum inclusion criteria rather than administrative records covering the universe of businesses.

5. The analysis here relies on the global innovation index constructed by Dutta et al. (2023). The authors implement a comprehensive innovation framework, including the institutional environment, the operational stability of businesses, entrepreneurship policies and culture, finance for start-ups, unicorn valuation, high-tech manufacturing, International Organization for Standardization 9001 quality (ISO 2015), creative goods exports, and GitHub commits. Refer to GII (Global Innovation Index) (dashboard), World Intellectual Property Organization, Geneva, https://www.wipo.int/global_innovation_index/en/.

6. Measured by data on global international patent families in sustainable technologies in 2000–19, the HICs were investing in green innovation during their transition to high income. As with overall innovation, the expansion in green innovation in the ECA HICs started before this transition, which suggests that successful countries raise investment in R&D and innovation as their per capita income is rising and not after they reach high-income status. Refer to PATSTAT (Patent Statistical Database), European Patent Office, Munich, https://www.epo.org/en/searching-for-patents/business/patstat#:~:text=PATSTAT%20contains%20 bibliographical%20and%20legal,or%20can%20be%20consulted%20online.

7. Croatia in 2008, Poland in 2009, and Romania in 2019; the available data do not cover Bulgaria, which was assessed to have reached the high-income threshold in 2023.

8. The most common interventions delivered by governments and innovation agencies include tax incentives for R&D (such as subsidies, tax exemptions, and tax credits); patent boxes (which operate as special tax regimes that lower the tax rate on revenues deriving from patents); R&D grants, loans, and subsidies; and policies that seek to increase human capital (Bloom, Van Reenen, and Williams 2019).

9. This analysis compares firms of similar scale operating in the same industry. Refer to WBES (World Bank Enterprise Surveys) (dashboard), World Bank, Washington, DC, https://www.enterprisesurveys.org/en /enterprisesurveys.

10. Cusolito et al. (2024) examine the counterfactual TFP gains achieved by removing financial distortions (if finance misallocation were reversed) relative to the corresponding gains in the United States.

11. Albania, Azerbaijan, Bulgaria, Croatia, Czechia, Estonia, Georgia, Hungary, Kyrgyz Republic, Lithuania, North Macedonia, Poland, Serbia, Slovenia, Türkiye, and Ukraine. Refer to WBES (World Bank Enterprise Surveys) (dashboard), World Bank, Washington, DC, https://www.enterprisesurveys.org/en/enterprisesurveys.

12. The Herfindahl-Hirschman index is computed as the sum of the squared market shares of each firm in the economy (or industry). A value equal to 1 means that the entire market share in the economy (or sector) is concentrated in one firm. As the value approaches 0, the market shares become more evenly distributed among competing firms.

13. Refer to LPI (Logistics Performance Index) (dashboard), World Bank, Washington, DC, https://lpi.worldbank.org/.

14. WDI (World Development Indicators) (dashboard), World Bank, Washington, DC, https://datatopics.worldbank.org/world-development-indicators/.

15. Productive capacities involve worker skills, management capacities, finance, innovation, access to modern equipment, high-quality imported inputs, and access to foreign markets.

16. The threshold in the definition of very large firms in this chapter is 500 or more employees.

17. Teal (2023) and Tybout (2014) test the missing middle hypothesis in African countries, India, Indonesia, Mexico, and the United States. Following Tybout (2014), Pareto-shape employment shares at each size plant class are computed as follows: $\hat{s}\left(l_i, l_j \mid k\right) = l_i^{-k} - l_j^{-k}$, where l_i and l_j are the lower and upper bound of each size class bin; and parameter k is chosen to minimize the Euclidean distance between the log of the vector of actual shares s and $\hat{s}$.

18. The results are robust to different definitions of "middle" and to comparisons against the employment distribution of US firms where firms with at least 500 employees account for 35 percent of employees in the US private sector, but only 5 percent in the ECA HICs and less than 2.5 percent in the ECA MICs.

19. Based on firm-level data and report team calculations.

20. The analysis identifies the top 100 firms in each ECA country and selected European countries based on data availability and average results across countries. Only firms with at least five employees are considered. Conclusions do not change if top 20 or top 50 firms are considered instead. Refer to Orbis (portal), Moody's, New York, https://www.moodys.com/web/en/us/capabilities/company-reference-data/orbis.html. Because of data availability, the ECA MICs included are Bosnia and Herzegovina, Bulgaria, Georgia, Montenegro, North Macedonia, Serbia, and Ukraine. The ECA HICs are Croatia, Poland, and Romania. The EU+United Kingdom countries (also referred to as Europe in this section) are Austria, Belgium, Czechia, Denmark, Estonia, Finland, Germany, Greece, Hungary, Ireland, Italy, Latvia, Lithuania, Luxembourg, Portugal, Slovak Republic, Slovenia, Spain, Sweden, Switzerland, and United Kingdom.

21. Intangible assets include patents, software, and intellectual property.

22. The Nomenclature of Territorial Units for Statistics is a geocode standard for referencing the administrative divisions of countries for statistical purposes. In those countries with no such taxonomy, the analysis relied on equivalent administrative divisions. Refer to NUTS Overview (Nomenclature of Territorial Units for Statistics: Overview) (dashboard), Eurostat, European Commission, Luxembourg, https://ec.europa.eu/eurostat/web/nuts.

23. The baseline specification includes various controls, such as the share of foreign-owned companies in the relevant market; a proxy of the level of competition level, that is, the Herfindahl-Hirschman index; value added and capital per worker, which control for capital accumulation and changes in market development; the year-on-year change in market size; the Olley-Pakes static covariance term, which measures the extent to which resources flow toward more productive firms; and market-level fixed effects because structural market characteristics may be associated with the presence of SOEs.

24. The results are available upon request.

25. SOE presence is measured as the percentage of firms (firm share) or the labor or market share of SOEs.

26. This is the share of firms entering and exiting each year.

27. This analysis can be performed only for a subset of ECA countries for which information is available on the year in which the business began operations.

28. The background analysis is based on firm-level data; the results are available upon request.

29. If the firm transitions to a higher size class five years later, it is recorded a score of 1, while, if it remains in the same size class or falls to a lower bin, it is recorded a score of 0.

30. Only 11 percent and 15 percent of ECA businesses with fewer than five employees and with five to nine employees, respectively, manage to move to superior bins. Thus, only a small share of microfirms become small, medium, or large.

31. Refer to Orbis (portal), Moody's, New York, https://www.moodys.com/web/en/us/capabilities/company-reference-data/orbis.html.

References

Abreha, Kaleb Girma, Xavier Cirera, Elwyn Adriaan Robin Davies, Roberto N. Fattal Jaef, and Hibret Belete Maemir. 2023. "A Missing Middle or Too Much Informality?" *Let's Talk Development* (blog), January 12, 2023. https://blogs.worldbank.org/en/developmenttalk/missing-middle-or-too-much-informality#:~:text=A%20%E2%80%9Cmissing%20middle%E2%80%9D%20indicates%20that,would%20imply%20a%20productivity%20gain.

Acemoglu, Daron, and Pascual Restrepo. 2018. "The Race between Man and Machine: Implications of Technology for Growth, Factor Shares, and Employment." *American Economic Review* 108 (6): 1488–1542.

Aghion, Philippe. 2017. "Entrepreneurship and Growth: Lessons from an Intellectual Journey." *Small Business Economics* 48 (1): 9–24.

Akcigit, Ufuk, and Sina T. Ates. 2021 "Ten Facts on Declining Business Dynamism and Lessons from Endogenous Growth Theory." *American Economic Journal: Macroeconomics* 13 (1): 257–98.

Akcigit, Ufuk, and William R. Kerr. 2018. "Growth Through Heterogeneous Innovations." *Journal of Political Economy* 126 (4): 1374–1443.

Akcigit, Ufuk, Jeremy G. Pearce, and Marta Prato. 2020. "Tapping into Talent: Coupling Education and Innovation Policies for Economic Growth." NBER Working Paper 27862 (September), National Bureau of Economic Research, Cambridge, MA.

Artola, Concha, and Veronique Genre. 2011. "Euro Area SMEs under Financial Constraints: Belief or Reality?" CESifo Working Paper 3650 (November), Munich Society for the Promotion of Economic Research, Center for Economic Studies, Ludwig Maximilian University and Ifo Institute for Economic Research, Munich.

Autor, David H., David Dorn, and Gordon H. Hanson. 2013. "The China Syndrome: Local Labor Market Effects of Import Competition in the United States." *American Economic Review* 103 (6): 2121–68.

Autor, David H., David Dorn, and Gordon H. Hanson. 2016. "The China Shock: Learning from Labor-Market Adjustment to Large Changes in Trade." *Annual Review of Economics* 8 (October): 205–40.

Baumol, William J. 1990. "Entrepreneurship: Productive, Unproductive, and Destructive." *Journal of Political Economy* 98 (5, Part 1): 893–921.

Beck, Thorsten, Asli Demirgüç-Kunt, and Vojislav Maksimovic. 2005. "Financial and Legal Constraints to Firm Growth: Does Firm Size Matter?" *Journal of Finance* 60 (1): 137–77.

Beck, Thorsten, Asli Demirgüç-Kunt, and María Soledad Martínez Pería. 2011. "Banking Financing for SMEs: Evidence across Countries and Bank Ownership Types." *Journal of Financial Services Research* 39 (1–2), 35–54.

Bernstein, Shai, Rebecca Diamond, Abhisit Jiranaphawiboon, Timothy McQuade, and Beatriz Pousada. 2022. "The Contribution of High-Skilled Immigrants to Innovation in the United States." NBER Working Paper 30797 (December), National Bureau of Economic Research, Cambridge, MA.

Bianchi, Nicola, and Michela Giorcelli. 2019. "Scientific Education and Innovation: From Technical Diplomas to University STEM Degrees." NBER Working Paper 25928 (June), National Bureau of Economic Research, Cambridge, MA.

Bloom, Nicholas, Raffaella Sadun, and John Michael Van Reenen. 2016. "Management as a Technology?" Working Paper 16-133 (June), Harvard Business School, Boston. https://www.hbs.edu/faculty/Pages/item.aspx?num=51154.

Bloom, Nicholas, Mark Schankerman, and John Michael Van Reenen. 2013. "Identifying Technology Spillovers and Product Market Rivalry." *Econometrica* 8 (4): 1347–93.

Bloom, Nicholas, and John Michael Van Reenen. 2010. "Why Do Management Practices Differ across Firms and Countries?" *Journal of Economic Perspectives* 24 (1): 203–24.

Bloom, Nicholas, John Michael Van Reenen, and Heidi L. Williams. 2019. "A Toolkit of Policies to Promote Innovation." *Journal of Economic Perspectives* 33 (3): 163–84. doi.org/10.1257/jep.33.3.163.

Brown, J. David, Gustavo A. Crespi, Leonardo Iacovone, and Luca Marcolin. 2016. "Productivity Convergence at the Firm Level: New Evidence from the Americas." In *Understanding the Income and Efficiency Gap in Latin America and the Caribbean*, edited by Jorge Thompson Araujo, Ekaterina Vostroknutova,

Konstantin M. Wacker, and Mateo Clavijo, 117–86. Directions in Development: Countries and Regions Series. Washington, DC: World Bank.

Caballero, Ricardo J., and Mohamad L. Hammour. 1994. "The Cleansing Effect of Recessions." *American Economic Review* 84 (5): 1350–68.

Cirera, Xavier, Sara Brolhato, and Antonio Soares Martins-Neto. 2023. "Businesses of the State in Brazil: Employment and Impact on Business Dynamism." Background paper for *The Business of the State*, World Bank, Washington, DC.

Cirera, Xavier, Diego A. Comin, and Marcio Cruz. 2022. *Bridging the Technological Divide: Technology Adoption by Firms in Developing Countries.* Washington, DC: World Bank.

Cirera, Xavier, Jaime Frías, Justin Hill, and Yanchao Li. 2020. *A Practitioner's Guide to Innovation Policy: Instruments to Build Firm Capabilities and Accelerate Technological Catch-Up in Developing Countries.* Washington, DC: World Bank. https://doi.org/10.1596/33269.

Cirera, Xavier, and William F. Maloney. 2017. *The Innovation Paradox: Developing-Country Capabilities and the Unrealized Promise of Technological Catch-Up.* Washington, DC: World Bank. doi.org/10.1596/978-1-4648-1160-9_ch1.

Criscuolo, Chiara, Peter N. Gal, and Carlo Menon. 2014. "The Dynamics of Employment Growth: New Evidence from 18 Countries." CEP Discussion Paper 1274, Centre for Economic Performance, London School of Economics and Political Science, London.

Cusolito, Ana Paula, Roberto N. Fattal-Jaef, Davide Salvatore Mare, and Akshat V. Singh. 2024. "The Role of Financial (Mis)allocation on Real (Mis)allocation: Firm-level Evidence for European Countries." Policy Research Working Paper 10811, World Bank, Washington, DC.

Cusolito, Ana Paula, and William F. Maloney. 2018. *Productivity Revisited: Shifting Paradigms in Analysis and Policy.* Washington, DC: World Bank.

Dall'Olio, Andrea Mario, Tanja K. Goodwin, Martha Martínez Licetti, Ana Cristina Alonso Soria, Maciej Drozd, Jan Orlowski, Fausto Andres Patiño Peña, and Dennis Sanchez-Navarro. 2022. "Are All State-Owned Enterprises Equal? A Taxonomy of Economic Activities to Assess SOE Presence in the Economy." Policy Research Working Paper 10262, World Bank, Washington, DC.

Decker, Ryan A., John C. Haltiwanger, Ron S. Jarmin, and Javier Miranda. 2020. "Changing Business Dynamism and Productivity: Shocks versus Responsiveness." *American Economic Review* 110 (12): 3952–90.

de Jong, Jeroen P. J., and Deanne N. den Hartog. 2007. "How Leaders Influence Employees' Innovative Behaviour." *European Journal of Innovation Management* 10 (1): 41–64. https://doi.org/10.1108/14601060710720546.

De Loecker, Jan K., Jan Eeckhout, and Gabriel Unger. 2020. "The Rise of Market Power and the Macroeconomic Implications." *Quarterly Journal of Economics* 135 (2): 561–644. https://doi.org/10.1093/qje/qjz041.

Didier, Tatiana, and Ana Paula Cusolito. 2024. *Unleashing Productivity Through Firm Financing: Evidence and Policies to Close the Finance Productivity Divide.* Washington, DC: World Bank.

Dutta, Soumitra, Bruno Lanvin, Lorena Rivera León, and Sacha Wunsch-Vincent, eds. 2023. *Global Innovation Index 2023: Innovation in the Face of Uncertainty,* 16th ed. Geneva: World Intellectual Property Organization.

EC (European Commission). 2008. *NACE Rev. 2: Statistical Classification of Economic Activities in the European Community.* Eurostat Methodologies and Working Papers Series. Luxembourg: Office for Official Publications of the European Communities.

Ederer, Florian, and Gustavo Manso. 2013. "Is Pay for Performance Detrimental to Innovation?" *Management Science* 59 (7): 1496–1513. http://dx.doi.org/10.1287/mnsc.1120.1683.

Ferrando, Annalisa, and Nicolas Griesshaber. 2011. "Financing Obstacles among Euro Area Firms: Who Suffers the Most?" Working Paper 1293 (February), European Central Bank, Frankfurt am Main.

Ferro, Esteban, and Fausto Andres Patiño Peña. 2023. "Private Sector Performance under the Pressure of SOE Competition: The Case of Ecuador." Background paper for *The Business of the State*, World Bank, Washington, DC.

Foster, Lucia, John C. Haltiwanger, and Chad Syverson. 2016. "The Slow Growth of New Plants: Learning about Demand?" *Economica* 83 (329): 91–129.

Garicano, Luis, Claire Lelarge, and John Michael Van Reenen. 2016. "Firm Size Distortions and the Productivity Distribution: Evidence from France." *American Economic Review* 106 (11): 3439–79.

Griffith, Rachel, Stephen Redding, and John Michael Van Reenen. 2004. "Mapping the Two Faces of R&D: Productivity Growth in a Panel of OECD Industries." *Review of Economics and Statistics* 86 (4): 883–95. https://doi.org/10.1162/0034653043125194.

Grover, Arti Goswami, Leonardo Iacovone, and Pavel Chakraborty. 2019. "Management Practices in Croatia: Drivers and Consequences for Firm Performance." Policy Research Working Paper 9067, World Bank, Washington, DC.

Haltiwanger, John C., Ron S. Jarmin, and Javier Miranda. 2013. "Who Creates Jobs? Small versus Large versus Young." *Review of Economics and Statistics* 95 (2): 347–61.

Herfindahl, Orris C. 1950. "Concentration in the U.S. Steel Industry." PhD dissertation, Columbia University, New York.

Hirschman, Albert O. 1964. "The Paternity of an Index." *American Economic Review* 54 (5): 761–62.

Hopenhayn, Hugo A. 1992. "Entry, Exit, and Firm Dynamics in Long Run Equilibrium." *Econometrica* 60 (5): 1127–50.

Hunt, Jennifer. 2011. "Which Immigrants Are Most Innovative and Entrepreneurial? Distinctions by Entry Visa." *Journal of Labor Economics* 29 (3): 417–57. https://doi.org/10.1086/659409.

Iacovone, Leonardo, Mariana De La Paz Pereira López, and Marc Tobias Schiffbauer. 2023 "Competition Makes IT Better: Evidence on When Firms Use IT More Effectively." *Research Policy* 52 (8): 104786.

Iacovone, Leonardo, Ferdinand Rauch, and L. Alan Winters. 2013. "Trade as an Engine of Creative Destruction: Mexican Experience with Chinese Competition." *Journal of International Economics* 89 (2): 379–92.

ISO (International Organization for Standardization). 2015. "Quality Management Systems: Requirements." International Standard ISO 9001:2015, 5th ed. (September), ISO, Geneva.

Keller, Wolfgang. 2000. "Do Trade Patterns and Technology Flows Affect Productivity Growth?" *World Bank Economic Review* 14 (1): 17–47.

Kerr, William R., and Sari Pekkala Kerr. 2020. "Immigration Policy Levers for U.S. Innovation and Startups." Working Paper 20-105, Harvard Business School, Boston.

Leiblein, Michael J., and Tammy L. Madsen. 2009. "Unbundling Competitive Heterogeneity: Incentive Structures and Capability Influences on Technological Innovation." *Strategic Management Journal* 30 (7): 711–35.

Melitz, Marc J., and Sašo Polanec. 2015. "Dynamic Olley-Pakes Productivity Decomposition with Entry and Exit." *RAND Journal of Economics* 46 (2): 362–75.

Murphy, Kevin. M., Andrei Shleifer, and Robert W. Vishny. 1991. "The Allocation of Talent: Implications for Growth." *Quarterly Journal of Economics* 106 (2): 503–30. https://www.jstor.org/stable/2937945.

Nanda, Ramana, and Matthew Rhodes-Kropf. 2016. "Financing Entrepreneurial Experimentation." In *Innovation Policy and the Economy*, vol. 16, edited by Josh Lerner and Scott Stern, 1–23. Cambridge, MA: National Bureau of Economic Research; Chicago: University of Chicago Press.

OECD (Organisation for Economic Co-operation and Development). 2018a. "OECD Product Market Regulation (PMR) Indicators: How Does Estonia Compare?" 2018 Product Market Regulation Country Note, OECD, Paris. https://issuu.com/oecd.publishing/docs/est_country_note_-_tot_final?fr=sNjJhOTkzNTk1MQ.

OECD (Organisation for Economic Co-operation and Development). 2018b. *OECD Science, Technology and Innovation Outlook 2018: Adapting to Technological and Societal Disruption.* Paris: OECD. https://doi.org/10.1787/sti_in_outlook-2018-en.

Schumpeter, Joseph Alois. 1942. *Capitalism, Socialism, and Democracy.* New York: Harper and Brothers.

Syverson, Chad. 2011. "What Determines Productivity?" *Journal of Economic Literature* 49 (2): 326–65.

Teal, Francis. 2023. "Firm Size, Employment, and Value Added in African Manufacturing Firms: Why Ghana Needs Its 1 percent." *Journal of African Economies* 32 (2): 118–36. http://hdl.handle.net/10.1093/jae/ejab015.

Toivanen, Otto, and Lotta Väänänen. 2016. "Education and Invention." *Review of Economics and Statistics* 98 (2): 382–96. https://doi.org/10.1162/REST_a_00520.

Tybout, James R. 2014. "The Missing Middle: Correspondence." *Journal of Economic Perspectives* 28 (4): 235–36.

Venturini, Alessandra, Fabio Montobbio, and Claudio Fassi. 2012. "Are Migrants Spurring Innovation?" MPC Research Report 2012/11, Migration Policy Centre, Robert Schuman Centre for Advanced Studies, European University Institute, San Domenico di Fiesole (FI), Italy.

What Works Centre for Local Economic Growth. 2015. "Innovation: Grants, Loans, and Subsidies." Evidence Review 9 (October), What Works Centre for Local Economic Growth, London. https://whatworksgrowth.org/wp-content /uploads/15-10-20-Innovation-Grants-Loans-Subsidies-Report.pdf.

World Bank. 2023. *The Business of the State*. Washington, DC: World Bank.

World Bank. 2024. "World Development Report 2024: Economic Growth in Middle-Income Countries, Concept Note." World Bank, Washington, DC.

Talent and Social Mobility

Country Case in Brief: Finland

A largely agrarian society before World War II, Finland witnessed significant changes to its economy and a rapid increase in population in the postwar period. Industrialization and rapid urbanization led to the growth of the Finnish middle class, which clamored for higher-quality education among children. The Finnish education system was reformed to improve education quality and access; provide an educated workforce for the increasingly industrialized, postagrarian economy; and respond to a desire for greater social equality.

Reform of the education system started in the 1960s with comprehensive changes in schooling that included a transition to a common, unified, and compulsory curriculum. The reforms transferred control of the school system from the central authorities to local municipalities and teachers and fostered a competitive teacher selection process. The gradual nature of the reforms was a key factor in their implementation. Nine years of education were made mandatory in the 1970s, and, in the 1980s, lower-secondary education became comprehensive through the merger of all educational tracks into one. As a result, the two-tier system of grammar and civic schools was replaced by free comprehensive schools accessible to all children regardless of socioeconomic background or location of residence. This change involved the expansion of secondary schooling and the postponement of educational track selection to age 16. The reform significantly improved learning outcomes among students whose parents had only basic educational attainment (Pekkala Kerr, Pekkarinen, and Uusitalo 2013).

From the 1970s to the 1990s, Finland transitioned from a middle- to a high-income competitive economy based on its well-educated and skilled workforce. Different waves of education reforms contributed to this transition. In the early 2000s,

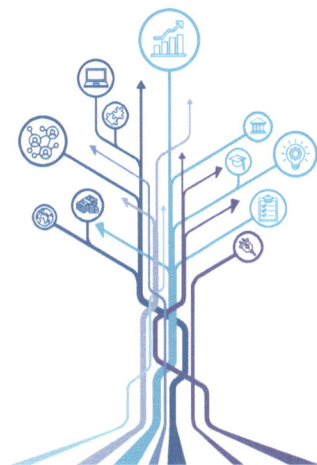

Finland ranked as the world's most competitive economy, with a high level of human capital, widespread adoption of information and communication technologies, and education and research institutions redesigned to foster innovation and research and development (R&D).

In education, standards increased, inequality declined, and attainment levels almost doubled. In the 2000s, Finland took nearly all the top spots in mathematics, scientific literacy, and reading globally. From 1965 to 2015, the number of students staying longer in education increased, and test scores improved by the equivalent of more than four years of additional learning. Finland also consistently ranked at the top of adult skills assessments. The reforms also improved intergenerational educational mobility. Finns with less well-educated parents are more likely to exhibit higher levels of literacy or numeracy than their international counterparts.

Finland's era of success remains a reference, although it has been followed by a period of decline. Finnish students who entered elementary school in the 1990s were the most well performing in the world. But their peers who followed them only a few years later were not nearly as successful. At the beginning of the Finnish miracle, the government centralized teacher training at major universities and employed national inspectorates to maintain school quality. Over time, more authority was devolved locally to trust educators, but this was also driven by budget pressure, and it is difficult to know whether the high scores of the early 2000s partly arose because of those discarded strategies (Daly 2024; Ripley 2013). The relative stagnation—although at high levels—in the quality of education in Finland in recent years also shows the importance of keeping up with good practices and ensuring a constant assessment of possible reforms.

Introduction

The earlier reforms of Finland's education system are among the best examples of the effectiveness of policy in transforming middle-income countries (MICs) into high-income, high-skill, innovation-centered economies.

This chapter attempts to answer the following questions:

- *How does ensuring equal access to opportunities among all segments of society contribute to optimal talent allocation and subsequently impact economic growth?* Technological progress is an essential driver of economic growth, and, for this to occur, countries require an increasing flow of well-trained, talented people. But, in socially immobile societies, where employment and education opportunities are not allocated by merit but by unrelated family circumstances, the flow may be weaker. This is particularly the case across countries in the ECA region, where an improvement in the indicators of mobility in access to higher education is associated with a rise in income.

- *In what ways do high-quality education systems foster innovation and human capital development, and how do these factors drive economic growth in an innovation-led model?* Research has found that cognitive skills among individuals are linked to a diverse set of innovation outcomes. Therefore, education systems that do not ensure that graduates are sufficiently proficient in basic skills will not help countries transition to innovation-led growth. Higher-education systems in ECA countries are fundamental in this process because they are one of the main centers of R&D in the region.

- *How does high-skill international migration impact a country's innovation capacity, human capital accumulation, and overall economic growth, and what policies might optimize the benefits of international migration while mitigating potential drawbacks?* The outflow of high-skill individuals may not undermine the development of homegrown talent if the proper incentives are in place. Remittances may support human capital development in origin countries, and returning migrants may improve productivity in the origin country by importing knowledge and best practices from the destination country. Bilateral migration agreements could allow destination countries to fund education and training programs in origin countries, thus achieving a more equal distribution of the benefits of migration across both sorts of countries.

- *How do expectations of social mobility influence public support for structural reforms, thereby overcoming the forces of preservation?* The more optimistic ECA citizens are about their own and their children's social mobility, the more they will be receptive to giving up part of their income to support educational reforms. This is particularly important in a context in which the middle class is becoming more vulnerable across the region. The less optimistic vulnerable households are about their future, the weaker will be their support for structural reforms to overcome the forces of preservation.

This chapter shows that innovation-led growth requires putting the right people on the right track. Innate ability is spread evenly throughout a population. Yet, not everyone has access to the same opportunities that would allow talent to flourish. A socially mobile, meritocratic society in which opportunities are not conditioned on family and social circumstances ensures that talent is not misallocated. But there is little to gain from equal access to education if the quality of education is low or if job opportunities are few.

Talent will flourish only if good education is available, only if basic education—primary and secondary education—provides foundational skills, and only if higher-education institutions produce innovation both in-house and in partnership with industry, thereby strengthening the forces of creation. If well managed, the flow of talented individuals across borders has the potential to boost innovation, human capital accumulation, and economic growth. Households also feature in this process, which requires the existence of a robust middle class that has the means and is effective in investing in the human capital of future generations.

Rewarding Merit: Social Mobility and Economic Growth in Europe and Central Asia

Creative destruction requires talent. Talented innovators drive creative destruction by developing novel ideas, technologies, and approaches to business that render old systems obsolete. Individuals need opportunities to develop their talents and an expectation that investment in their talents will improve their lives (World Bank 2024b). In socially immobile societies in which employment and education opportunities are not allocated by merit but by unrelated family circumstances, individuals may be denied the chance to develop their talent and put it to work. This stifles innovation and economic growth.

In the ECA region, educational mobility is decreasing among younger generations. Without government involvement, low intergenerational mobility will perpetuate cross-generational income inequality, reducing the chances that talented children in poor households will succeed. Merit- and ability-based policies are needed to boost mobility among talented children with disadvantaged backgrounds. Societies in which talented individuals are not engaged in the labor market miss the opportunities represented by productive populations. Addressing the barriers to labor force participation, particularly among women, migrants, refugees, and disadvantaged groups, is critical. Policies should focus on combating discrimination, challenging restrictive social norms, and providing equal labor market access to maximize the potential of talent.

Declining Mobility in Education among Younger Generations in the ECA Region

If a society's talent potential is realized, the labor market becomes more efficient and jobs become more plentiful, leading to more rapid economic growth. Technological progress is an essential driver of economic growth and improvements in living standards. Yet, greater spending on R&D alone may be insufficient to fuel breakthrough scientific innovations, which also require a rising flow of well-trained, talented people (Romer 2000).

The levels of intergenerational mobility in education reflect how well societies allocate talent. The size of investment in a child's education depends on parental income and parental human capital. More well-educated parents tend to earn more but also tend to be more effective at raising children's human capital. The complementarity between parental human capital and investments in children means that wealthier parents invest more than poor parents in the human capital of their children (Becker et al. 2018; Heckman and Mosso 2014).

Without government involvement, the intergenerational transmission of educational attainment will perpetuate cross-generational income inequality, effectively reducing the chances that talented children in poor households will succeed (Corak 2013; van der Weide et al. 2023). By drawing such children into science and innovation, policies designed to improve intergenerational mobility could quadruple the number of inventors and significantly boost economic growth (Bell et al. 2019). Evidence from Europe shows that subnational regions with higher intergenerational mobility enjoy better innovation outcomes (McNamara, Neidhöfer, and Lehnert 2024).

Talented individuals can fully realize their abilities only in societies with high social mobility. A study of recipients of a merit-based scholarship for graduate studies in Italy found that individuals in households with lower socioeconomic status were more likely to apply and win the scholarship if they came from provinces with high social mobility (Nano, Panizza, and Viarengo 2024). Moreover, applicants from provinces with low social mobility tended to come from more well-off households, indicating that individuals with disadvantaged backgrounds face barriers, particularly in settings with low social mobility.

The ECA region's average intergenerational mobility is equal to or greater than the world average depending on the measure used. Intergenerational mobility in education may be measured in an absolute or relative sense. Absolute mobility measures whether the level of education of an individual is higher than the level of education of his or her parents. Relative mobility measures whether the relative position of an individual in the education distribution is higher than the relative position of his or her parents in the education distribution to which they belong. The analysis here relies on three measures of absolute mobility: (1) the share of individuals who have achieved higher educational attainment relative to their parents; (2) the upward mobility gap, which weights the share of individuals who have achieved higher educational attainment relative to their parents by the difference in educational attainment between the generations (Foster and Rothbaum 2018); and (3) the probability of upward mobility in higher education, defined as the share of individuals with tertiary education born to parents without tertiary degrees (Torre, Lokshin, and Foster 2025).

The two indicators of relative mobility are (1) the *intergenerational correlation*, defined as the correlation between the education of an individual and the education of his or her parents, and (2) *intergenerational persistence*, defined as the additional years of education that an individual has attained for every year of education that his or her parents have achieved. For these two indicators, higher values imply lower relative mobility. The ECA region's absolute intergenerational mobility in education is similar to the world average (refer to figure 3.1, panel a), but its relative mobility is considerably higher than the world average (refer to figure 3.1, panel b) among individuals in birth cohorts with approximately 10 years of education.

Younger generations in the ECA region experience lower absolute mobility in education relative to older generations. The number of additional school years with respect to parents is smaller among younger cohorts than among older

FIGURE 3.1 ECA: absolute mobility is similar to, but relative mobility is greater than the world average

a. Share of population with education
higher than education of their parents
(cohorts with approximately 10 years of education)

Share of children with higher educational
attainment than their parents (%)

b. One minus intergenerational persistence
(cohorts with approximately 10 years of education)

Intergenerational persistence
(one minus)

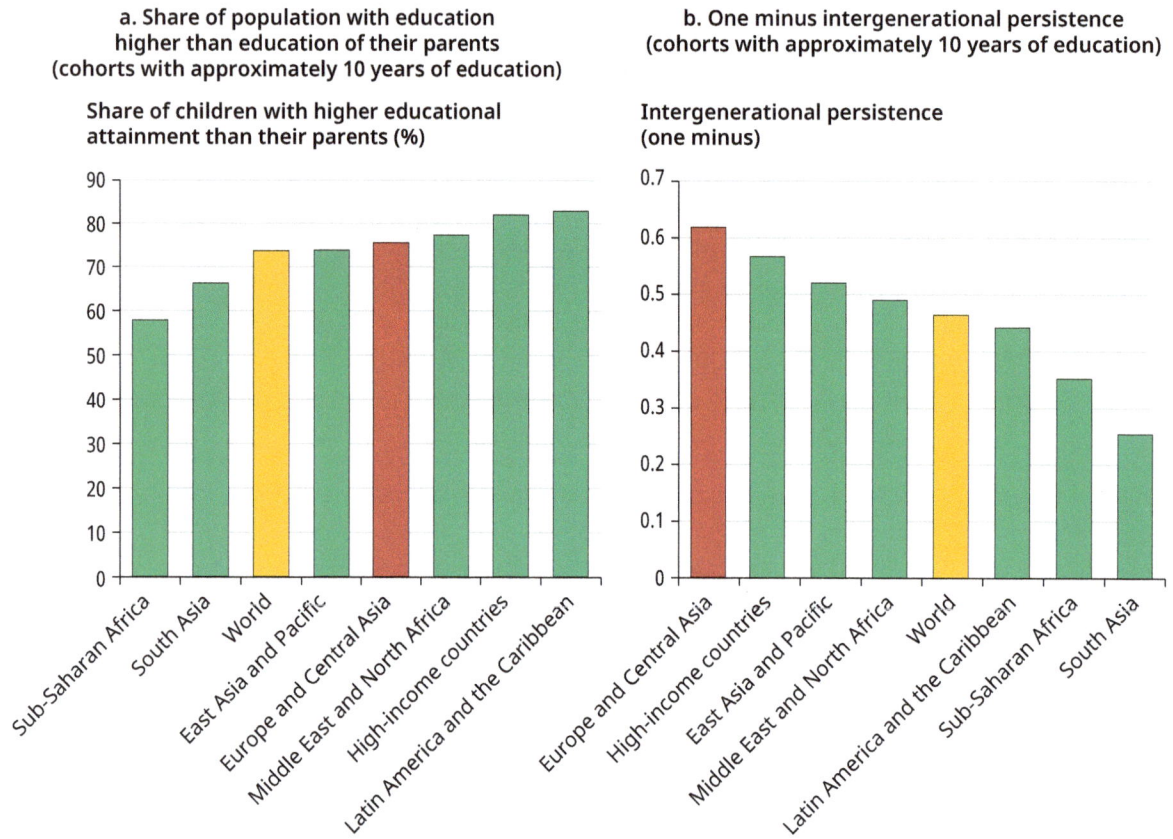

Source: van der Weide et al. 2023.

Note: A higher value indicates greater mobility. The values for each region correspond to birth cohorts with approximately 10 years of education. In ECA and high-income countries, this is the 1950s birth cohort. In the remaining regions, it is the 1980s birth cohort, although, in the case of Sub-Saharan Africa (6.5 years) and South Asia (7.4 years), the average education of the most well-educated cohort does not reach 10 years. One minus intergenerational persistence is plotted to preserve the directional sense of higher values, implying greater mobility. The average values of intergenerational persistence are 0.47 in ECA countries and 0.52 in the world. The average values of one minus intergenerational persistence are 0.53 in ECA countries and 0.48 in the world.

cohorts, largely because of substantial increases in educational attainment over the years (Torre, Lokshin, and Foster 2025). For almost every country, upward educational mobility is lowest among younger generations and highest among older generations (refer to figure 3.2). Median upward mobility was about 40 percent less among the cohort born in the 1990s than among the cohorts born in the 1930s or 1940s. The country with the largest difference in upward mobility between individuals born in the 1930s and 1990s is Kazakhstan, where upward mobility was almost 85 percent lower among the youngest generation than among the oldest generation. Meanwhile, in Kosovo and Türkiye, upward mobility is greater among younger generations.

FIGURE 3.2 Absolute upward educational mobility has declined among younger generations, ECA

Average upward mobility gap among children relative to their mothers

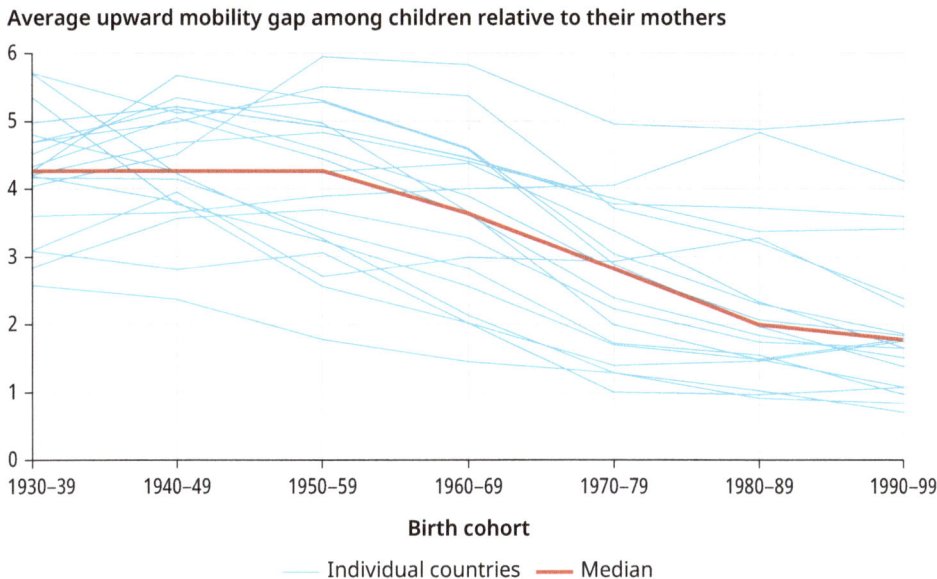

Birth cohort

—— Individual countries   —— Median

Sources: Torre, Lokshin, and Foster 2025; LiTS (Life in Transition Survey) (dashboard), European Bank for Reconstruction and Development, London, http://www.ebrd.com/what-we-do/economic -research-and-data/data/lits.html.

Note: The figure plots the average upward mobility gap among birth cohorts across all waves of the Life in Transition Survey.

The declining trend in upward mobility across generations in most countries can be explained by a drop-off in the share of upward movers and a narrowing in the average difference in years of schooling affecting upward movers. About 70 percent of individuals born in the 1940s attained more years of education than their mothers. The median difference was more than six years of education. Among individuals born in the 1990s, the median share of upward movers (relative to their mothers) was 42 percent, with a median difference of 4.3 years of education (refer to figure 3.3). A similar pattern holds for the mobility measures calculated relative to the father's education. The decrease in absolute mobility could also be related to ECA's high levels of schooling, the so-called "ceiling effect" (Narayan et al. 2018).

Upward mobility in higher education—defined as the probability of the attainment of higher education among individuals whose parents did not attain it— is growing. Among the generation born in the 1930s, the probability was only 10 percent, while, among the cohort born in the 1990s, it was close to 20 percent (refer to figure 3.4). In some countries, such as Albania, the increase was greater: from about 10 percent to more than 40 percent over the same period.

FIGURE 3.3 **Upward mobility in education has declined across generations, ECA**

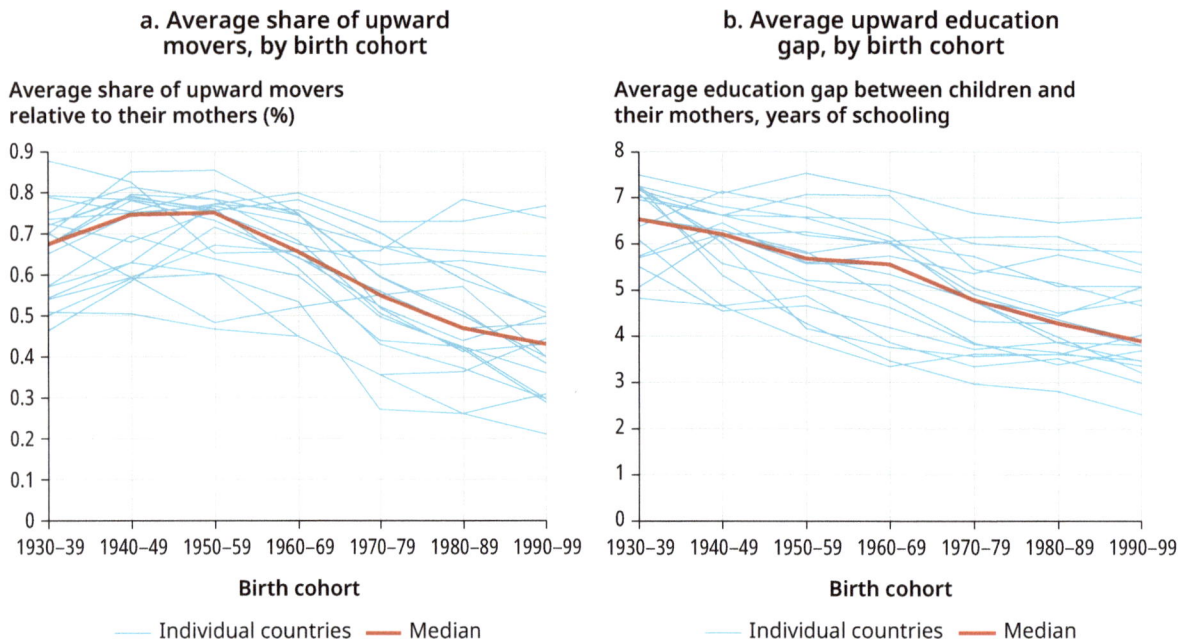

a. Average share of upward movers, by birth cohort

Average share of upward movers relative to their mothers (%)

b. Average upward education gap, by birth cohort

Average education gap between children and their mothers, years of schooling

——— Individual countries ——— Median

Sources: Torre, Lokshin, and Foster 2025; LiTS (Life in Transition Survey) (dashboard), European Bank for Reconstruction and Development, London, http://www.ebrd.com/what-we-do/economic-research-and-data/data/lits.html.

Note: The gray lines plot the values for individual countries.

FIGURE 3.4 **Upward mobility in higher education has increased among younger generations, ECA**

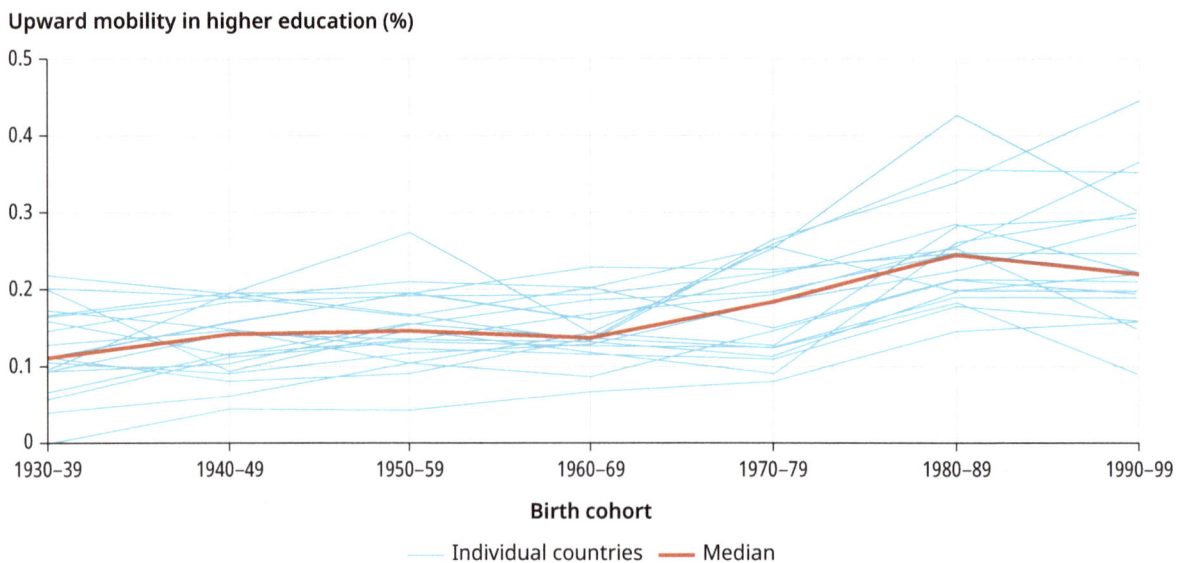

Upward mobility in higher education (%)

——— Individual countries ——— Median

Sources: Torre, Lokshin, and Foster 2025; LiTS (Life in Transition Survey) (dashboard), European Bank for Reconstruction and Development, London, http://www.ebrd.com/what-we-do/economic-research-and-data/data/lits.html.

Note: Upward mobility in higher education is measured as the probability in a birth cohort that an individual will attain tertiary education if his or her mother does not have tertiary education.

Relative mobility is lower among younger generations, although the changes across birth cohorts are small. Depending on the measure, relative mobility has been either stable or shows a U-shape across generations (refer to figure 3.5). The values of intergenerational persistence in the median country do not change substantially across birth cohorts. Some countries, however, experienced significant intercohort variation. For example, in Türkiye, mobility is much greater among the older generation relative to the younger generation. In North Macedonia, the opposite is true, albeit at smaller magnitude. The changes in intergenerational correlation across cohorts in the median country exhibit a somewhat inverted U-shape, that is, the correlation is lower among the oldest cohorts and among the youngest cohorts.

Upward mobility in higher education is associated with higher gross domestic product (GDP) per capita. A panel data analysis of trends in GDP per capita and educational mobility in 23 ECA countries in 2000–20 shows that, of all the mobility indicators, only the probability of upward mobility in higher education is associated with higher country incomes (refer to figure 3.6). A 1 standard deviation (SD) increase in the probability of upward mobility in higher education is associated with an approximately 0.50 SD rise in GDP per capita. The indicators of relative mobility are not associated with higher incomes per capita. The ECA patterns contrast with those reported by Neidhöfer et al. (2024) in Latin America, where both relative and absolute mobility indicators are associated significantly with regional GDP per capita.

FIGURE 3.5 **Relative mobility may exhibit a U-shape across generations**

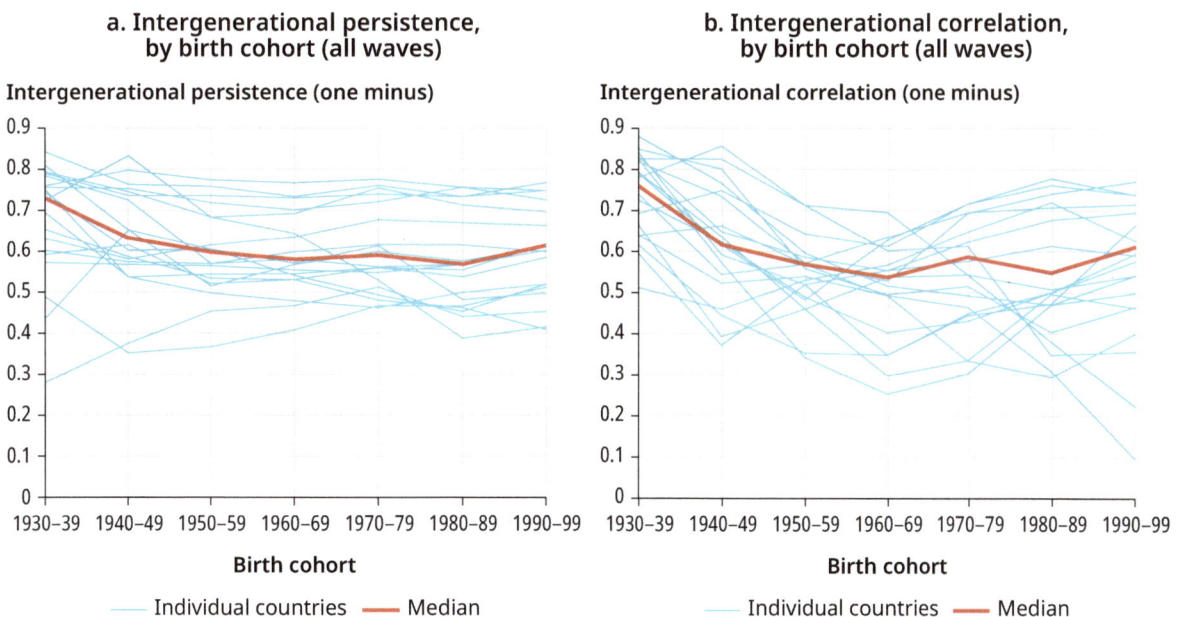

a. Intergenerational persistence, by birth cohort (all waves)

b. Intergenerational correlation, by birth cohort (all waves)

Sources: Torre, Lokshin, and Foster 2025; LiTS (Life in Transition Survey) (dashboard), European Bank for Reconstruction and Development, London, http://www.ebrd.com/what-we-do/economic-research-and-data/data/lits.html.

FIGURE 3.6 Upward mobility in higher education is associated with higher incomes, ECA, 2000–20

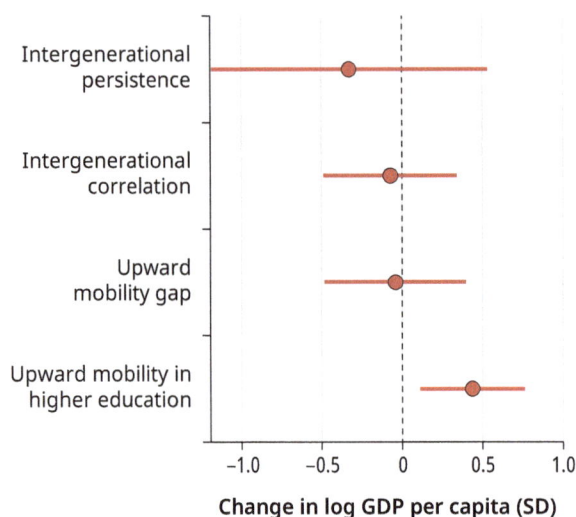

Change in log GDP per capita (SD)

Sources: Torre, Lokshin, and Foster 2025; LiTS (Life in Transition Survey) (dashboard), European Bank for Reconstruction and Development, London, http://www.ebrd.com/what-we-do/economic-research-and-data/data/lits.html.

Note: The figure plots the change in log GDP per capita associated with a 1 SD increase in each of four mobility measures. The underlying estimations correspond to regressions that include country-year-level controls (Gini index of inequality, log population, log population squared), cohort-level controls (average years of education, SD of years of education), cohort-specific initial conditions (log GDP per capita at decade of birth, population at decade of birth, infant mortality rate at decade of birth), country fixed effects, and year fixed effects. Standard errors are clustered at the country level. SD = standard deviation.

Improving Labor Market Participation among Women and Disadvantaged Groups

Because society cannot benefit from well-educated, talented individuals unless the talents are applied, an important dimension of the allocation of talent in society is the labor force participation rate. Societies in which talented individuals do not have jobs miss the potential represented by more productive individuals. This issue is especially so in the case of women, who tend to be more well educated than men in the ECA region, and in the case of disadvantaged groups, who may otherwise be less productive.

The average female labor force participation rate in the region is relatively high but heterogeneous. Some countries, such as Azerbaijan, Kazakhstan, and Moldova, exhibit a far higher rate—exceeding 60 percent of the female population ages 15 or older—than might be predicted based on income. Other countries have a lower rate, including Kosovo, which has, at 16 percent, among the lowest rates in the world, as well as Bosnia and Herzegovina, North Macedonia, Romania, Tajikistan, Türkiye, and Uzbekistan, with rates below 45 percent (refer to figure 3.7).

The low female labor force participation rate in some ECA countries is not explained by differences in skills but may be related to social norms. A study of six Western Balkans countries—a subregion with lower female labor force participation than the rest of the ECA region—found no clear evidence that gaps by sex in skills or payoffs for skills affect women in labor markets (World Bank 2018). Women do not have lower levels of skills relevant to the labor market, nor are women disadvantaged in how skills and education pay off. Yet, there is evidence that norms, perceptions of employers, and approaches to recruitment

FIGURE 3.7 The female labor force participation rate is heterogeneous, ECA, 2022

Women in the labor force as a share of the female population ages 15 or older (% × 100)

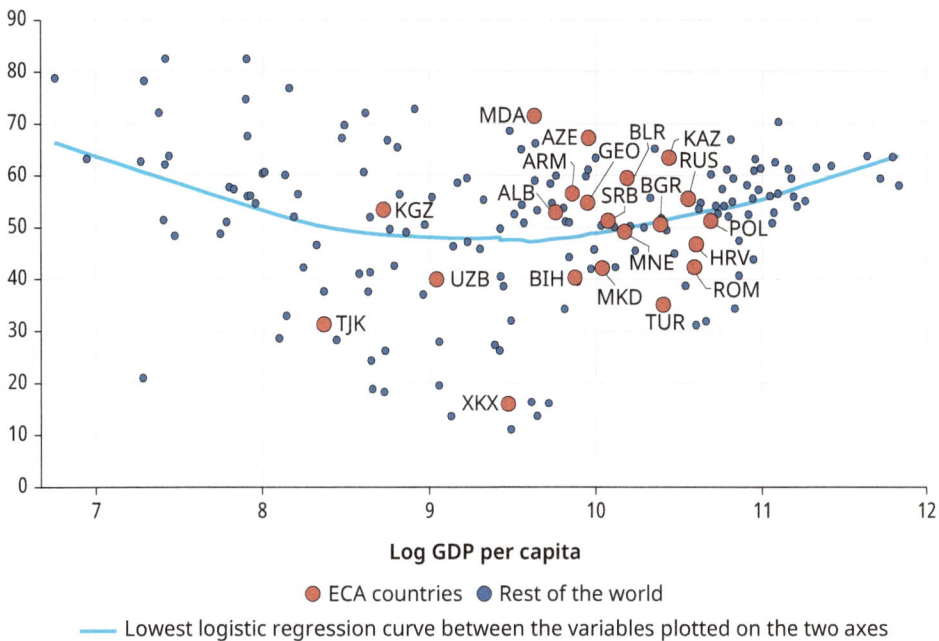

Source: Labour Force Statistics (LFS, STLFS, RURBAN databases), International Labour Organization, Geneva, https://ilostat.ilo.org/methods/concepts-and-definitions/description-labour-force -statistics/#elementor-toc__heading-anchor-1.

Note: For country abbreviations, refer to International Organization for Standardization (ISO), https://www.iso.org/obp/ui/#search.

may be responsible for the worse outcomes experienced by women in the labor market in the region.

Disadvantaged groups also face challenges. The Roma population in the Western Balkans exhibits extremely low labor force participation rates—as low as 19 percent in Montenegro—and lower than the rates among non-Roma at similar income levels (Robayo-Abril and Millán 2019). Moreover, returns to education among Roma are low, at 0 percent–3 percent (depending on the country) per year of education versus 4 percent–8 percent among non-Roma. These figures likely stem from discrimination and unequal treatment. Unless the barriers are also removed, narrowing the human capital accumulation gap between Roma and non-Roma may not be sufficient to allow Roma a fair chance on the labor market.

Migrants and refugees also face restrictions in putting their talents to work. Many ECA countries have become, for the first time in many years, a destination for migrants. The number of foreign citizens living in the four ECA countries that are part of the European Union (EU)—Bulgaria, Croatia, Poland, and Romania—rose from about 236,000 in 2013 to 802,000 in 2023.[1] Other ECA countries, such as Türkiye and some Western Balkans countries, have also seen large increases in foreign migrants. Ukrainian migrants have the right to work and freedom of mobility across the EU (Bossavie, Sánchez, and Makovec 2024). Other migrants in other countries face more restrictions. Excessive restrictions on the right to work of migrants limit the productivity of their talent pools, and these may have negative consequences for the host countries.

The Forces of Creation: Better Education and Innovation

ECA governments need to build a larger pool of talent with advanced skills and unleash the forces of creation. This work requires that relevant authorities in MICs substantially upgrade education systems, particularly higher education (World Bank 2024b). The constraints in many countries include the deteriorating quality of basic education and the dismal performance of secondary vocational schools. Secondary vocational education systems, which cater disproportionately to students with disadvantaged backgrounds and deliver neither professional nor foundational skills, need drastic reform. Ensuring the learning of foundational skills throughout basic education should be a priority.

ECA countries, including several of the ECA high-income countries (HICs), also underperform in the quality of higher education, undermining innovation. Higher education in the region needs to be improved by enhancing institutional management and accountability, aligning research and the provision of skills more tightly, and strengthening the links to industry to promote innovation. Facing dwindling enrollment, public universities might consider consolidation as a response.

The Quality of Basic Education Is Trending Downward

The quality of education is fundamental to long-term economic growth. Relative to educational attainment, educational quality is much more closely associated with higher incomes (Hanushek 2020; Hanushek and Woessmann 2015). Keeping students in classrooms while ineffectively teaching them does not lead to better outcomes for society in the long run.

The quality of secondary education has been trending downward in the median country in the ECA region in the past decade or so and lags the quality among the best performers in the East Asia and Pacific region (refer to figure 3.8). The median mathematics scores in the Programme for International Student Assessment (PISA) evaluation among 15-year-olds in a group of ECA countries declined from 441 to 427 points in 2012–22, while the median scores among EU countries slipped from 490 to 475 points (refer to figure 3.8).[2] Scores among top performers, such as Finland and Poland, fell by 30 points in the same period. This decrease is equivalent to a loss of one or two years of schooling (Avvisati and Givord 2021). The education quality gap in PISA mathematics scores between the ECA countries and the best performers in the East Asia and Pacific region rose

FIGURE 3.8 **PISA mathematics scores have been declining in the ECA region since 2015**

Mathematics score

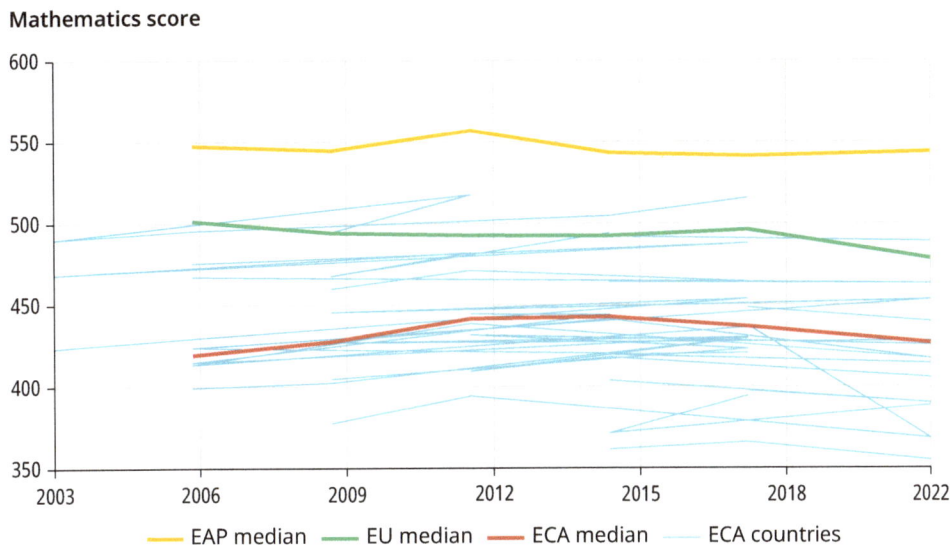

Source: Data from PISA (Programme for International Student Assessment) (dashboard), Organisation for Economic Co-operation and Development, Paris, http://www.oecd.org/pisa /pisaproducts/.

Note: Eight ECA countries—Albania, Bulgaria, Croatia, Kazakhstan, Montenegro, Poland, Romania, and Türkiye—have participated in all PISA rounds since 2006. Other ECA countries have participated in fewer of the study evaluations. The participants in EAP are Hong Kong SAR, China; Japan; Republic of Korea; Macao SAR, China; Singapore; and Taiwan, China. EAP = East Asia and Pacific.

slightly, from 114 points in 2012 to 117 points in 2022, equivalent to about four and a half years of schooling.[3] The drop in student performance in the ECA countries was significant even among the region's top performers after the COVID-19 pandemic.

The quality of basic education among students with disadvantaged backgrounds is poor. These students are disproportionately streamed into vocational education, undermining their acquisition of foundational skills. Proponents have argued that vocational education programs promote youth employment, instill technological knowledge, equip students with marketable skills, and produce mid-level technicians. Yet, vocational education does not necessarily lead to better labor market outcomes (refer to box 3.1).

Vocational education students in the ECA region are overwhelmingly from disadvantaged backgrounds. Vocational education focuses on the acquisition of professional skills, but the students enrolled in this type of program perform poorly in basic subjects, such as reading and mathematics, which are skills in wide demand by employers (refer to figure 3.9). The lack of foundational skills puts students enrolled in vocational education in a vulnerable position in the labor market because the professional skills they acquire can quickly become obsolete as technologies change, and the labor market advantage that vocational education

BOX 3.1 Vocational Education and Training in Europe and Central Asia Need to Be Better

Vocational education and training (VET) systems are popular among policy makers worldwide (Crawfurd et al. 2021). Europe and Central Asia (ECA) has a sizable VET footprint. On average, 45 percent of its upper-secondary students are enrolled in vocational programs. This figure contrasts with 22 percent in the rest of the world. In some ECA countries, the enrollment exceeds 70 percent (World Bank, UNESCO, and ILO 2023).

The popularity of VET systems in the region stems from the belief that they improve employment outcomes, particularly among youth and disadvantaged groups. But the evidence is mixed. Postsecondary VET courses have a positive impact on labor market outcomes (Ghisletta, Kemper, and Stöterau 2021), although the mechanisms differ across countries at varying income levels, and design characteristics are important. Secondary VET systems struggle, meanwhile, to keep up with evolving labor market demands. Secondary VET graduates who pursue no additional education may perform the same type of jobs that their peers performed two decades ago, while the nature of jobs for the rest of the labor force has changed greatly. Jobs in Europe have become more intensive in social and nonroutine, cognitive tasks, while typical jobs held by secondary VET graduates have remained as intensive in manual and routine tasks as they were 20 years ago (Dalvit et al. 2023).

Secondary VET is generally of two broad types: classroom based or workplace based. Systems focusing on work-based learning and apprenticeships are associated with more seamless entry into the labor market, heavily involving private firms in providing education, as seen over centuries of tradition. However, this tradition did not formerly exist in most European countries, and vocational schools were typically created from scratch by governments without a strong link to private firms. This practice was also the case in planned economies, in which vocational education was mostly classroom based (Cedefop 2004).

While vocational graduates do slightly better from a labor market perspective in countries where the VET system is mostly work based, classroom-based VET may not be detrimental to labor market outcomes if foundational skills are provided. In Finland, in which students are among the best performers in Europe on the PISA evaluation and in which vocational education is mostly classroom based, although entry occurs at a later age (16–17), vocational-track graduates do well in the labor market relative to their academic-track peers (Silliman and Virtanen 2022). If vocational education systems do not involve private firms in the provision of professional skills or do not supply the foundational skills students may be lacking, the labor market outcomes among VET graduates may be underwhelming (World Bank, UNESCO, and ILO 2023).

VET systems in many ECA countries are failing to provide graduates with professional skills useful in the labor market, instead playing, imperfectly, a social policy role because they cater disproportionately to students with disadvantaged backgrounds. Unless countries can mirror the successful cases of apprenticeship-type systems, with the extensive involvement of private firms and a strong base of foundational skills, the rationale for investment in VET systems the ECA region will remain weak.

FIGURE 3.9 Vocational-track students perform significantly worse than general-track students

Share of students at or above level 2 proficiency in mathematics (%)

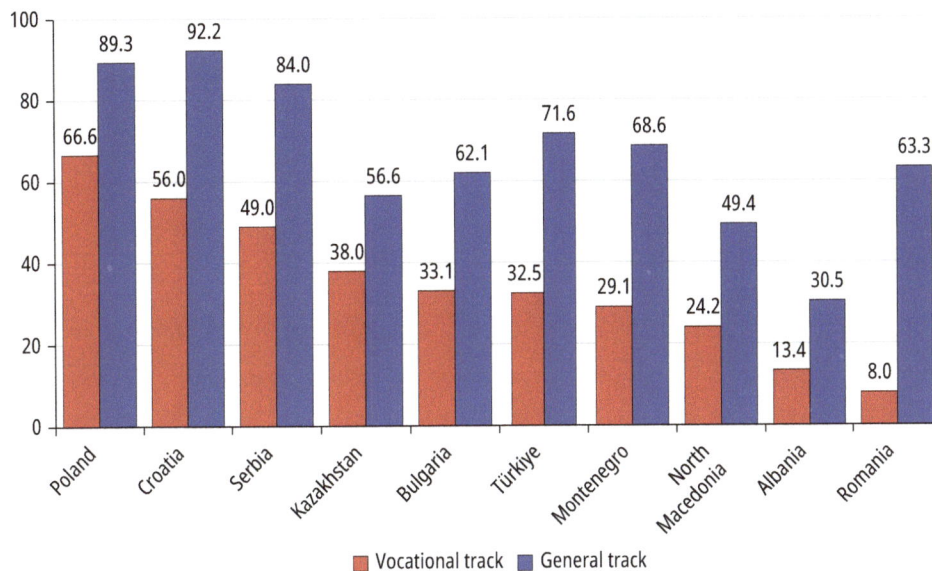

■ Vocational track ■ General track

Source: World Bank estimates based on the 2022 evaluation of PISA (Programme for International Student Assessment) (dashboard), Organisation for Economic Co-operation and Development, Paris, http://www.oecd.org/pisa/pisaproducts/.

Note: Only countries with a meaningful sample of upper-secondary vocational-track students (10 percent of the total student sample) are included.

graduates have at the start of their professional lives can soon dissipate (Dalvit et al. 2023; Hanushek et al. 2017).

Early selection into vocational education results in higher costs and lower benefits and induces higher inequality relative to academic secondary schooling. This leads to inequality in academic and labor market outcomes by channeling poor and minority students into the less prestigious vocational track, while reinforcing ethnic inequalities (Foster 1965; Psacharopoulos 1987, 1991). Tracking contributes little to the efficiency (learning) of an education system. The effect of tracking on inequality is significantly positive, indicating that tracking increases the inequality in the education system (Terrin and Triventi 2023). Moreover, students streamed into vocational studies are sometimes not allowed to switch to another program and, later, enjoy only limited opportunities to enter tertiary education.

A comprehensive basic education system that does not sort students into different program tracks early on improves the academic and labor market performance of the students. Education reforms improve outcomes if they delay or eliminate the selection of students into separate programs at an early age (14 or younger) and if they introduce nationally unified curricula and comprehensive schooling. Cross-country comparisons demonstrate that, for the same mean values, the variance in test scores is higher in countries in which track sorting takes place early, suggesting a higher degree of inequality (Hanushek and Woessmann 2006). The reason is that, in academic schooling, students spend more time on tasks that are the focus of greater expectations, they spend more hours learning subjects that are tested, and they benefit from the opportunity to move on to higher education. Moreover, reforms of track sorting lead to more schooling and earnings among students with low socioeconomic backgrounds, as shown in Finland, Norway, and Poland (Aghion et al. 2023; Jakubowski et al. 2016; Meghir and Palme 2005; Ollikainen 2021; Pekkala Kerr, Pekkarinen, and Uusitalo 2013; Pekkarinen, Uusitalo, and Pekkala Kerr 2009).

The Worrisome Low Quality of Higher Education in the Region

To move from adoption to innovation, countries need to be able to rely on solid higher-education institutions. The higher-education system is a main determinant of innovation. In countries in the Organisation for Economic Co-operation and Development (OECD), the higher-education sector accounts for more than three-quarters of all basic research (OECD 2017). While comparable data on ECA countries are not available, this share should be understood only as an upper bound, given the limited investment in R&D in the region by the private sector.

The poor quality of higher education in the region is especially worrisome. In most ECA countries, the quality of higher education is lower not only relative to global standards but also relative to the quality of basic education in the region (refer to figure 3.10).

The lower quality of higher education is mirrored by poor performance in cognitive skills among adults with tertiary degrees. An analysis comparing the skills proficiency of adults possessing tertiary degrees with the quality of higher education shows a significant correlation between the two. In countries in which the quality of higher education is lower, adults with tertiary degrees perform less well in literacy, numeracy, and problem solving (refer to figure 3.11). This issue is particularly concerning because substantial evidence demonstrates that cognitive skills are linked to innovation (Bell et al. 2019).

There is also a notable disconnect between the skills taught in tertiary education institutions and the needs of the labor market. Employers frequently report that graduates lack essential soft skills, such as communication and teamwork abilities, as well as technical skills specific to the industry of employment. This skills mismatch may result in graduate underemployment and overqualification and may also lead to a drain on human resources. Many universities in the region still instruct according to Soviet-era curricula that focus more on rote learning than on critical thinking and practical skills (Huisman, Smolentseva, and Froumin 2018). Reliance on outdated curricula fails to equip students with the skills required to compete and thrive in a dynamic job market.

FIGURE 3.10 ECA: higher education is worse than expected given the quality of basic education

Quality of higher education (university quality score)

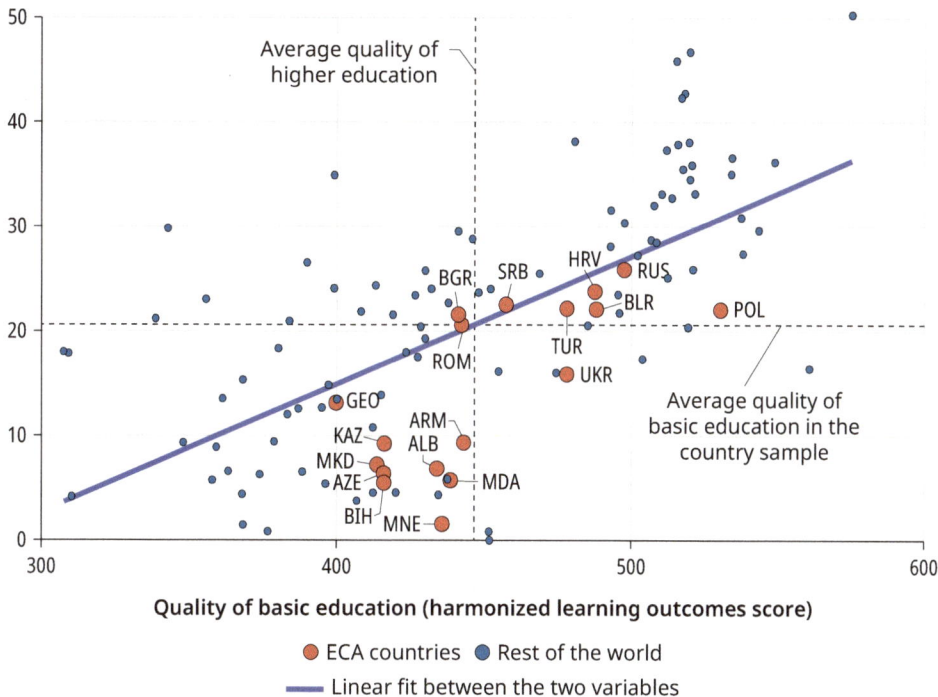

Quality of basic education (harmonized learning outcomes score)

● ECA countries ● Rest of the world
— Linear fit between the two variables

Sources: Demirgüç-Kunt and Torre 2022; HLO (Harmonized Learning Outcomes) Database, World Bank, Washington, DC, https://datacatalog.worldbank.org/search/dataset/0038001; Human Capital (Data Portal), World Bank, Washington, DC, https://humancapital.worldbank.org/en/home.

Note: The quality of basic education is proxied by the harmonized learning outcomes score by country (refer to the sources). The quality of higher education is proxied by the aggregate university quality score as calculated by Demirgüç-Kunt and Torre (2022). For country abbreviations, refer to International Organization for Standardization (ISO), https://www.iso.org/obp/ui/#search.

Insufficient funding for tertiary education leads to inadequate infrastructure and poor learning environments. Many institutions struggle with inadequate infrastructure, including poorly maintained buildings and outdated equipment.

Academic capture undermines education standards and deprives talented students of fair learning opportunities. The phenomenon occurs if corruption and conflict of interest compromise education standards, affecting the quality of many higher-education institutions in the ECA region. Close relationships between education institutions and political or business elites often erode academic integrity because decisions become based on personal or political interests rather than educational merit. The corruption damages the credibility of higher-education institutions and devalues the degrees these institutions offer. Talented students who might otherwise benefit from a robust education are deprived of fair, high-quality learning opportunities (Milovanovitch, Denisova-Schmidt, and Anapiosyan 2018).

FIGURE 3.11 The lower quality of higher education translates into low skill proficiency among adults

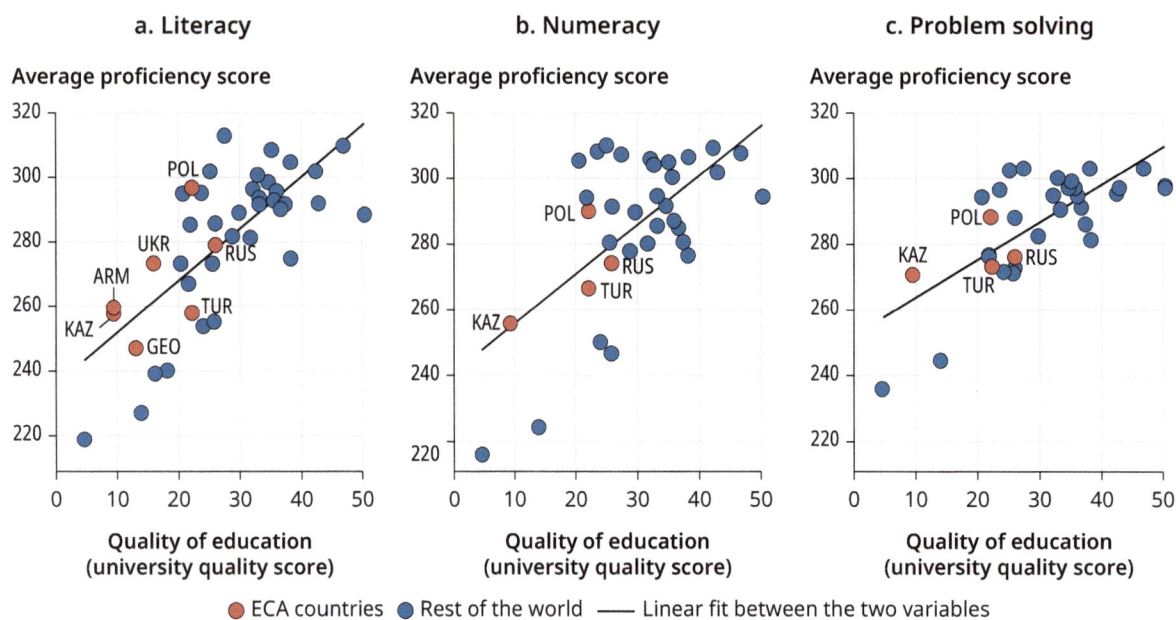

a. Literacy

Average proficiency score

b. Numeracy

Average proficiency score

c. Problem solving

Average proficiency score

● ECA countries   ● Rest of the world   —— Linear fit between the two variables

Sources: World Bank estimates based on Demirgüç-Kunt and Torre 2022; PIAAC Data and Methodology (dashboard), Program for the International Assessment of Adult Competencies, Organisation for Economic Co-operation and Development, Paris, https://www.oecd.org/en/about/programmes/piaac/piaac-data.html.

Note: The panels plot the country-level average skills proficiency scores for tertiary graduates (vertical axes) against the country-level quality of higher education (horizontal axes). The quality of higher education is proxied by the aggregate university quality score calculated by Demirgüç-Kunt and Torre (2022). For country abbreviations, refer to International Organization for Standardization (ISO), https://www.iso.org/obp/ui/#search.

Poor management, too, has been associated with weaker university performance. A study in the United Kingdom found that management quality in universities is heterogeneous across institutions and also within institutions, where some departments are much more well managed than others. Well-managed departments also perform better in conducting research and instruction and in student satisfaction (McCormack, Propper, and Smith 2014). The features of management that matter the most in university performance seem to be related to the provision of incentives, such as rewards for top performers, the removal of poor performers, attracting and retaining talent, and the management of general operations.

ECA university systems are facing dwindling enrollments. In Poland, for example, the number of students dropped by 28 percent in 2013–22, while the decline was about 20 percent in Bulgaria and around 10 percent in Romania.[4] In Moldova, tertiary enrollment fell from 128,000 in 2006/07 to 56,700 in 2022/23, a decrease of over 41 percent (Mazur 2022). The decline in student enrollment across the ECA was not matched by a reduction in the size of the higher-education system in the region. In 2017–18, Poland had more than 10.0 higher-education institutions per million inhabitants, while Ukraine had 7.7 (World Bank 2019b). This finding contrasts with fewer than 5.0 in Germany and less than 2.0 in Spain. These trends have sparked discussions about consolidating universities, that is, merging two or more institutions. Consolidation can be a strategic response to demographic challenges and a way to avoid university closures that are costly for students. Many countries in the region have only limited resources for higher education. The extra resources resulting from the efficiency gains associated with merging institutions could be critical in maintaining and enhancing education quality.

In research performance, ECA universities lag universities in the East Asia and Pacific region, Europe, and the United States. Only 9 universities in the ECA region rank among the global top 500 universities, well below the number in the East Asia and Pacific region (116), the EU (154), the United Kingdom (55), and the United States (107) (refer to table 3.1). No ECA country appears in the top 50, and only 1 ECA university is in the top 100.

Although investment is low, higher-education institutions are major centers of R&D in the ECA region, relatively more so than in other global regions, accounting for about 30 percent of R&D investment in the ECA. This outcome also reflects the weak R&D efforts of the ECA private sector. The shares of higher-education institutions in total R&D investment range from more than 50 percent in Bosnia and Herzegovina and North Macedonia (although low in absolute terms) to around 40 percent in Kazakhstan; 30 percent in Poland, Serbia, and Türkiye; 25 percent in Romania;

TABLE 3.1 Number of universities in the global top 500 of the Times Higher Education ranking

Region, country	Universities in the global top 500
Europe and Central Asia	9
Russian Federation	6
Türkiye	3
European Union	154
United Kingdom	55
East Asia and Pacific	116
Australia	32
China	31
Japan	10
Korea, Rep. of	13
Rest of region	30
United States	107

Source: World Bank compilations based on 2024 data of THE (Times Higher Education) World University Rankings (dashboard), Times Higher Education, London, https://www.timeshighereducation.com/world-university-rankings.

and less than 10 percent in Bulgaria.[5] These shares are generally higher than the EU average of about 22 percent.[6] The relevance of universities to R&D spending in the ECA exceeds that in Japan (12 percent), the United States (10 percent), the Republic of Korea (9 percent), and China (8 percent). Still, university investment in R&D per inhabitant in the ECA, which is highest in Poland, at €81, and lowest in Bulgaria, at €6, does not match the corresponding investment in Japan (€132), Korea (€133), the EU (€172), or the United States (€214).

Lack of infrastructure and support hinders innovation in the ECA countries. Shortfalls are evident, for example, in research labs, technology parks, and the institutional support for intellectual property rights, venture capital, and pro-entrepreneurial policies. Without such support, it is difficult to concretize new ideas and bring them to market, and creative and groundbreaking efforts are easily discouraged. Part of this lack and shortfall may also derive from the characteristics of ECA higher education, which, unlike the higher education in the Anglo-American model, appears to fail in developing commercially viable research outputs, especially because research centers are not tightly associated with institutions of higher learning (refer to box 3.2).

BOX 3.2 Research and Higher Education: Germany, the United Kingdom, and the United States

The higher-education systems in Germany, the United Kingdom, and the United States have distinct approaches to integrating research and education and nurturing and identifying talent. The United Kingdom and the United States have historically emphasized embedding research within universities. These systems have developed robust mechanisms for identifying and nurturing talent, often through competitive admissions processes and specialized honors programs. In contrast, the German system relies on a dual structure whereby universities focus on teaching and basic research, while specialized institutions, such as the Max Planck Society, concentrate on applied research and industry collaboration. This model, followed by several European countries and most postcommunist nations, often identifies talent through performance in rigorous secondary education systems and develops talent through specialized academic tracks.

Universities in the United Kingdom and the United States often rank at or near the top globally and are able to attract high-quality faculty and abundant resources. They also serve as talent magnets, drawing in high-achieving students from across the world. The German system excels in identifying and nurturing talent in specific technical fields through the dual education system, which combines vocational training and academic learning.

Continued

BOX 3.2 **Research and Higher Education: Germany, the United Kingdom, and the United States** *(Continued)*

The higher-education system in former Soviet Union countries presents another dual structure model, with centralized control, specialized institutions, free education, limited institutional autonomy, and an emphasis on applied sciences and engineering (Smolentseva 2003). Talent is often identified early through specialized schools and competitions, with an emphasis on mathematics and sciences. Still, the rigid separation between research and teaching institutions often leads to a disconnect between cutting-edge research and classroom instruction. This system has produced highly skilled specialists in specific fields, but has struggled to develop a more diverse range of talent.

The US system encourages institutional autonomy, fosters innovation, and integrates research and teaching, unlike the post-Soviet model. The US system's flexibility and responsiveness to market demands contrast with the often rigid and slowly adapting post-Soviet institutions (Urquiola 2020). It is not clear, however, how easily the US model can be replicated in other societies.

Many postcommunist countries have been reforming their systems to align more with Western models. The steps they are following include integrating research into universities, introducing private universities and tuition fees, increasing institutional autonomy, and participating in the Bologna Process, the series of ministerial meetings and agreements among European countries to ensure comparability in the standards and quality of higher-education qualifications. Yet, challenges remain in funding, the modernization of curricula, and finding a balance between historical strengths and the need for reform and international integration (Huisman, Smolentseva, and Froumin 2018).

Talent on the Move: High-Skill Migration from and to ECA Countries

High-skill emigration raises worries in most ECA countries, although it may not undermine the development of homegrown talent. Emigration can incentivize education investment, and remittances can support human capital development in origin countries. Returning migrants may improve productivity in the origin country by importing expertise and best practices from the destination country. Bilateral migration agreements could allow destination countries to fund education and training programs in origin countries, thus achieving a more equal distribution of the benefits of migration across both types of countries.

How the Emigration of High-Skill Workers Can Hinder Development

A concern across ECA countries is the emigration of talented workers. Worldwide, migrants tend to have higher educational attainment than the population in the countries of origin of the migrants. But, in some countries in the ECA region, the share of individuals with higher education who migrate is quite high, exceeding a third in Albania, Bosnia and Herzegovina, Kazakhstan, and Moldova and more than a quarter in Armenia, Bulgaria, Croatia, the Kyrgyz Republic, and North Macedonia (refer to figure 3.12). Countries with fewer higher-education graduates experience the highest emigration rates among this group. A nontrivial share of high-school graduates also emigrate to study abroad, reflecting the low quality of universities in the region: 17.2 percent of individuals ages 20–24 who migrated to the EU from ECA countries in 2022 did so for reasons of education.[7]

The emigration of highly skilled workers can be an obstacle to development if the costs to the origin society from losing a highly qualified worker outweigh the benefits from the remittances and knowledge spillovers the worker generates during emigration and following return (World Bank 2023). In countries in which education is publicly funded, the emigration of individuals with higher-education

FIGURE 3.12 **Small shares of university graduates may mean high emigration rates among graduates**

Population with tertiary education that has emigrated (%)

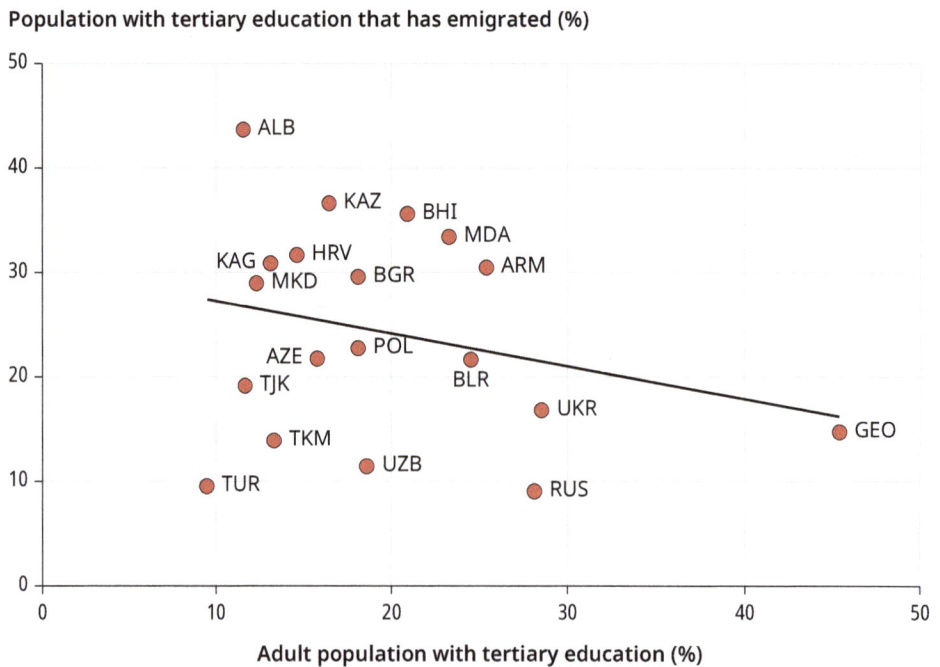

Source: World Bank elaboration based on Migration Data Portal, World Bank, Washington, DC, https://www.migrationdataportal.org/international-data?i=stock_abs_&t=2024.

degrees represents the transfer of a subsidy from the origin country (typically an MIC) to the destination country (typically an HIC).

Pull factors, such as proximity to the EU, and push factors, such as limited job opportunities in some specialized professions in the origin countries, help explain outward migration. Origin countries can do little about the pull factors, but they can try to diminish the influence and strength of push factors (World Bank 2019a). They can, for instance, raise the competitiveness of wages in critical high-skill occupations. Smaller countries could focus on developing niche sectors, such as personal and health services for tourists, which may become a magnet for qualified workers once the niche sectors reach a critical mass (World Bank 2023).

Origin countries could also establish bilateral agreements with HICs to ensure that the benefits of migration are shared evenly. Global skills partnerships are a model of collaboration whereby the government or the private sector of the destination country finances training among potential migrants in the origin country before emigration (Acosta et al. 2025). Such training would benefit students who stay home and enter the domestic labor force, reducing the adverse effects of the drain on human resources (World Bank 2023).

How the Emigration of High-Skill Workers Can Promote Development

The emigration of highly skilled individuals does not necessarily erode the development of talent in origin countries. First, the prospect of emigration may incentivize individuals to invest in their own education even if they do not ultimately emigrate. For example, in Fiji, an increase in high-skill emigration to Australia, Canada, and New Zealand led to an increase in human capital investment—particularly, tertiary educational attainment—among the population that did not emigrate, generating a net rise in tertiary educational attainment even after accounting for those who emigrated (Chand and Clemens 2023).

Second, the budget constraints on households that receive remittances in the origin countries from the emigrants may be relaxed. If child labor is not the norm or is not fungible for adult labor, relaxed household constraints generally lead to a boost in household human capital investment. In Bosnia and Herzegovina, for instance, households receiving remittances tended to invest more in children's education than households without migrants (Oruc, Jackson, and Pugh 2018). Because high-skill migrants may remit more income and may originally be from households that do not rely on farmwork, high-skill migration may not be completely detrimental to talent development in the origin country (Bollard et al. 2011). Still, as Gao, Kikkawa, and Kang (2021) find in the Kyrgyz Republic, this positive remittance impact may be offset by the missing adult labor effect, which can be significant if child labor is a substitute for adult labor, as in households dependent on farmwork.

The belief that high-skill emigration always has a detrimental effect on innovation is unfounded. There is substantial evidence that migrant inventors promote innovation in destination countries, although it is unclear whether the innovation in the destination countries would have occurred in the origin countries had the inventors not emigrated (Bahar, Choudhury, and Rapoport 2020). The channels of knowledge diffusion may thus be important in driving innovation if high-skill migrants establish such channels between the destination and origin countries, which may boost innovation in the latter. Agrawal et al. (2011) label this the "knowledge access effect." Their study documents the role of such an effect in the most important inventions in India, explained by the activities of diaspora inventors.

High-skill emigrants may create productive connections to global sources of knowledge, capital, and goods. Returning migrants may improve productivity in origin countries by importing knowledge and best practices from the destination countries (Pekkala Kerr et al. 2016). This issue was particularly the case for returning high-skill migrants in Bosnia and Herzegovina who moved back to their country after staying in Germany in the early 1990s (Bahar et al. 2024). Even when remaining abroad, the diaspora can result in increased investment back home, as shown, for instance, by the Diaspora Invest Project, also in Bosnia and Herzegovina (World Bank 2024a). The diaspora can play a role in the discussion of economic development plans back home, as is currently the case in Korea and Viet Nam (World Bank 2023).

In destination countries, high-skill immigrants contribute decisively to better innovation outcomes (Bahar, Choudhury, and Rapoport 2020; Bahar and Rapoport 2018; Hunt and Gauthier-Loiselle 2010; Ozgen, Nijkamp, and Poot 2011). Likewise, foreign graduate students have been shown to contribute to innovation in the United States (Chellaraj, Maskus, and Matoo 2008; Stuen, Mobarak, and Maskus 2012). ECA's higher-education policy makers should see the internationalization of their student pools as a strategy for improving innovation outputs.

Weakening the Forces of Preservation: Perceptions of Mobility and Support for Reform

Preservation is an antagonist of creation because it is also an antagonist of destruction (World Bank 2024b). To spark a process of creative destruction, MICs need to overcome the forces that preserve the status quo. This implies structural reform. But such reform fails if households are not optimistic about the gains from reform. This section shows that expectations of social mobility significantly influence public support for structural reform.

Individuals optimistic about their own or their children's prospects are thus more likely to support higher taxes for education. This section also shows that vulnerability to poverty is eroding the middle class in many ECA countries. ECA countries should thus protect and strengthen the middle class and foster its economic security, promote fair socioeconomic mobility, and carefully design reforms to garner public support, especially in areas such as education, that are associated with long-term payoffs.

How Household Perceptions of Social Mobility Affect Support for Reform

The transition to innovation-led growth requires a solid middle class that will invest in human capital and support the reforms needed to level the playing field and foster growth. The middle class is the backbone of democracy (Alesina and Rodrik 1994; Birdsall 2010; Stewart 2001). It helps produce economic benefits and foster economic development (Easterly 2001). The entrepreneurial activities that originate in the middle class lead to employment creation and productivity enhancements, incentivizing investments in education and health, contributing to human capital accumulation and growth in consumption and savings, and creating a virtuous circle that expands the middle class (Acemoglu and Zilibotti 1997; Banerjee and Duflo 2008; Szymańska 2019; Zilibotti and Doepke 2007).

The effects of structural reform and investment in human capital are not instantaneous. They take time—maybe even a generation—to materialize. In low-income countries, upgrading education systems focuses on issues related to expanding access to primary and secondary education. In contrast, in MICs, the education reforms necessary to advance to high-income status require complex and longer-term investments in upgrading vocational and tertiary education that are critical to R&D (Doner and Schneider 2016). And, in HICs, the reforms focus on tertiary and postgraduate education.

Expectations for the future influence people's support for reform. In deciding whether to support tax-financed investments in education, many individuals assess the probability of benefiting—individually or through household members—from the outcomes of such reforms and compare the discounted value of the benefits against the current consumption forgone because of higher tax outlays. Individuals with high socioeconomic status today, as well as those who expect to be upwardly mobile in the future, may be more likely to see the benefit of supporting investments in education if they expect their children to take advantage of tertiary education, while also having a greater capacity to sustain higher tax outlays today. Individuals with low socioeconomic status, or those who expect to be downwardly mobile in the future, may perceive a lower value in such investments or be less able to forgo current consumption. Yet, given that the future is uncertain for everyone, more risk-averse individuals will discount the future more heavily, which, at the margin, would decrease their support for structural reforms.

Beliefs about social mobility are important in driving support for increased tax investment in education. A study by Cojocaru, Lokshin, and Torre (2024) shows that ECA countries in which expectations of future mobility (within the same generation) are more positive exhibit a higher share of the population willing to pay a part of their income or pay more taxes to support investments in education (refer to figure 3.13, panel a). A similar pattern is manifest between more positive beliefs about the life prospects of children born today (relative to the current generation) and greater willingness to finance education investments (refer to figure 3.13, panel b).

The pattern across countries is reproduced across individuals: more positive expectations of one's own future social mobility are associated with a greater willingness to support investments in education. According to estimates using the latest round of the Life in Transition survey, a 1 SD increase in expected future mobility is associated with a 2.3 percentage point rise in support for education

FIGURE 3.13 **Optimism about social mobility is linked to greater willingness to invest in education**

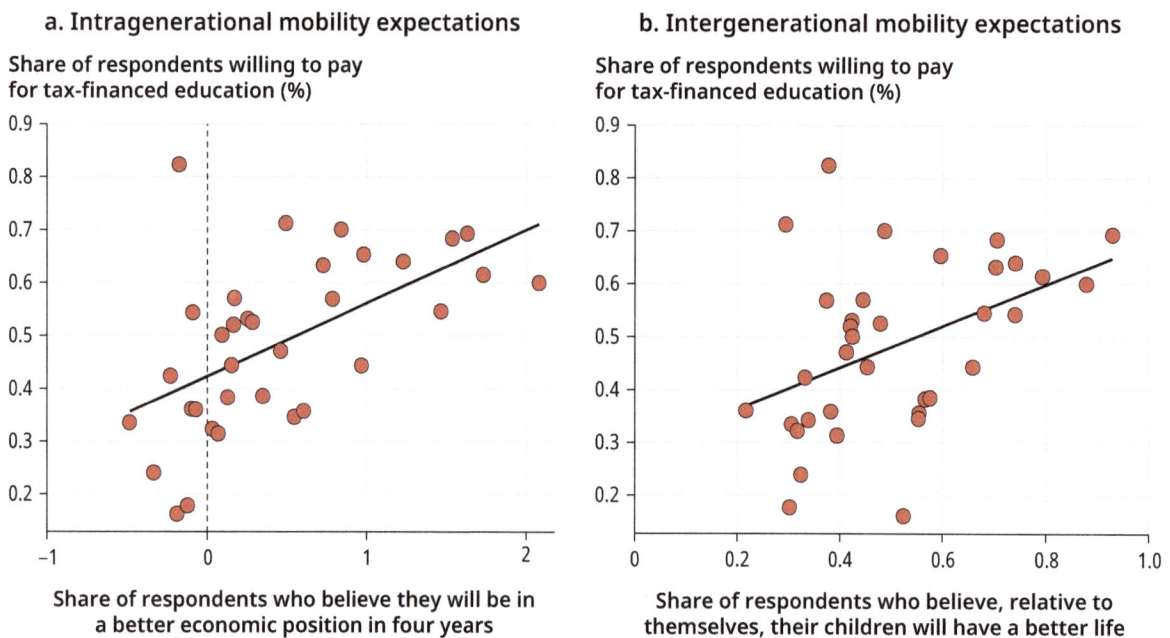

a. Intragenerational mobility expectations

Share of respondents willing to pay
for tax-financed education (%)

Share of respondents who believe they will be in
a better economic position in four years

b. Intergenerational mobility expectations

Share of respondents willing to pay
for tax-financed education (%)

Share of respondents who believe, relative to
themselves, their children will have a better life

Source: Cojocaru, Lokshin, and Torre 2024.

Note: Respondents were asked to imagine a 10-step ladder. On the bottom, the first step, stand the poorest 10 percent of the population. On the highest step, the 10th step, stand the richest 10 percent of the population. Panel a plots responses to the question, "Where on the ladder do you believe your household will be four years from now?" Panel b plots whether respondents agree or disagree with the statement "Children who are born now will have a better life than my generation." The values in each panel scale the responses.

investments, controlling for main sociodemographic characteristics and one's current position on the income ladder (Cojocaru, Lokshin, and Torre 2024).[8] More positive expectations with respect to the life prospects of children born today are similarly positively correlated with a greater willingness to support investments in education. Among survey respondents who agree with the statement that "children who are born now will have a better life than my generation," support for education investments is 4.1 percentage points higher in the latest Life in Transition Survey round (2022–23) and as much as 7.3 percentage points higher in the 2016 survey round.

The effect of expectations of mobility on support for reforms is also mediated by a belief in fairness. As the study by Cojocaru, Lokshin, and Torre (2024) shows, respondents who believe that success in their society is meritocratic or determined by a combination of hard work, intelligence, and skills are more likely to forgo part of their income to invest in the education system. Individuals with a greater degree of tolerance toward losses may also be more optimistic about their mobility prospects. A belief in fairness and a level of risk aversion can be interacted with expectations of mobility in a model to assess whether the relationship between mobility expectations and support for reforms is moderated by these factors. The results show that, holding beliefs about fairness constant, the predicted support for reforms is higher among individuals who have a lower aversion to risk and is higher among those who expect to be upwardly mobile.

Support for education reforms is greatest among individuals with low risk aversion, who believe that success is generally fairly obtained, and who expect to be upwardly mobile in the future. It is the lowest among those who are averse to risk, believe that success in their society is not meritocratic, and have no expectations of upward mobility.

Middle-Class Vulnerability to Falling into Poverty

Income and welfare security—also understood as a lack of vulnerability to falling into poverty—are important aspects of middle-class identity. The concept of the middle class encompasses more than the opinion that one is able to afford a particular standard of living. One of the hallmarks of the concept is a sense of stability and economic security, often achieved through asset ownership, a high level of education and skills, or working in certain professions (Atkinson and Brandolini 2013). This sense of stability and security can be defined as the absence—or exceptionally low level—of the risk of falling into poverty (López-Calva and Ortiz-Juárez 2014).

In recent years, however, vulnerability to poverty has increased, meaning that some households with an income that would have previously been considered middle class are now vulnerable to falling into poverty. The permanent income needed to avoid vulnerability rose, on average, from about $42.50 a day in 2008 to

$46.00 a day in 2020 in a sample of 17 high-income European countries (Bussolo et al. 2025). The predicted income associated with the lower-middle-class threshold between 2005–08 and 2017–20 jumped, for instance, from $30 to $53 a day in Bulgaria (refer to figure 3.14). Bolch et al. (2023) also find an increase in the income needed to be safely out of poverty in other lower-middle-income and upper-middle-income countries. This increase in the income level may be interpreted as an insurance premium to maintain the same level of protection against the risk of poverty. Households that do not pay this premium and remain at the level of income of the previous period thus face a higher risk of falling into poverty.

The composition of the middle class in high-income Europe has changed, and higher levels of education are needed to safely stay out of poverty. Changes in the income thresholds that define the middle class have consequences for the composition of the middle class. In 2017–20, the composition of human capital needed to generate an income sufficient to insulate a household from the risk of poverty and remain in the middle class shifted toward higher levels of education and more professional or more management-oriented occupations. Households with lower levels of education and skills were more likely to fall into poverty in the later period than in the earlier period. In 2005–08, for example, nearly one household in four in the middle class had a head with only primary education; by 2017–20, this share had dropped to less than one

FIGURE 3.14 **The income needed to avoid vulnerability has increased over time**

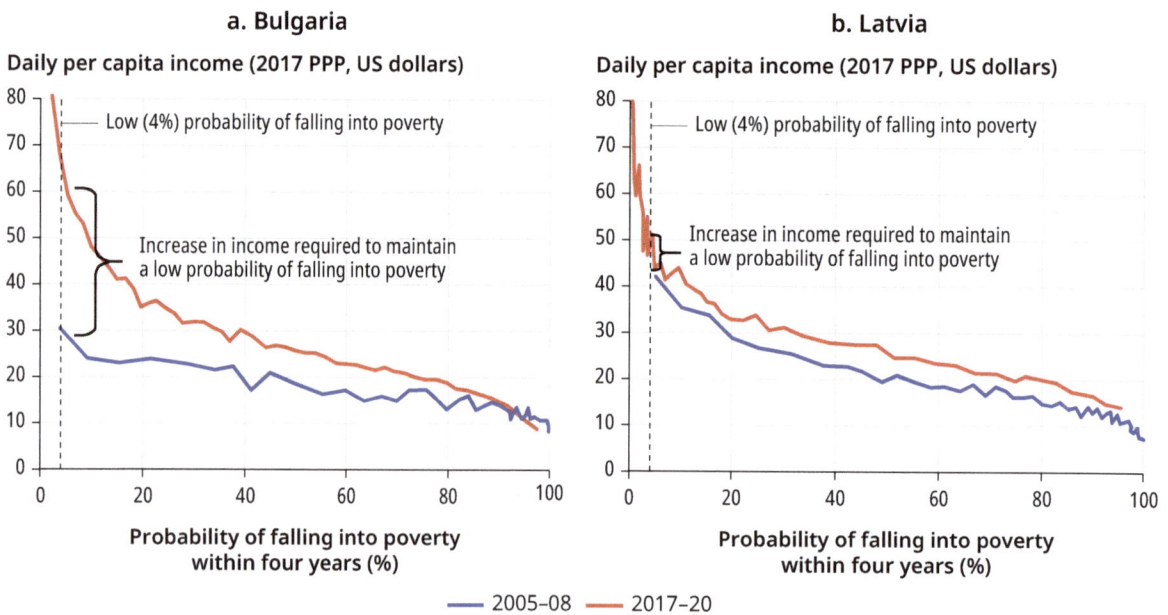

a. Bulgaria

Daily per capita income (2017 PPP, US dollars)

Low (4%) probability of falling into poverty

Increase in income required to maintain a low probability of falling into poverty

Probability of falling into poverty within four years (%)

b. Latvia

Daily per capita income (2017 PPP, US dollars)

Low (4%) probability of falling into poverty

Increase in income required to maintain a low probability of falling into poverty

Probability of falling into poverty within four years (%)

—— 2005–08   —— 2017–20

Source: Bussolo et al. 2025.

Note: PPP = purchasing power parity.

household in seven, and nearly one household head in three at the threshold had tertiary education.

The existence of a large pool of households that is neither poor nor middle class casts some doubt on the volume of social support that strong, growth-enhancing reforms may enjoy in the ECA region. The share of the population that is not poor, but not safely out of poverty, is 20 percent in ECA lower-middle-income countries, 28 percent in ECA upper-middle-income countries, and 29 percent in ECA HICs (Bolch et al. 2023; Bussolo et al. 2025). Individuals in this group are particularly exposed to income shocks that can push them into poverty and may thus be less willing to incur risky tradeoffs that could put their welfare in danger.

Conclusions and Policy Recommendations

The transition to high-income status requires that talent be nurtured and that misallocations arising from inequality of opportunity and preservation of outdated education structures be reduced. The ECA countries need a high-skill labor force, and good-quality education is fundamental to such a labor force. The quality of basic education in the region has been showing a declining trend. The region also underperforms markedly in the quality of higher education. In any case, good-quality education is not sufficient if opportunities are not available to all and if merit is not rewarded. A high level of social mobility ensures that talent is not misallocated and wasted and that talented children from all backgrounds can fully flourish for their own benefit and the benefit of society.

To achieve these goals, governments and stakeholders in the ECA region need to consider several options.

- *Promote merit-based policies that help overcome barriers to entry and ensure equal access to higher education to all strands of society.* Education subsidies that fund talented individuals from disadvantaged backgrounds to pursue higher-education degrees may be more effective than only expanding enrollment, particularly in research-oriented programs (Akcigit, Pearce, and Prato 2024; Londoño-Vélez et al. 2023). Such policies should not, however, come at the expense of not rewarding merit. Selection for any education program and successful graduation should ultimately be determined by ability.

- *Facilitate the broader participation of women in the labor market and reduce job restrictions and other obstacles facing migrants.* In ECA countries with low female labor force participation, social norms play a fundamental role in depressing the prospects of women in the labor market. Norms change only slowly, but broadbased education and information interventions have been shown to help in weakening patriarchal norms (World Bank 2024b). Migrants may also represent a pool of talent that may be relied on, particularly in the context of a shrinking population. Legal restrictions on work prevent migrants and, especially, refugees from fully contributing to host economies and societies.

- *Reform vocational education and training systems extensively.* Delaying vocational school tracking to the end of lower-secondary education will undoubtedly help reduce talent misallocation by improving the opportunities and academic outcomes among children with disadvantaged backgrounds. The ECA countries should support the development of strong foundational skills among students in vocational education and involve the private sector in providing work-based learning and apprenticeships. These countries should, too, consider resizing vocational education systems.

- *Integrate research centers and universities and strengthen higher-education–industry links to foster innovation.* Integrating research centers into the higher-education system can improve the quality and relevance of the system. Higher-education–industry links should be promoted to stimulate innovation. Governments should also reassess the needs in advanced research capacity required among institutions to participate in the global science network.

- *Consolidate universities to make better use of resources and improve the management and accountability of institutions of higher education.* University consolidation could address the decline in the number of students, improve education quality, and achieve significant cost savings by eliminating duplicate administrative structures and optimizing infrastructure. The resulting concentration of talent would enhance interdisciplinary collaboration and open funding opportunities. University funding should be linked to performance evaluations. Universities should compete on quality by increasing their reliance on competitive grants, enhanced competition for students and faculty, and yardstick competitions (which often involve assessment exercises).

- *Develop bilateral migration agreements between origin and destination countries to support the more efficient allocation of migrant talent.* Bilateral migration agreements could allow destination countries to fund education and training programs in origin countries, thus achieving a more equal distribution of the benefits of migration across both types of countries. To improve the allocation of talent, destination countries should enhance the recognition of migrant qualifications, provide refugees with the right to work, and improve or establish demand pathways for workers.

- *Implement adaptive and shock-responsive social safety nets to reduce the vulnerability of the middle class.* Protecting and developing a stronger middle class would ensure broad support for reforms, including tax-financed investment in costly education reforms. Such measures could also compensate for the lasting effects of the previous transition to a market economy, which may have decreased support for broad, structural reforms.

The appropriate mix of policy recommendations for each country depends on the specific context. For this purpose, as in the previous chapter, countries are placed into four groups: (1) EU member states (Bulgaria, Croatia, Poland, Romania), (2) EU candidates (Georgia, Moldova, Ukraine, Western Balkans), (3) Türkiye, and (4) Central Asia and the South Caucasus (Armenia, Azerbaijan, Kazakhstan, Kyrgyz Republic, Tajikistan, Turkmenistan, Uzbekistan). Table 3.2 provides the relative priorities for each set of countries.

- For EU members, the key priority areas are related to the development of bilateral migration agreements to support the more efficient allocation of migrant talent, the implementation of adaptive and integrated social safety nets, and the provision of childcare services to increase female labor force participation.

- For the EU candidates, the key priority areas are related to the need to reform the vocational education system by delaying tracking and increasing the role of the private sector. Expanding affordable childcare and improving the opportunities of students with disadvantaged backgrounds are also important.

TABLE 3.2 Talent and mobility: summary of recommendations

Recommendation	EU members	EU candidates	Türkiye	Central Asia and South Caucasus
Improve the quality of education in a holistic way				
Delay tracking into vocational education	Medium	High	Medium	Medium
Consolidate higher-education systems	Low	Medium	Medium	High
Integrate research institutes with universities	Medium	Medium	Medium	High
Promote merit across society				
Establish transparent, merit-based university admission systems	Medium	Medium	Medium	High
Implement needs-based scholarship programs for students from disadvantaged backgrounds	Low	High	Low	Medium
Align skills and research with the labor market				
Increase the role of the private sector in vocational education	Medium	High	Medium	Medium
Strengthen university–industry partnerships	Medium	Medium	High	High
Develop bilateral migration agreements to improve the allocation of migrant talent	High	High	Medium	Medium
Ensure inclusivity				
Implement adaptive, shock-responsive, and integrated social safety nets	High	Medium	Medium	High
Expand affordable childcare services to increase female labor force participation	High	High	High	Medium

Source: World Bank.

● For Türkiye, the key priority areas are related to strengthening university–industry partnerships to improve R&D and expanding affordable childcare services to increase female labor force participation.

● For the countries of Central Asia and the South Caucasus, the key priorities are related to improving the higher-education system by consolidating large systems, establishing transparent and merit-based admission systems, integrating research institutes with universities, and strengthening partnerships between institutions of higher learning and industry. Implementing adaptive social safety nets is also a priority.

Notes

1. Refer to Migration and Asylum (dashboard), Eurostat, European Commission, Luxembourg, https://ec.europa.eu/eurostat/web/migration-asylum.

2. Albania, Bulgaria, Croatia, Kazakhstan, Montenegro, Poland, Romania, and Türkiye have participated in all PISA rounds since 2006. Other ECA countries have participated in fewer of the study evaluations.

3. The median reading score in ECA countries participating in PIRLS (Progress in International Reading Literacy Study) among fourth graders—Azerbaijan, Bulgaria, North Macedonia, Poland, Russia, and Türkiye—fell from 547 in 2006 to 518 in 2021, while, among EU countries, it declined from 542 to 526. Refer to PIRLS (dashboard), International Association for the Evaluation of Educational Achievement, Amsterdam, https://www.iea.nl/studies/iea/pirls.

4. Refer to Education and Training (database), Eurostat, European Commission, Luxembourg, https://ec.europa.eu/eurostat/web/education-and-training/overview.

5. Total R&D expenditure was estimated at about €38 million (57 percent executed by higher-education institutions) in Bosnia and Herzegovina in 2021 and at about €49 million (65 percent executed by higher-education institutions) in North Macedonia in 2022.

6. Refer to Education and Training (database), Eurostat, European Commission, Luxembourg, https://ec.europa.eu/eurostat/web/education-and-training/overview.

7. These values correspond to citizens of ECA countries who obtained their first permit of residence in any EU country in 2022. Citizens of Bulgaria, Croatia, Poland, and Romania are excluded. Refer to Migration and Asylum (dashboard), Eurostat, European Commission, Luxembourg, https://ec.europa.eu/eurostat/web/migration-asylum.

8. LiTS (Life in Transition Survey) (dashboard), European Bank for Reconstruction and Development, London, http://www.ebrd.com/what-we-do/economic-research-and-data/data/lits.html.

References

Acemoglu, Daron, and Fabrizio Zilibotti. 1997. "Was Prometheus Unbound by Chance? Risk, Diversification, and Growth." *Journal of Political Economy* 105 (4): 709–51.

Acosta, Pablo, Çaglar Özden, Jeremy Lebow, Limon Rodriguez, and Evelina Dahlgren. 2025. *Global Skill Partnerships for Migration: Preparing Tomorrow's Workers for Home and Abroad.* Washington, DC: World Bank.

Aghion, Philippe, Ufuk Akcigit, Ari Hyytinen, and Otto Toivanen. 2023. "Parental Education and Invention: The Finnish Enigma." NBER Working Paper 30964 (February), National Bureau of Economic Research, Cambridge, MA.

Agrawal, Ajay K., Devesh Kapur, John McHale, and Alexander Oettl. 2011. "Brain Drain or Brain Bank? The Impact of Skilled Emigration on Poor-Country Innovation." *Journal of Urban Economics* 69 (1): 43–55.

Akcigit, Ufuk, Jeremy G. Pearce, and Marta Prato. 2024. "Tapping into Talent: Coupling Education and Innovation Policies for Economic Growth." *Review of Economic Studies.* Published ahead of print, April 18, 2024. https://doi .org/10.1093/restud/rdae047.

Alesina, Alberto Francesco, and Dani Rodrik. 1994. "Distributive Politics and Economic Growth." *Quarterly Journal of Economics* 109 (2): 465–90.

Atkinson, Anthony B., and Andrea Brandolini. 2013. "On the Identification of the 'Middle Class'." In *Income Inequality: Economic Disparities and the Middle Class in Affluent Countries,* edited by Janet C. Gornick and Markus Jäntti, 77–100. Stanford, CA: Stanford University Press.

Avvisati, Francesco, and Pauline Givord. 2021. "How Much Do 15-Year-Olds Learn over One Year of Schooling? An International Comparison Based on PISA." OECD Education Working Paper 257 (October), Organisation for Economic Co-operation and Development, Paris.

Bahar, Dany, Prithwiraj Choudhury, and Hillel Rapoport. 2020. "Migrant Inventors and the Technological Advance of Nations." *Research Policy* 49 (9): 103947.

Bahar, Dany, Andreas Hauptmann, Cem Özgüzel, and Hillel Rapoport. 2024. "Migration and Knowledge Diffusion: The Effect of Returning Refugees on Export Performance in the Former Yugoslavia." *Review of Economics and Statistics* 106 (2): 287–304.

Bahar, Dany, and Hillel Rapoport. 2018. "Migration, Knowledge Diffusion, and the Comparative Advantage of Nations." *Economic Journal* 128 (612): F273–F305.

Banerjee, Abhijit Vinayak, and Esther Duflo. 2008. "What Is Middle Class about the Middle Classes around the World?" *Journal of Economic Perspectives* 22 (2): 3–28.

Becker, Gary Stanley, Scott Duke Kominers, Kevin M. Murphy, and Jörg L. Spenkuch. 2018. "A Theory of Intergenerational Mobility." *Journal of Political Economy* 126 (S1): S7–S25.

Bell, Alexander M., Raj Chetty, Xavier Jaravel, Neviana Petkova, and John Michael Van Reenen. 2019. "Who Becomes an Inventor in America? The Importance of Exposure to Innovation." *Quarterly Journal of Economics* 134 (2): 647–713.

Birdsall, Nancy. 2010. "The (Indispensable) Middle Class in Developing Countries." In *Equity and Growth in a Globalizing World,* edited by Ravi Kanbur and Michael Spence, 157–87. Washington, DC: Commission on Growth and Development, World Bank.

Bolch, Kimberly B., Lidia Ceriani, Indermit Singh Gill, and Luis F. López-Calva. 2023. "Measuring the Global Middle Class." Paper presented at the 10th meeting of ECINEQ, Society for the Study of Economic Inequality, Aix-en-Provence, France, July 10–12, 2023. https://www.ecineq.org/wp-content/uploads/2023/06/EcineqAMSE-339 .pdf.

Bollard, Albert, David J. McKenzie, Melanie Morten, and Hillel Rapoport. 2011. "Remittances and the Brain Drain Revisited: The Microdata Show That More Educated Migrants Remit More." *World Bank Economic Review* 25 (1): 132–56.

Bossavie, Laurent Loic Yves, Daniel Garrote Sánchez, and Mattia Makovec. 2024. *The Journey Ahead: Supporting Successful Migration in Europe and Central Asia.* Europe and Central Asia Studies Series. Washington, DC: World Bank.

Bussolo, Maurizio, Jonathan Karver, Michael Lokshin, Luis F. López-Calva, and Iván Torre. 2025. "Growing Vulnerability: What Happened to Europe's Middle Class in the Course of a Decade?" Policy Research Working Paper 11047, World Bank, Washington, DC.

Cedefop (European Center for the Development of Vocational Training). 2004. *Towards a History of Vocational Education and Training (VET) in Europe in a Comparative Perspective: Proceedings of the First International Conference, October 2002, Florence,* 2 vols. Cedefop Panorama Series. Luxembourg: Publications Office of the European Communities.

Chand, Satish, and Michael A. Clemens. 2023. "Human Capital Investment under Exit Options: Evidence from a Natural Quasi-Experiment." *Journal of Development Economics* 163 (June), 103112.

Chellaraj, Gnanaraj, Keith E. Maskus, and Aaditya Mattoo. 2008. "The Contribution of International Graduate Students to US Innovation." *Review of International Economics* 16 (3): 444–62.

Cojocaru, Alexandru, Michael Lokshin. and Iván Torre. 2024. "Perceptions of Economic Mobility and Support for Education Reforms." Policy Research Working Paper 10966, World Bank, Washington, DC.

Corak, Miles. 2013. "Income Inequality, Equality of Opportunity, and Intergenerational Mobility." *Journal of Economic Perspectives* 27 (3): 79–102.

Crawfurd, Lee, Susannah Hares, Ana Minardi, and Justin Sandefur. 2021. "Understanding Education Policy Preferences: Survey Experiments with Policymakers in 35 Developing Countries." Working Paper 596 (December), Center for Global Development, Washington, DC.

Dalvit, Nicolò, Rafael E. de Hoyos, Leonardo Iacovone, Ioanna Pantelaiou, Aleksandra Peeva, and Iván Torre. 2023. *The Future of Work: Implications for Equity and Growth in Europe.* Washington, DC: World Bank.

Daly, Tim. 2024. "The Rise and Fall of Finland Mania, Part Two: Why Did Scores Plummet?" *Flypaper* (blog), January 18, 2024. https://fordhaminstitute.org/national/commentary/rise-and-fall-finland-mania-part-two-why-did-scores-plummet#_edn3.

Demirgüç-Kunt, Asli, and Iván Torre. 2022. "Measuring Human Capital in Middle Income Countries." *Journal of Comparative Economics* 50 (4): 1036–67.

Doner, Richard F., and Ben Ross Schneider. 2016. "The Middle-Income Trap: More Politics than Economics." *World Politics* 68 (4): 608–44.

Easterly, William Russell. 2001. "The Middle Class Consensus and Economic Development." *Journal of Economic Growth* 6 (4): 317–36.

Foster, James E., and Jonathan Rothbaum. 2018. "The Mobility Curve: Measuring the Impact of Income Changes on Welfare." Unpublished paper, Department of Economics and Institute for International Economic Policy, George Washington University, Washington, DC.

Foster, Philip J. 1965. "The Vocational School Fallacy in Development Planning." In *Education and Economic Development*, edited by C. Arnold Anderson and Mary Jean Bowman, 142–66. Chicago: Aldine.

Gao, Xin, Aiko Kikkawa, and Jong Woo Kang. 2021. "Evaluating the Impact of Remittances on Human Capital Investment in the Kyrgyz Republic." ADB Economics Working Paper 637 (May), Asian Development Bank, Manila.

Ghisletta, Andrea, Johanna Kemper, and Jonathan Stöterau. 2021. "The Impact of Vocational Training Interventions on Youth Labor Market Outcomes: A Meta-Analysis." Working Paper 20 (July), Chair of Education Systems, Department of Management, Technology, and Economics, Federal Institute of Technology, Zurich.

Hanushek, Eric Alan. 2020. "Quality Education and Economic Development." In *Anticipating and Preparing for Emerging Skills and Jobs: Key Issues, Concerns, and Prospects*, edited by Brajesh Panth and Rupert Maclean, 25–32. Education in the Asia-Pacific Region: Issues, Concerns and Prospects Series 55. Manila: Asian Development Bank; Singapore: Springer.

Hanushek, Eric Alan, Guido Schwerdt, Ludger Woessmann, and Lei Zhang. 2017. "General Education, Vocational Education, and Labor-Market Outcomes over the Life-Cycle." *Journal of Human Resources* 52 (1): 48–87.

Hanushek, Eric Alan, and Ludger Woessmann. 2006. "Does Educational Tracking Affect Performance and Inequality? Differences-in-Differences Evidence across Countries." *Economic Journal* 116 (510): C63–C76.

Hanushek, Eric Alan, and Ludger Woessmann. 2015. "The Economic Impact of Educational Quality." In *Handbook of International Development and Education*, edited by Pauline Dixon, Steve Humble, and Chris Counihan, 6–19. Cheltenham, UK: Edward Elgar Publishing.

Heckman, James J., and Stefano Mosso. 2014. "The Economics of Human Development and Social Mobility." *Annual Review of Economics* 6 (August): 689–733.

Huisman, Jeroen, Anna Smolentseva, and Isak D. Froumin, eds. 2018. *25 Years of Transformations of Higher Education Systems in Post-Soviet Countries: Reform and Continuity.* Palgrave Studies in Global Higher Education Series. Cham, Switzerland: Palgrave Macmillan.

Hunt, Jennifer, and Marjolaine Gauthier-Loiselle. 2010. "How Much Does Immigration Boost Innovation?" *American Economic Journal: Macroeconomics* 2 (2): 31–56.

Jakubowski, Maciej, Harry Anthony Patrinos, Emilio Ernesto Porta, and Jerzy Wiśniewski. 2016. "The Effects of Delaying Tracking in Secondary School: Evidence from the 1999 Education Reform in Poland." *Education Economics* 24 (6): 557–72.

Londoño-Vélez, Juliana, Catherine Rodriguez, Fabio Sanchez, and Luis E. Álvarez-Arango. 2023. "Elite Colleges as Engines of Upward Mobility: Evidence from Colombia's Ser Pilo Paga." NBER Working Paper 31737 (September), National Bureau of Economic Research, Cambridge, MA.

López-Calva, Luis F., and Eduardo Ortiz-Juárez. 2014. "A Vulnerability Approach to the Definition of the Middle Class." *Journal of Economic Inequality* 12 (1): 23–47.

Mazur, Jana. 2022. "The Activity of Higher Education Institutions in the Academic Year 2022/23." *Comunicates* (blog), December 19, 2022. https://statistica.gov.md/index.php/en/the-activity-of-higher-education-institutions-in-the-academic-year-202223-9454_60176.html.

McCormack, John, Carol Propper, and Sarah Louise Smith. 2014. "Herding Cats? Management and University Performance." *Economic Journal* 124 (578): 534–64.

McNamara, Sarah, Guido Neidhöfer, and Partick Lehnert. 2024. "Intergenerational Mobility of Education in Europe: Geographical Patterns, Cohort-Linked Measures, and the Innovation Nexus." ZEW Discussion Paper 24-004, Leibniz Centre for European Economic Research, Mannheim, Germany.

Meghir, Costas, and Mårten Palme. 2005. "Educational Reform, Ability, and Parental Background." *American Economic Review* 95 (1): 414–24.

Milovanovitch, Mihaylo, Elena Denisova-Schmidt, and Arevik Anapiosyan. 2018. "Conflict of Interest in Eastern Europe: 'Academic Capture'." *International Higher Education* 92 (Winter): 29–30.

Nano, Enrico, Ugo Gianluigi Panizza, and Martina Viarengo. 2024. "Merit-Based Scholarships for University Graduates: A Generation of Italian Economists." *Labour Economics* 90 (October), 102569.

Narayan, Ambar, Roy van der Weide, Alexandru Cojocaru, Christoph Lakner, Silvia Redaelli, Daniel Gerszon Mahler, Rakesh Gupta N. Ramasubbaiah, and Stefan Thewissen. 2018. *Fair Progress? Economic Mobility across Generations around the World.* Equity and Development Series. Washington, DC: World Bank.

Neidhöfer, Guido, Matías Ciaschi, Leonardo Gasparini, and Joaquín Serrano. 2024. "Social Mobility and Economic Growth." *Journal of Economic Growth* 29 (2): 327–59. https://doi.org/10.1007/s10887-023-09234-8.

OECD (Organisation for Economic Co-operation and Development). 2017. *OECD Science, Technology, and Industry Scoreboard 2017: The Digital Transformation.* Paris: OECD.

Ollikainen, Jani-Petteri. 2021. "Comprehensive School Reform and Labor Market Outcomes over the Lifecycle: Evidence from Finland." *Labour Economics* 68 (January): 101952.

Oruc, Nermin, Ian Jackson, and Geoffrey Pugh. 2018. "The Effects of Remittances on Education in a Post-Conflict Society: Evidence from Bosnia-Herzegovina." *Journal of Balkan and Near Eastern Studies* 21 (1): 90–103.

Ozgen, Ceren, Peter Nijkamp, and Jacques Poot. 2011. "Immigration and Innovation in European Regions." IZA Discussion Paper DP 5676 (April), Institute of Labor Economics, Bonn, Germany.

Pekkala Kerr, Sari, William R. Kerr, Çağlar Özden, and Christopher Robert Parsons. 2016. "Global Talent Flows." *Journal of Economic Perspectives* 30 (4): 83–106.

Pekkala Kerr, Sari, Tuomas Pekkarinen, and Roope Uusitalo. 2013. "School Tracking and Development of Cognitive Skills." *Journal of Labor Economics* 31 (3): 577–602.

Pekkarinen, Tuomas, Roope Uusitalo, and Sari Pekkala Kerr. 2009. "School Tracking and Intergenerational Income Mobility: Evidence from the Finnish Comprehensive School Reform." *Journal of Public Economics* 93 (7–8): 965–73.

Psacharopoulos, George. 1987. "To Vocationalize or Not to Vocationalize? That Is the Curriculum Question." *International Review of Education* 33 (2): 187–211.

Psacharopoulos, George. 1991. "Vocational Education Theory, Voced 101: Including Hints For 'Vocational Planners.'" *International Journal of Educational Development* 11 (3): 193–99.

Ripley, Amanda. 2013. *The Smartest Kids in the World: And How They Got That Way.* New York: Simon and Schuster.

Robayo-Abril, Monica, and Natalie Millán. 2019. *Breaking the Cycle of Roma Exclusion in the Western Balkans.* March. Washington, DC: World Bank.

Romer, Paul Michael. 2000. "Should the Government Subsidize Supply or Demand in the Market for Scientists and Engineers?" NBER Working Paper 7723 (June), National Bureau of Economic Research, Cambridge, MA.

Silliman, Mikko, and Hanna Virtanen. 2022. "Labor Market Returns to Vocational Secondary Education." *American Economic Journal: Applied Economics* 14 (1): 197–224.

Smolentseva, Anna. 2003. "Challenges to the Russian Academic Profession." *Higher Education* 45 (4): 391–424.

Stewart, Frances. 2001. "Horizontal Inequalities: A Neglected Dimension of Development." WIDER Annual Lecture 5, United Nations University–World Institute for Development Economics Research, Helsinki, December 14, 2001. https://www.wider.unu.edu/event/wider-annual-lecture-5-horizontal-inequality-neglected-dimension -development.

Stuen, Eric T., Ahmed Mushfiq Mobarak, and Keith E. Maskus. 2012. "Skilled Immigration and Innovation: Evidence from Enrolment Fluctuations in US Doctoral Programmes." *Economic Journal* 122 (565): 1143–76.

Szymańska, Anita. 2019. "The Structure of Income Inequality with Particular Emphasis on the Economic Middle Class." *Social Inequalities and Economic Growth* 60 (April): 45–60.

Terrin, Éder, and Moris Triventi. 2023. "The Effect of School Tracking on Student Achievement and Inequality: A Meta-Analysis." *Review of Educational Research* 93 (2): 236–74.

Torre, Iván, Michael Lokshin, and James Stephen Foster. 2025. "Does Social Mobility Affect Economic Development? Cross-Country Analysis Using Different Mobility Measures." Policy Research Working Paper 11056, World Bank, Washington, DC.

Urquiola, Miguel. 2020. *Markets, Minds, and Money: Why America Leads the World in University Research.* Cambridge, MA: Harvard University Press.

van der Weide, Roy, Christoph Lakner, Daniel Gerszon Mahler, Ambar Narayan, and Rakesh Gupta. 2023. "Intergenerational Mobility around the World: A New Database." *Journal of Development Economics* 166 (January), 103167.

World Bank. 2018. "Is There a Gender Gap in Skills in the Western Balkans? Summary Note Based on the Skills towards Employability and Productivity (STEP) Surveys." Conference Version, March 13, Poverty and Equity Global Practice, Europe and Central Asia Region, World Bank, Washington, DC.

World Bank. 2019a. *Migration and Brain Drain.* Europe and Central Asia Economic Update (Fall). Washington, DC: World Bank.

World Bank. 2019b. *Review of the Education Sector in Ukraine: Moving toward Effectiveness, Equity, and Efficiency.* RESUME3, Final Report. Washington, DC: World Bank.

World Bank. 2023. *World Development Report 2023: Migrants, Refugees, and Societies.* Washington, DC: World Bank.

World Bank. 2024a. *Retaining the Growth Momentum.* Western Balkans Regular Economic Report 26 (Fall). Washington, DC: World Bank.

World Bank. 2024b. *World Development Report 2024: The Middle-Income Trap.* Washington, DC: World Bank.

World Bank, UNESCO (United Nations Educational, Scientific, and Cultural Organization), and ILO (International Labour Organization). 2023. *Building Better Formal TVET Systems: Principles and Practice in Low- and Middle-Income Countries.* Washington, DC: World Bank; Paris: UNESCO; Geneva: ILO.

Zilibotti, Fabrizio, and Matthias Doepke. 2007. "Occupational Choice and the Spirit of Capitalism." CEPR Discussion Paper DP6405, Centre for Economic Policy Research, London.

Energy

Country Case in Brief: The United Kingdom

As countries embark on a transition to lower carbon emissions and clean energy, the United Kingdom stands out among the high-income countries (HICs) because it has fundamentally shifted its energy mix several times. It has undergone three historical transitions in primary energy source: from wood to coal in the nineteenth century; from coal to oil and, mainly, natural gas in the twentieth century; and, in the twenty-first century, from fossil fuels to renewables.

The First Transition: From Wood to Coal

Why did the industrial revolution of the eighteenth century begin in the United Kingdom rather than in some larger, more populous, and richer nation of the period? Contemporary observers believed the answer was obvious. "Coal," wrote one French official sent to uncover the secret of the country's industrial strength in 1738 (Allen 2009). Modern scholarship corroborates the visiting official's verdict: the combination of high real wages and an abundance of cheap, easily exploitable energy in the form of high-quality black coal. The high wages provided a compelling incentive to economize on labor. Cheap coal meant that it was cost-effective to do so by substituting new, energy-intensive machinery. Other countries enjoyed one or other of these conditions. None enjoyed both, at least initially.

Coal was the feedstock for the coke blast furnaces with which Abraham Darby revolutionized iron smelting at the pioneering Coalbrookdale iron works in 1709. Coal fueled the first commercial steam engine, invented by Thomas Newcomen in 1712. Coal-powered steam turned Richard Arkwright's spinning jenny into the

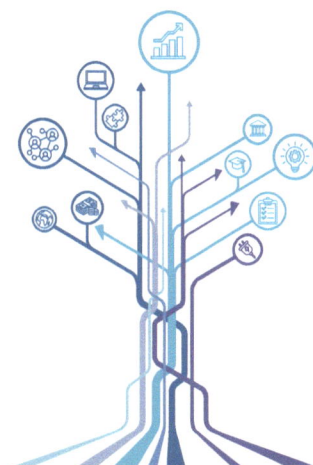

basis of the factory system of cotton production, the parent of all subsequent manufacturing. And, in the nineteenth century, coal became the soul not only of manufacturing, but of a modern services sector, too.

The Second Transition: From Coal to Natural Gas

According to the prevailing wisdom after World War II, the fundamental economic importance of the energy sector rendered nationalization and the vertical integration of production and supply the only reasonable ways to organize the sector. Though initially successful, this structure became problematic as oil gained position as the dominant input for industrial and transport technologies. By the early 1970s, the United Kingdom's dependence on the domestic coal industry for nearly half of the country's primary energy requirements had become a weakness. Costs were high; fractious industrial relations led to disruptive supply shortages; and a growing reliance on imported oil and gas after successive price hikes by the Organization of the Petroleum Exporting Countries contributed to the country's need for an International Monetary Fund bailout in 1976.

The situation was transformed by three related developments. The first was the discovery of exploitable oil and gas in the United Kingdom's area of the North Sea in the mid-1970s. The second was the radical restructuring of the economy from low-end manufacturing to services following the election of Prime Minister Margaret Thatcher's Conservative government in 1979, which led to a dramatic downward revision of the trajectory of UK energy demand. In 1970, it had been predicted that the country would require 100 gigawatts of electricity-generating capacity by 1995; in fact, only a little over half of that was needed (Brown 1971). The third was the parallel reorganization of the UK energy industry. Large state-owned enterprises (SOEs) were privatized from 1986 to 1994, accompanied by price incentives for competing, private companies in energy markets, supervised by independent regulatory agencies in determining investment, production, and consumption (Rhodes, Hough, and Butcher 2014).

Together, these three developments transformed the United Kingdom's energy use. Between 1970 and 2010, coal's share of the country's primary energy mix fell from 44 percent to 14 percent, while the contribution of natural gas rose from 5 percent to 40 percent. In the power sector, the transition from coal to natural gas was especially rapid. After 1990, the share of UK power generated from coal dropped by half, to slightly more than 30 percent in 2010, while the contribution of natural gas from mostly domestic sources grew from near zero to slightly less than 40 percent.

The economic impact of the transition from coal to natural gas was huge. The final energy costs among households and industry fell; the United Kingdom's external accounts improved dramatically; and new tax revenues were spawned. There was also a major environmental dividend: the country's per capita territorial carbon dioxide emissions dropped by 30 percent from 1970 to 2010. More than half the decline was derived from the lower carbon intensity of the new primary energy mix. Pollution plunged by almost 80 percent, creating a substantial health dividend (Tiseo 2024).

The Third Transition: From Fossil Fuels to Renewables

By the turn of the millennium, shrinking the energy sector's environmental impact was becoming a central policy objective. The 2008 Climate Change Act legislated an 80 percent reduction in the country's overall territorial carbon emissions by 2050, a target later widened to require net-zero carbon emissions. Fully decarbonizing the power sector became subject to a more ambitious deadline of 2035. This set the stage for the United Kingdom's third energy transition, from fossil fuels to renewables.

The United Kingdom's strategy has once again been to harness the power of liberalized, but regulated, energy markets to incentivize private investment in an abundant domestic primary energy resource—this time, wind—using new regulatory and financial instruments, such as carbon credits and auctions of guaranteed long-term offtake prices. With rapidly declining prices for renewable energy, the results have been impressive. By 2022, renewables provided nearly 20 percent of the UK's primary energy, up from less than 5 percent in 2010. In the power sector, renewables have overtaken natural gas as the largest source of electricity generation. In 2020, the United Kingdom became the first G20 economy to cut carbon emissions by half.

Yet, the country's third transition is far from complete. Formidable technological obstacles exist in substituting fossil fuels in industrial uses, domestic heating, and transport. In the power sector, policy makers are grappling with the trade-offs between decarbonization and the competing policy objectives of security in supply (given the intermittency of wind energy) and affordability (because of the scale of investment required). As in the earlier transition from coal to gas, the United Kingdom's regulatory framework has had to adapt to unexpected technological and geopolitical changes.

Lessons from the United Kingdom's Energy Transitions and the Main Questions for Europe and Central Asia

The UK experience offers several useful lessons for the countries of the Europe and Central Asia (ECA) region. The first lesson revolves around the fundamental role the energy sector plays in a country's evolution toward a sustainable, secure, high-income future. The transition of the United Kingdom from wood to coal underpinned the industrial revolution, and the transition from coal to natural gas occurred as the economy was undergoing substantial structural change. Without that change, facilitated by government policies and by markets, such an energy transition would not have been possible.

A second lesson is that, with abundant resources, a country can use natural gas as an important fuel on the road to net-zero carbon emissions because of the technology options available for producing lower greenhouse gas emissions, which also results in less air pollution. The Russian Federation's invasion of Ukraine has altered the way energy security is perceived, however, and this assessment has been profoundly revised. In most ECA countries, already highly reliant on natural gas, the lack of domestic gas sources means that natural gas consumption may have peaked or is about to peak. Most ECA countries are preparing to transition to cleaner energy sources directly rather than using natural gas as an intermediate fuel. Still, natural gas will be essential in high value added areas in the region for at least another two decades (World Bank 2024c).

A third lesson is that diversification in primary energy sources is crucial. In the United Kingdom, the shift to renewables has returned primary energy supply to domestic sources, but the intermittency of these sources challenges the security of supply, at least until connectivity and storage at scale become more affordable.

The fourth, overriding lesson is that policy matters and must be adaptable. The United Kingdom's historical experience demonstrates how choices over policy priorities, industrial organization, market design, and regulatory institutions drive outcomes: privatization and liberalization in the 1980s and decarbonization policy in the 2000s and 2010s. Yet, there are no once-and-for-all solutions. In the United Kingdom policy experience, the only constant has been change—and sound policy making.

This chapter addresses the question of how the ECA countries can achieve high-income status, while managing the transition to lower emissions and affordable, abundant, and secure energy. The shift toward the more efficient use of energy and lower carbon emissions involves the infusion of foreign technologies, capital, and expertise and fundamental transformations in the structure of economic activity. These changes offer many opportunities for substantial savings among households and enterprises, thereby allowing room to scale up production, boost growth, and achieve more rapid convergence. The pinnacle of these overlapping transitions is the participation of firms in the ECA countries in global value chains for technologies that improve energy efficiency and lower emissions. This participation will depend on the pace of structural change and the availability of skilled labor at home.

Introduction

Building on the above history, this chapter is focused on the following questions.

First, are ECA countries reducing carbon emissions, while ensuring abundant, affordable, and secure energy supply? Supported by a profound structural shift from manufacturing to services and from state-run to more market-oriented economies, ECA countries have greatly slowed the pace of carbon emissions growth, even in an environment of robust economic expansion. In these countries, an increase in gross domestic product (GDP) of 103 percent between 2000 and 2020 led to a rise in carbon emissions of 9 percent over the same period, whereas, among the middle-income countries (MICS), an increase in income of 178 percent led to a rise in carbon emissions of 134 percent, and, among HICs, an increase in income of 41 percent led to a reduction in emissions of 12 percent during the same period. Nonetheless, the region's economic expansion has been largely driven by fossil fuels, extensive emissions, and declining, but still high energy intensity. However, a shift toward abundant renewable energy and modern transmission grids as aging energy assets are replaced, combined with improvements in energy efficiency, should ultimately lead to a sizable decline in carbon emissions and energy intensity in the region.

Second, does the transition to affordable, more secure, and lower-emission energy represent an opportunity for the MICs in the region to boost economic growth and transition to high-income status? The positive impact of lower-emission innovation on GDP growth is visible in China, Europe, and the United States, but not so much in the ECA region. It is most visible in the ECA countries in which the transition to a market economy and integration with global markets has advanced the most and in which the pressure of incumbent firms is more well contained and young and dynamic firms enjoy a level playing field. The ECA region is the most energy-intensive developing world region, largely because of its historical reliance on heavy industry and fossil fuels. It also has some of the world's highest energy subsidies, and the average age of coal plants in 13 ECA countries is more than 30–35 years.[1] Innovations in energy efficiency and reductions in emissions—linked, notably, with the infusion of foreign technologies—offer ample growth opportunities. However, policy barriers, underdevelopment of markets and regulations, and the resistance of incumbents often hinder the move to energy efficiency. If these can be overcome (generally through more competitive markets and prices, continued structural transformation, greater macroeconomic stability, and training and retraining), some ECA countries could become low-emission technology adopters, while others could lead in innovation.

Third, have the MICs in the region strengthened the forces of creation sufficiently to ensure that the transition to lower emissions and increased energy efficiency will support the growth to high income? The infusion of lower-emission technologies is much slower among the MICs in the region and among other emerging and developing countries than among HICs, with the exception of the take-up of solar and wind in the ECA Convergers—Croatia, Poland, and Romania—and in Türkiye.[2] Raising the share of energy generated by solar and wind to more than 15 percent in 2022, these are the only ECA countries with solar and wind penetration above the global average of 12 percent. Most ECA countries will also encounter problems in participating in lower-emission global value chains and will be, at least in the near term, largely consumers rather than producers or innovators of greener technologies. How to become part of these value chains is a top challenge facing policy makers.

Fourth, have the MICs in the region weakened the forces of preservation that raise obstacles to the more-efficient and lower-emission energy needed along the path to high-income status and beyond? Powerful SOEs are an element of the energy transition, but, in the region, they control 100 percent of energy transmission, more than 80 percent of fossil fuel generation, and more than 65 percent of electricity distribution, though they are less present in low-carbon technologies. The region's high natural gas and coal subsidies are also tilting the playing field in favor of fossil fuel technologies. Subsidies for fossil fuels are among the greatest market disincentives for decarbonization and the green transition. Eliminating them is a key step to more efficient, lower-carbon, and cleaner energy. These subsidies also raise barriers to economic growth through the associated misallocation of human, physical, and financial capital to less productive sectors.

Carbon Emissions and Energy Intensity

The region has a unique development experience in energy use and carbon emissions. Owing to natural endowments and the economic organization of the Soviet Union and its satellite states, most ECA countries were exhibiting high rates of energy and carbon intensity by the 1990s. Abundance (and the subsidized pricing) of fossil fuels fostered energy systems that relied almost exclusively on oil, natural gas, and economic specialization in energy-intensive sectors, such as heavy industry. Meanwhile, at the time, no one worried about carbon emissions.

Emissions per dollar of GDP have been on a steeply declining trend since the mid-1990s. Emissions per unit of primary energy have been declining slowly in the ECA region, in contrast to lower-middle-income and upper-middle-income countries, which have been on an upward trajectory (refer to figure 4.1, panels a and b). Emissions per capita in the region have shown a slight increase relative to HICs and in absolute terms since 2000, but the increase has been greater in countries in other income groupings (refer to figure 4.1, panel c).

In 2000, countries in the ECA region were about 35 percent more energy intensive than upper-middle-income countries and more than 65 percent more energy intensive than HICs (refer to figure 4.2). By 2009, energy intensity in the region was substantially lower than the energy intensity of upper-middle-income countries, but was still greater than the energy intensity among the HICs back in 2000. Energy intensity leveled off in the ECA region after 2015, which is a source of concern.

FIGURE 4.1 Carbon and energy emissions intensity and emissions per capita

a. Carbon emissions intensity

CO$_2$ emissions, kilograms per 2021 PPP US dollar of GDP

b. Energy emissions intensity

CO$_2$ emissions per unit of primary energy

c. Emissions per capita

CO$_2$ emissions per metric ton per capita

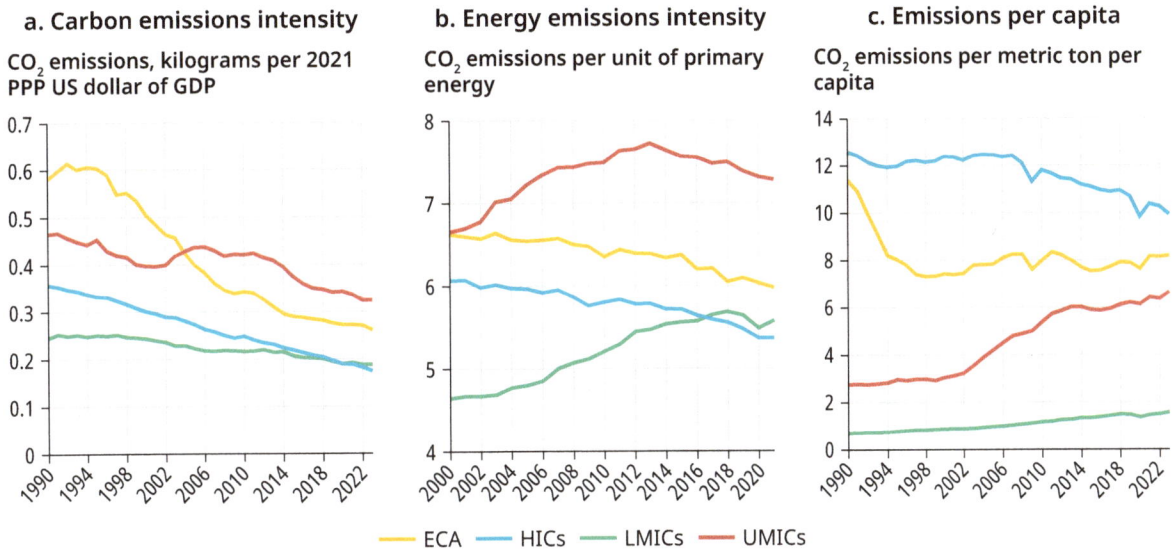

ECA — HICs — LMICs — UMICs

Source: WDI (World Development Indicators) (dashboard), World Bank, Washington, DC, https://datatopics.worldbank.org/world-development-indicators/.

Note: LMICs = lower-middle-income countries; PPP = purchasing power parity; UMICs = upper-middle-income countries.

There is a tight correlation between GDP and energy use across countries and over time (refer to figure 4.3). Only among the HICs and the ECA Convergers has there been some decoupling between average GDP and average energy use since the global financial crisis of 2007–09. Among the MICs in the ECA region and other developing regions, energy demand has continued to grow along with GDP.

Per capita emissions in the ECA region changed little between 2000 and 2020, after declining 36 percent in the 1990s, when the transition from planned to market economies was initiated. The broad stability in per capita emissions after 2000 contrasted with increases in the MICs and declines in the HICs (refer to figure 4.4, panel a). Even with the decline in the 1990s, the ECA region is still among the world's largest carbon emitters per capita, at about 7.6 metric tons of CO$_2$ per inhabitant in 2020, or 71 percent more than the world average. Per capita carbon emissions can be decomposed into a product of three factors: per capita economic growth, energy intensity (energy use per unit of output) to account for energy efficiency, and the emissions intensity of energy (carbon emissions per unit of energy used) to account for the role of energy sources (refer to figure 4.4, panels b, c, and d). Several messages are thus embedded in the decomposition.

FIGURE 4.2 **Energy intensity, primary energy**

Energy intensity, megajoules per 2017 PPP
US dollar of GDP

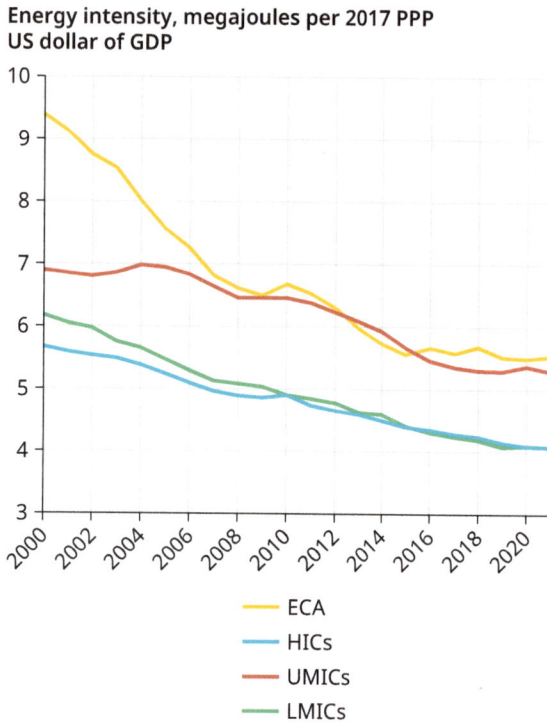

— ECA
— HICs
— UMICs
— LMICs

Source: WDI (World Development Indicators) (dashboard), World Bank, Washington, DC, https://datatopics.worldbank .org/world-development-indicators/.

Note: PPP = purchasing power parity.

FIGURE 4.3 **GDP and energy use, ECA and comparators, 2000–19**

Primary energy demand, exajoules, logarithm

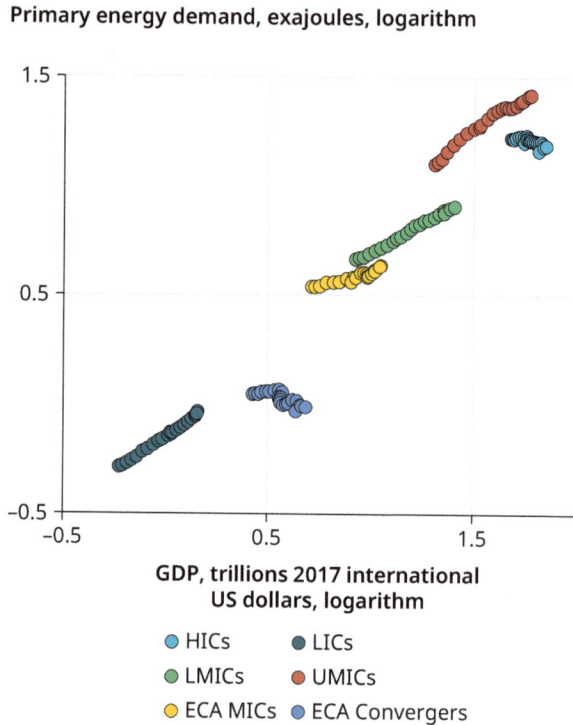

GDP, trillions 2017 international
US dollars, logarithm

● HICs   ● LICs
● LMICs   ● UMICs
● ECA MICs ● ECA Convergers

Source: World Bank calculations based on Data and Statistics (dashboard), International Energy Agency, Paris, https://www.iea.org/data-and-statistics.

Despite substantial improvements in energy intensity in the ECA region since 2000, more efficient use of energy—that is, lower intensity per unit of GDP—is still required. The region has reduced energy intensity more quickly relative to other regions because of the structural transformation of the ECA countries during the transition from planned economies to market economies. Most of the reduction in the region occurred before 2015 (refer to figure 4.4, panel c). Energy intensity declined by 40 percent from 2000 to 2015. Yet, despite the reduction, energy intensity is still greater in the ECA region than in the MICs. To produce a unit of GDP, the region requires 1.4 times more energy relative to South Asia and more than 1.6 times more energy than Latin America and the Caribbean. Compared with the European Union (EU), the ECA region consumes 1.9 times more energy to produce a unit of output.

FIGURE 4.4 Decomposing per capita carbon emissions, index, 2000 = 100

a. CO_2 emissions per capita

b. GDP per capita

c. Energy intensity

d. CO_2 emissions per energy used

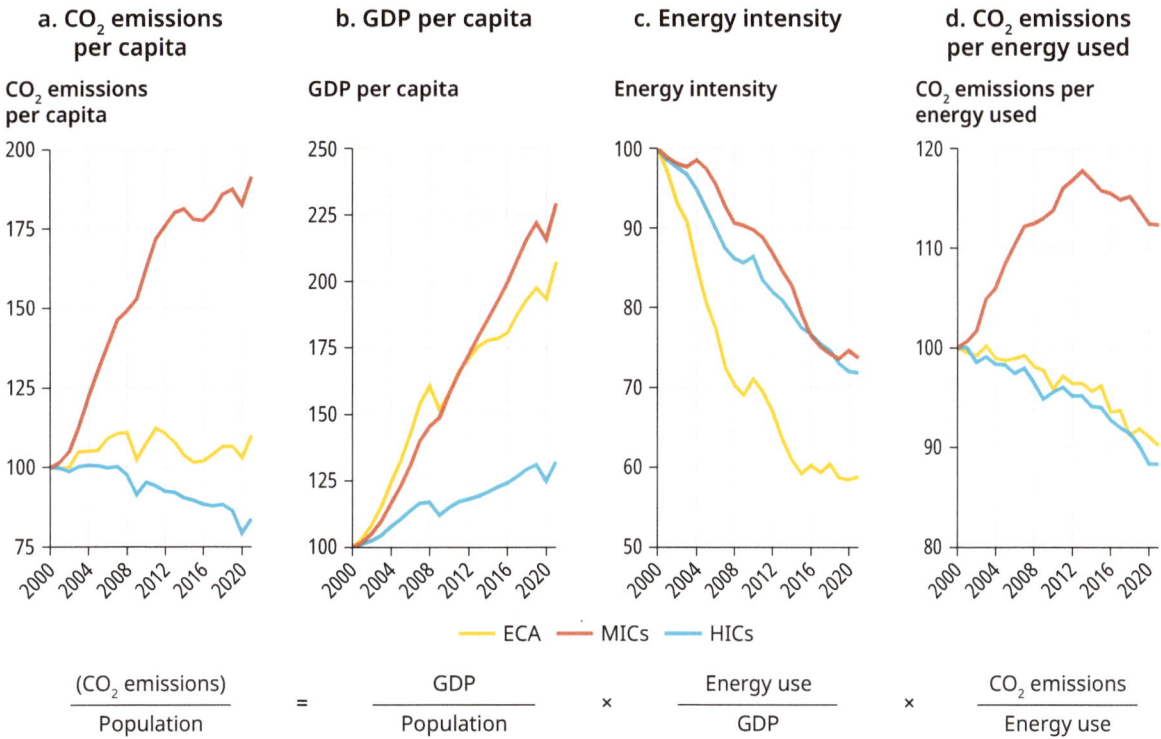

$$\frac{(CO_2 \text{ emissions})}{\text{Population}} = \frac{\text{GDP}}{\text{Population}} \times \frac{\text{Energy use}}{\text{GDP}} \times \frac{CO_2 \text{ emissions}}{\text{Energy use}}$$

Source: World Bank calculations using data from WDI (World Development Indicators) (dashboard), World Bank, Washington, DC, https://datatopics.worldbank.org/world-development-indicators/.

The region reduced the emissions intensity of energy in 2000–20 by about 10 percent, or as much as the HICs, although from a higher level. The reduction contrasts with an increase in the emissions intensity of energy among MICs around the world (until 2013), also starting from quite different levels, however. Regardless of the overall reduction in the emissions intensity of energy, coal still accounts for an oversized share of primary energy demand in the region, especially in electricity generation (refer to figure 4.5, panel b). Moreover, several countries in the region have experienced substantial increases in the emissions intensity of energy since 2000 even as their energy intensity declined.

Large energy subsidies are an important incentive behind the high carbon intensity of energy and the continued substantial dependence on fossil fuels in the region. Subsidies support lower prices among final consumers, but also represent a lifeline for thermal power generation, mostly linked to SOEs. Fossil fuel subsidies in the region amounted to an oversized $110 billion in 2020 (3.6 percent of regional GDP), even before the surge in subsidies, along with prices, in 2022 (World Bank 2024b).

FIGURE 4.5 The changing structure of electricity production

a. From renewables, excluding hydropower

Percent of total power production

b. From coal

Percent of total power production

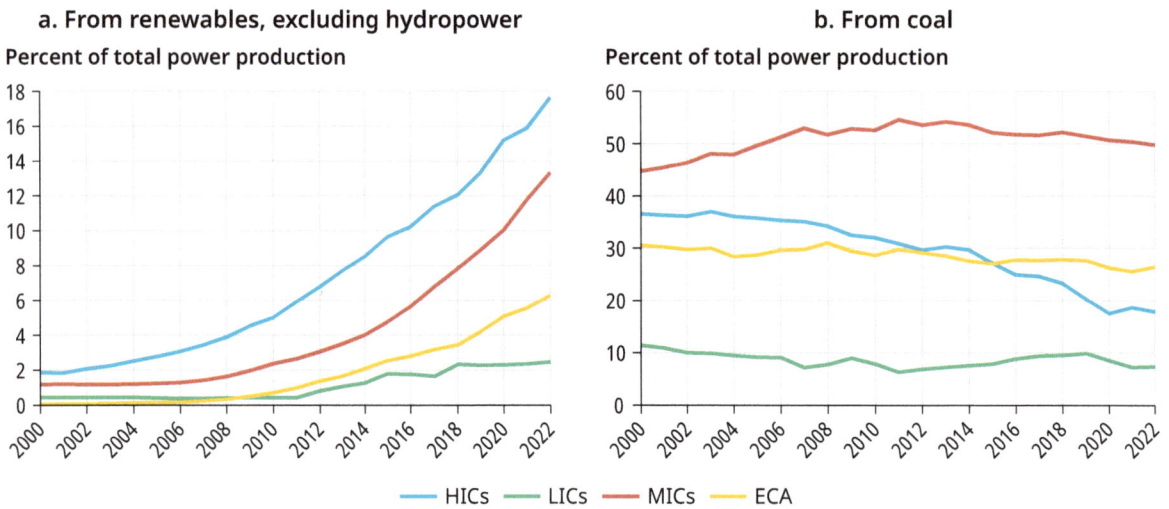

HICs — LICs — MICs — ECA

Source: World Bank 2024b.

ECA Transitions and Foundations

The transitions among the ECA MICs demand deliberate policy choices to ensure that the policies are complementary and the transitions smooth. The first transition—to affordable, secure energy—was more difficult because of the largest supply shock ever experienced in natural gas markets worldwide. The shock was associated with the surge in the prices of natural gas and wholesale electricity in 2022 following Russia's invasion of Ukraine. The impact was exacerbated by the heavy reliance on Russian natural gas and the coupling of Asian and European markets. The energy shock underscored the need to (1) diversify the sources of energy supply, (2) heavily cut dependence on imported oil and natural gas, (3) dramatically improve energy efficiency, and (4) utilize domestic low-cost renewables. Energy security is now a top policy priority in many countries in the region and around the world.

The second transition—to lower emissions—involves the infusion of modern foreign technologies and products. It should be complemented with efforts to decarbonize transportation, heating, industry, and other sectors through energy efficiency, behavioral changes, and technology shifts, starting with electrification. The investment needs associated with the adoption of the new technologies—as with the adoption of any new technology—are projected to be substantial and will be accompanied by losses mostly in stranded state-owned fossil fuel generation assets. The International Energy Agency estimate of global energy transition investment needs is $4 trillion per year until 2030, or about 4 percent of global 2023 GDP (IEA 2023b, 2023c). The World Bank Climate

Change and Development Reports on the ECA region indicate that the additional investment needs in reducing carbon emissions to net zero may be up to 2 percent of GDP a year (World Bank 2023a).

These transitions must support economic growth and foster the shift to high-income status. Facilitating the ongoing structural transformation of ECA economies will help bind enterprises more tightly into global markets and buttress the infusion of the new capital, technologies, and management expertise that are required to shift away from productivity stagnation to productivity gains across the region. Creating or completing markets and allowing energy prices to reflect the true underlying cost should help households and enterprises become more energy efficient, the latter benefiting from a bump in profitability. Increased energy security should underpin a more predictable business environment and facilitate new business entry, especially in countries where unreliable power supply and frequent outages are damaging business prospects. Additional investment in transmission should help improve reliability and ultimately reduce power costs, although this is a development with a longtime lag.

The cost of additional investment is substantial, but will be similar to the requirements accompanying any technological change, including the adoption of automobiles, computers, and mobile phones. It must also be considered against the cost of inaction: the rising economic cost of air pollution, stepped-up health spending, and adaptation. Climate change damage in the region is already estimated to account for 1 percent to 2 percent of GDP a year in Azerbaijan, Kazakhstan, and Romania and over 10 percent of GDP in Uzbekistan.

How would the transition to more secure, more energy efficient, and cleaner technologies aid economic growth? The positive impact of the transition derives from the higher energy efficiency, lower energy costs, and reduced externalities associated with lower emissions. These positive impacts will all help companies scale up the production of existing products or services or introduce new product lines, thereby creating new job opportunities and stimulating innovation across sectors. As with every technological transition, however, higher initial investment costs will be borne by consumers, enterprises, and the government. The transition will change all parts of the economy that produce or consume energy. In all ECA countries, large infusions of foreign capital, technology, and expertise will be needed to make the transition to lower energy intensity and lower emissions a reality.

Strengthening the Forces of Creation

The bulk of the new investment in greater energy efficiency and lower carbon emissions is expected to be realized by the private sector. Critical to the success of this endeavor will be the ability of firms to integrate more closely into the global economy and infuse new foreign technologies, expertise, and capital. Entrepreneurs must also be able to identify new opportunities and to innovate. The foundations of these efforts include contestable markets in energy, public transport, housing, and, indeed, in all sectors of the economy that produce, transport, or utilize energy. The continued integration of domestic firms into global markets will help reshape enterprises and make them more energy efficient. How to become part of the global value chains related to the green transition, with a huge impulse for innovation and economic growth, is both a challenge and a priority for the ECA MICs. Past technological transitions reveal an accelerating pace of technology diffusion from advanced to developing countries, but countries need to be ready and to have established adequate foundations.

Competitive Markets and Prices

The first foundation requires competitive markets for energy inputs and outputs and prices that provide the appropriate signals to households and firms about the true cost of products. Fossil fuel subsidies should be phased out, and administered energy prices must be rationalized to cover costs and avoid quasi-fiscal deficits. Market mechanisms, including carbon taxes, can help internalize externalities and contribute to changing consumer and firm behavior.

Carbon Pricing

Explicit carbon pricing that reflects the negative externalities of emissions and pollution can encourage efforts to reduce carbon emissions. Two types of explicit carbon pricing exist: a carbon tax, that is, a tax on the carbon content of fuels, and an emissions trading system (ETS). Under the more widespread version of an ETS (cap-and-trade), an overall level of emissions is set for regulated entities.[3]

Carbon pricing instruments cover almost one-fourth of global emissions, though most systems fail to price carbon at a level consistent with achieving the temperature goals of the Paris Agreement (World Bank 2023d). In the ECA region, besides the four EU member states, other countries have moved more slowly on introducing carbon pricing instruments. Given the trade relations with the EU and the accession aspirations of several ECA countries, the EU ETS may be the most relevant instrument for them.[4] Türkiye, Ukraine, and the countries of the Western Balkans are either planning, considering, or implementing ETSs.

The carbon policies of EU trading partners will be affected by the introduction of the EU Carbon Border Adjustment Mechanism in 2026, which will coincide with the phaseout of the allocation of free allowances under the EU ETS. The impact of the mechanism, especially in the initial stages, on the exports and GDP of individual countries is likely to be modest, as the countries will probably quickly adjust their production and exports. For example, a recent report estimated the negative impact on GDP at about 3.7 percent of GDP in Bosnia and Herzegovina and 0.2 percent in Serbia (World Bank 2023e).

Among the EU candidate countries, adopting an EU-aligned carbon trading system will be an important accession requirement. The other ECA countries may decide in favor of other carbon pricing models, for example, the model of California, which uses carbon pricing as a backstop if other climate policies fail to deliver the expected reductions. Türkiye plans to launch an ETS in 2025. Indications are that it will involve an economy-wide carbon price that rises from $11 to $211 per metric ton of CO_2 equivalent by 2040. These prices are consistent with the ECA energy futures report's shadow carbon price for a 2060 net-zero scenario (ESMAP et al. 2024).

Carbon pricing or higher taxation on fossil fuels should be implemented after a substantial reduction or, better, elimination of fossil fuel subsidies. In practice, this sequencing has been difficult to achieve. Most subsidies are long-standing, though some were introduced during the pandemic, and others were introduced during the 2022 energy crisis and have yet to be lowered. The subsidies, which are substantial, offset the impact of carbon pricing or of other efforts aimed at reducing the use of high-emission technologies (refer to the discussion on fossil fuel subsidies that follows).

Continued Structural Transformation

The second foundation is the continued structural transformation of enterprises and the progressively tighter integration of firms into global markets. Despite the substantial heterogeneity across the ECA region, the main challenges to business dynamism are similar across the region. Countries will need to upgrade the competitive environment, dramatically boost the quality of education, and strengthen the availability of finance. Deepening trade and investment integration is crucial to accelerating the adoption of modern technologies and strengthening the ability of firms to overcome the limits they face to potential growth because of the small size of many economies in the region.

Sustained structural transformation will lead to more links with global value chains and open avenues for greater investment and infusion of foreign knowledge. The resulting reduction in inefficiencies—including in the use of energy and the energy mix—and the profound misallocations in the economy should result in an acceleration investment. Investment growth at a more rapid pace will help revamp the capital stock with machines and equipment that are more productive and energy efficient (refer to chapter 2).

In terms of the economic structure, industry accounts for about 20 percent of carbon emissions in the region, and the infusion of new capital and technologies holds the key to reducing both emissions and energy intensity. Besides continued structural transformation and integration into the global economy, measures in this direction include the promotion of energy management systems such as the

ISO 50001; capacity building and training for industrial energy auditors and managers; targeted research and development (R&D) incentives; the use of automation, software, robotics, and artificial intelligence; and the availability of financing programs.[5] Regulatory instruments could also be deployed (such as mandatory audits) and target and performance setting (Dobrotkova, Lukas, and Singh 2018; World Bank 2023b).

Macroeconomic Stability and the Cost of Capital

The third foundation is macroeconomic stability and investor certainty. Given the huge funding entailed in implementing the transition to lower and, ultimately, zero emissions and the long horizons involved, domestic and foreign investors require certainty that their property rights will be respected and that the macroeconomic environment will be supportive of their engagement. The effort to de-risk economies through prudent macroeconomic and financial policy should help improve the credibility of countries in international capital markets and the availability of finance. Some ECA countries face macroeconomic obstacles, including the incomplete market transition, the still outsized role of the state, and the inadequate rule of law. These should be addressed to ensure that private capital flows in to finance energy efficiency and the green transition.

The cost of capital for clean energy projects is higher in most ECA countries than in advanced economies, often deterring investment given the high up-front costs that most greener technologies require. The regional average cost of capital in advanced economies is between 4.4 percent (Europe) and 5.4 percent (North America), but 5.6 percent in East Asia and the Pacific and 6.9 percent in Latin America.

Energy Efficiency

Improving energy efficiency is the first mile of the agenda on lowering emissions and achieving more rapid economic growth. It is the most important and lowest cost option in providing affordable energy services, reducing carbon emissions, and realizing the climate commitment of countries. Improved energy efficiency will contribute to better energy security; enhanced competitiveness; the easing of budget constraints on households, businesses, and governments; reduced burdens on power systems; and, of course, reduced carbon emissions. The International Energy Agency (IEA) has estimated that, among single energy sources, energy efficiency has made the greatest contribution in meeting energy demand since the 1970s (IDA 2024; IEA 2022b).

Regulatory policies, including mandates for energy efficiency, are essential. These also include structural changes to energy demand in the heating sector through retrofitting, housing building codes, and improved standards on appliances. The global use of LED lightbulbs in 2017 alone, for instance, reduced carbon emissions by 570 million metric tons, or nearly 2 percent of total emissions (World Bank 2023f).

About one-fourth of energy demand in the region is for space heating. Improving energy efficiency in this area will have a marked impact. Almost three-fourths of that heating is for residential housing, and more than four-fifths is produced from fossil fuels, both coal and natural gas. Enhancing the energy efficiency of heating in buildings, along with decarbonizing the sources of heat and replacing them with cleaner sustainable heating sources, must be a top priority among policy makers (IDA 2024).

Green Subsidies and Industrial Policy

Many green industries are still in the early stages of maturity. Their development thus creates positive spillovers that are not fully captured by the original investors, which may lead to underinvestment (Rodrik 2014). Green technology adoption and innovation may not arise on their own because of market failures and various externalities, including the cost of carbon emissions or pollution, that are not internalized in energy prices.

Subsidies are one response. A key issue is whether industrial policy is another response to help economies advance in the green transition. China, the EU, the United States, and other advanced economies are, by a large margin, the leaders in implementing industrial policies and are using generous tax incentives, support for R&D, and other measures, including subsidies. Some MICs, too, in recent years have begun to pursue industrial policy interventions, the number of which rose from a low level in 2011 to nearly 1,600 in 2022 (Juhász, Lane, and Rodrik 2023).

Another argument for the deployment of subsidies or engagement in industrial policy by ECA governments is the dearth of innovation in the private sector in many countries. But will subsidies augment the modest private sector effort or crowd it out? It is also important to consider whether subsidies should be offered for frontier innovations or for the infusion of green technologies or whether SOEs should be eligible to receive subsidies. Spending scarce public resources on such policy interventions should be carefully weighed against alternative policies and alternative uses for these resources. These include the need to improve the quality of education, the opportunities for firms to connect with global value chains, and the broader business environment for attracting foreign investment.

A crucial question in designing today's green industrial policies is whether the spread of such policies in China and advanced economies will hurt MICs by limiting the scope for MICs to participate in global green value chains. In such an environment, MICs will likely face more difficulties in producing intermediate products and in learning by doing. This may slow decarbonization in MICs because they will be increasingly troubled by the cost of investment in green technologies to which they cannot contribute. Governments in many smaller MICs are worried that they will be saddled with substantial debt if they import technologies wholesale without the opportunity to be part of the production process.

The Cost of Scaling-Up Renewables and Other Clean Technologies

The transition to renewable power generation and other clean technologies will require substantial investment. A recent IEA report estimated that about $1.1 trillion globally was invested in unabated fossil fuel supply and power (IEA 2023c). About $1.7 trillion was invested in renewable energy. Another IEA report concludes that, worldwide, reaching net-zero emissions by 2050 will require the investment of $10 in clean energy for each $1 invested in fossil fuels (IEA 2023a). Focusing only on low-income countries and MICs and excluding China, a recent World Bank report indicated that power sector investment "must quadruple from an average of $240 billion annually in 2016–20 to $1 trillion in 2030" (World Bank 2023c, iv).

Regional ECA investment needs are huge, too. These range from 5.2 percent of GDP by 2030, excluding energy efficiency, to 4.0 percent of GDP per year by 2060, including energy efficiency (Rozenberg and Fay 2019; World Bank 2024c). These needs, however, must be calibrated based on the complementary reforms governments will introduce. Countries with functioning energy markets and no fossil fuel subsidies will certainly require less additional investment. Kazakhstan's private and public sectors are likely to need an estimated $1.15 trillion in 2025–60 (6 percent of cumulative discounted GDP) to reach net-zero emissions by 2060, and Türkiye, about $644 billion (around 4.8 percent of cumulative discounted GDP) to reach net zero by 2053 (World Bank 2022a, 2022b).

Globally, the private sector is expected to account for 70 percent to 80 percent of the total investment in decarbonization (Ananthakrishnan et al. 2023; IEA 2021). In the ECA region, the estimates are broadly similar: about 60 percent to 90 percent of all investment needs are likely to come from the private sector, and a larger share of the investments will reflect inflows of foreign direct investment and other capital in countries that are more well integrated in global markets.

Globally, the scale-up of renewable electricity generation technologies has been rapid, and the decline in the prices of the technologies has been substantial. In 2023, the world added 50 percent more renewable generation capacity than it had added in 2022 (IEA 2023a, 2024). This is reshaping how government authorities think about energy security, energy production, and economic growth. Because the energy transition begins with the decarbonization of electricity production, this remarkable progress is welcome news. The share of electricity produced by renewables reached 30.0 percent in 2022, up from 21.3 percent in 2012. Within this rise, there have been significant increases in generation from solar photovoltaics and wind energy driven by supportive policies in many regions (Arkolakis and Walsh 2023).

The economic growth benefits of creative destruction occurring because of the emergence of solar photovoltaics and wind technology have been particularly notable in China, Denmark, Germany, and the United Kingdom (Hasna et al. 2023).

China has become a global leader in photovoltaics and wind turbine manufacturing, relying on its large-scale production capabilities to innovate and drive down costs. The United States has witnessed substantial growth in the domestic solar industry, particularly in solar panel installation and innovation. California has led the way in solar adoption, creating thousands of jobs and fostering a robust solar market.[6] Germany's early and sustained investment in solar power, driven by the Energiewende (energy transition) policy, has made the country a leader in solar technology and installation, while Türkiye has leapfrogged many other countries in solar panel manufacturing (refer to box 4.1), and Poland has become one of the world leaders in adopting heat pumps (refer to box 4.2).

BOX 4.1 Solar Panel Manufacturing in Türkiye

Türkiye is the fourth-largest manufacturer of solar panels in the world, benefiting from years of policy support, a large domestic market, and strong domestic demand. Installed capacity grew from 250 megawatts in 2015 to 12,200 megawatts in early 2024.

The Turkish government created incentives for the domestic production of solar panels in 2010 by providing bonus payments on top of the regular feed-in tariffs if modules had a certain share of domestic content (most recently, 55 percent). This arguably led to the establishment of the first wave of domestic panel manufacturers in 2011–13. In 2016, the first Chinese manufacturer, the state-owned enterprise HT Solar Energy, built a factory in Istanbul's Tuzla Free Trade Zone, which produced mainly for export.

To protect its emerging technologies from low-cost modules from China, the Turkish government introduced import tariffs on solar modules. While the introduction of more protection has been paralleled with a surge in new manufacturers, it is not yet clear whether these manufacturers will be competitive given that the export of Turkish solar panels is restricted to Europe and the Middle East. Joint ventures with East Asian firms may also have helped create Türkiye's technical capacity.

In the next phase of foreign market expansion, one manufacturer in 2023 announced a factory opening in Romania, and two firms will build factories in the United States. However, Turkish manufacturers—still unable to compete against the prices offered by Chinese companies—have indicated that the domestic-content credits offered by the Inflation Reduction Act of 2022 in the United States have facilitated their investment.

Sources: World Bank elaboration based on Bellini 2023; *Daily Sabah* 2020; Ernst 2023; IRENA 2023; Kesikli 2020; Stantec 2021.

BOX 4.2 Poland's Rapid Adoption of Heat Pumps

Domestic sales of heat pumps grew rapidly in Poland in 2018–22, from 25,000 units to more than 200,000 units, almost as many as the 236,000 sold in Germany that year. Poland's global share of heat pump manufacturing more than tripled, to 2.3 percent, in 2020–21.

This robust growth has been enabled by a raft of government support programs. The €25 billion Clean Air Program is the main one. Launched in 2018, it aims to help households enhance energy efficiency by replacing old coal heaters with modern systems through the provision of subsidies of up to Zl 66,000 (€14,420) per home. The government has more recently added heat pumps as supportable technology under the My Electricity Program, which provides the equivalent of up to €12,322 per home. The government also developed a heat-specific program in 2021—Moje Ciepło—that supports the purchase and installation of heat pumps in new single-family homes, with up to €4,711 in subsidies.[a]

The expectation that demand in Poland would grow prompted Daikin, a Japanese multinational that is the world's largest manufacturer of air conditioners, to invest €300 million in a factory that employs around 1,000 people and started production in 2025. Likewise, Bosch, a German multinational engineering and technology company, invested €255 million in a factory that employs around 500 people and will start production at the end of 2025 or early 2026.

Sources: World Bank based on IEA 2022a; Kurmayer 2024; Ptak 2023.

a. Refer to Moje Ciepło Program (dashboard), National Fund for Environmental Protection and Water Management, Warsaw, https://mojecieplo.gov.pl/o-programie/.

The cost of installing renewable energy has plunged. The costs of electricity production from solar and wind are now among the lowest among all potential energy sources in many parts of the world (refer to figure 4.6, panels a and b). Prices are likely to continue to decline with the ongoing surge in capacity, innovation, and the infusion of knowledge into previously less highly saturated markets.

In the ECA region, the adoption of solar and wind technologies has advanced quickly in a few countries. Hydropower accounts for 20 percent of electricity generation, although its contribution is constrained by periodic water shortages. The other renewable sources have been growing rapidly, but extensive development is so far concentrated in the few countries with a favorable policy framework, principally the four EU member states and Türkiye. Among the ECA solar and wind frontrunners (Croatia, Poland, Romania, and Türkiye), the share of renewable energy in electricity generation has risen to 15 percent, in line with the global average, though it is below the 30 percent share of the global frontrunners, including Germany and the United Kingdom.

FIGURE 4.6 **Solar energy and onshore energy costs**

a. Total installed project cost, solar photovoltaics
US$1,000 per kilowatt

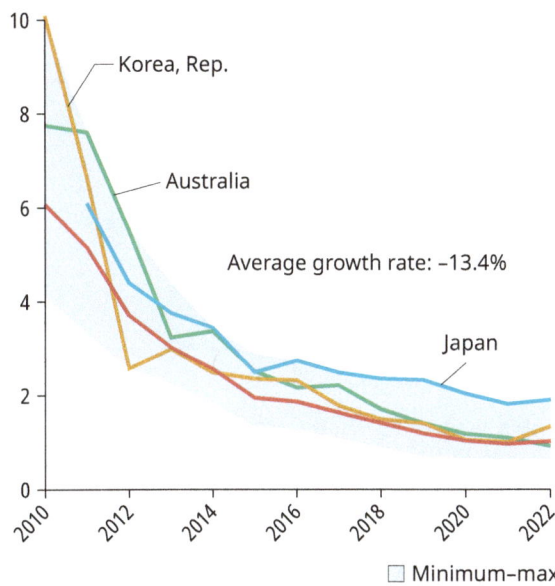

Korea, Rep.

Australia

Average growth rate: –13.4%

Japan

b. Total installed project cost, onshore wind
US$1,000 per kilowatt

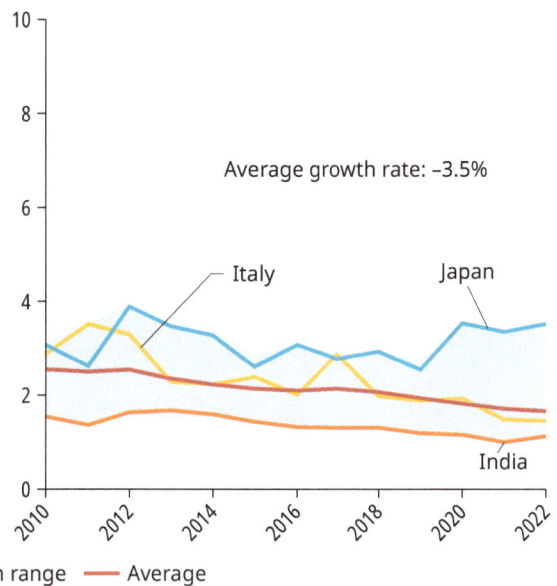

Average growth rate: –3.5%

Italy

Japan

India

☐ Minimum–maximum range ── Average

Sources: Hallegatte et al. 2024; IRENA 2023; World Bank 2023c.

Note: The sample includes Australia, Canada, China, France, Germany, India, Italy, Japan, Republic of Korea, Spain, the United Kingdom, and the United States.

Lower marginal costs in the generation and rapid spread of renewable energy do not automatically translate into lower prices among final consumers or an opportunity to boost economic growth. To accomplish these goals, a large scale-up in energy storage, including battery storage, is necessary. While there has been substantial progress in battery storage, the technologies are still not sufficiently mature. Transmission and distribution grids also need to be modernized.

Policies for Accelerating the Adoption of Renewables

At the top of the concerns of policy makers is an acceleration in the adoption of renewable technologies, some that are mature and some that will still evolve. Both are useful in their own right, but bare separate risks (that is, path dependence and obsolescence). And it is likely that, among ECA countries that do not yet participate in global value chains, the technologies will need to be imported and adapted by local service providers who will need to install, embed, and maintain the new technologies. Policies will initially have to support infusion (that is, adoption and diffusion) of the new technologies and later innovate. Policies that strengthen markets, sustain structural reforms, and foster integration into global markets are the foundation of these efforts. These policies may be categorized as supply-side and demand-side policies (refer to table 4.1).

TABLE 4.1 Policies to support the adoption of green technologies

Foundational policies	Sector-specific policies
	Supply side
	• Provide innovation support for sector-specific R&D
	• Set sectoral standards, for example, in efficiency
• Create competitive markets	• Establish sectoral regulations, such as open access, and develop regional markets for electricity
• Improve efficiency and effectiveness in the judiciary	• Train workers on specific technologies
• Regulate investment	• Get energy prices right
• Educate and upskill the workforce	• Phase out fossil fuel subsidies
	• Introduce a carbon price
• Discipline incumbent SOEs	*Demand side*
• Improve SOE governance and harden budget constraints	• Procure energy through feed-in tariffs and auctions
	• Establish energy efficiency regulations, for instance, on housing stock, appliances, industry, and transport
	• Establish consumer incentives for technology replacement, for example, financing and subsidies
	• Educate consumers about specific programs

Source: World Bank.

Note: Sector-specific policies refer to sectors that are most relevant for the green energy transition. This includes sectors that produce or deliver energy (such as oil and gas extraction, electricity generation, gas, and electricity networks) and energy-consuming sectors (such as industry, transport, housing, and agriculture). SOEs = state-owned enterprises.

A simple, transparent, and predictable energy transition policy package and regulatory environment can reduce risks and the cost of capital. The cost of capital reflects the risks perceived by independent power producers once their mitigants, such as targeted public support or risk-mitigation instruments, are accounted for (World Bank 2024d).

Complementary sectoral regulations may be needed to support success in additional interventions and to overcome barriers erected by incumbent firms. The substantial presence of SOEs in the economy—a set of usually powerful incumbents that may not be supportive of change and investments in lower-carbon technologies—is important. These incumbents are often a powerful force against change, influencing government policy and limiting reforms in regulation or the competitive environment. Rules on access to the electricity grid are thus needed to allow the developers of renewable technologies to connect to the market. This frequently closely depends on the capacity of the transmission system and the views of incumbents on new entrants who may disrupt the profitability of their businesses.

On the demand side, support can be provided for the procurement of green technologies to overcome incorrect economic pricing. For example, electricity generated from sources of renewable energy could be purchased through feed-in tariffs (only in the case of less mature technologies or if the projects are small) or through competitive auctions. The European Commission's guidelines on state aid offer an example of support schemes provided for renewable technologies at various stages of maturity.[7] Consumer incentives may be needed to replace older equipment, such as removing a gas-fired boiler to install a heat pump. This support might involve financing, including on-bill financing, or subsidies whereby the subsidy is justified because of the existence of incorrect economic pricing or to protect vulnerable customers. Information and consumer education are needed to attract support for green technologies and programs.

On the sector-specific supply side, inadequate regulatory policies are a key obstacle. Policies should include efforts to unbundle integrated electricity and natural gas systems, asset decommissioning, and enhancement of the quality of climate-related data to help investors make climate-related decisions. Such policies would result in better governance and greater efficiency among utilities, as well as better emissions tracking. Mandates should be established on energy efficiency, such as structural changes in energy demand in the heating sector (through retrofitting and development of residential building codes) and improved standards for appliances. A better policy framework for public–private partnerships and independent power producers is crucial to enhancing competition.

Training and Retraining

Investment policies will alter the nature of labor demand, shifting labor from sectors intensive in greenhouse gas emissions to lower-carbon sectors. Because the skills required by the two types of jobs differ, workers will need to be retrained, and training in new skills will need to be offered. Active labor market programs to retrain workers whose skill sets are ill matched to the requirements of green jobs will be required.

Weakening the Forces of Preservation

The ECA MICs have not yet weakened the forces of preservation that often stymie the production of lower-emission energy. The dominant SOEs in the region benefit from some of the world's highest fossil fuel subsidies. In several countries, SOEs still fix prices below cost recovery. The influence of SOEs hampers the scale-up of low-carbon technologies and incentivizes the continued inefficient use of energy. To protect them from closing, many ECA governments assign preference to generation by state-owned coal producers with higher marginal costs than generation using renewable resources. This results in the substantial misallocation of human, physical, and financial capital, operational inefficiencies, and market distortions.

Fossil Fuel Subsidies

Subsidies for fossil fuels are among the worst market disincentives for reducing energy intensity and emissions. They promote underpricing in two ways. First, the market prices paid for fossil fuels do not account for externalities, including damage from greenhouse gas emissions and local air pollutants. Second, in many countries, exploration, production, and consumption subsidies artificially lower the costs of supply or of prices paid for fossil fuels and key related products: electricity, diesel fuel, and gasoline. These subsidies increase the attractiveness of investing in fossil fuels and using these sources rather than clean energy alternatives.

Fossil fuel subsidies in the region are among the world's highest. They reached $110 billion in 2020, equivalent to 3.6 percent of regional GDP.[8] Russia accounted for $78 billion of these subsidies (5.2 percent of GDP), while Azerbaijan, Kazakhstan, and Ukraine all provided energy subsidies of more than 4.0 percent of GDP in the same year. By comparison, the EU countries, excluding Poland, spent 0.2 percent of GDP. In 2022, governments in the ECA region and the EU raised energy subsidies in response to surging energy prices, but started to reduce them by mid-2023 thanks to the mild winter of 2022–23. On average, among the ECA HICs, explicit subsidies were under 1 percent of GDP in both 2019 and 2022, while subsidies in the ECA upper-middle-income countries and lower-middle-income countries were higher (refer to figure 4.7).

FIGURE 4.7 Explicit and implicit subsidies, ECA region

Percent of GDP

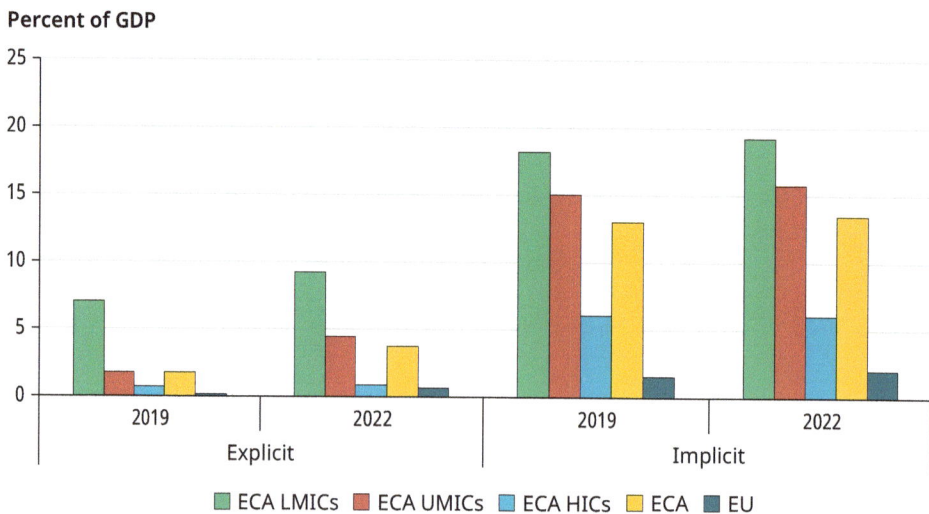

Source: Black et al. 2023.

Note: ECA HICs = Bulgaria, Croatia, Poland, and Romania. Group aggregates are calculated as total subsidies, divided by total GDP for each group. The ECA sample includes 20 economies. LMICs = lower-middle-income countries; UMICs = upper-middle-income countries.

Despite significant declines in gas subsidies over the previous decade, the ripple effects of the European energy crisis resulted in a sharp increase in 2021–22. The rise of natural gas subsidies was especially pronounced in 2022, when the market price of gas (against which subsidy rates are calculated) reached high levels. Even countries with few or no subsidies, such as Croatia, Poland, and Ukraine, adopted measures to protect consumers from damaging price spikes amid the energy crisis.

Currently, natural gas is the backbone of the ECA energy system, accounting for 46 percent of primary energy supply—far higher than the EU's 24 percent—and accompanied by the highest subsidy allocation among energy sources. The orderly removal of fossil fuel subsidies is a precondition for leveling the playing field for low-carbon emission technologies.

State-Owned Enterprises

SOEs account for an oversized ownership share in energy markets in the region. SOEs own all transmission networks, more than 80 percent of fossil fuel generation, nearly 75 percent of hydropower generation, and more than 65 percent of distribution networks. The SOE presence is even more extreme in the energy sector than in the broader economy, where enterprises in which the state has a share are active in more than half the sectors of the economy in more than half the countries (refer to figure 4.8).[9] In solar and wind, however, SOEs account for less than one-fourth of ownership.

FIGURE 4.8 The state is present in many economic sectors, ECA region

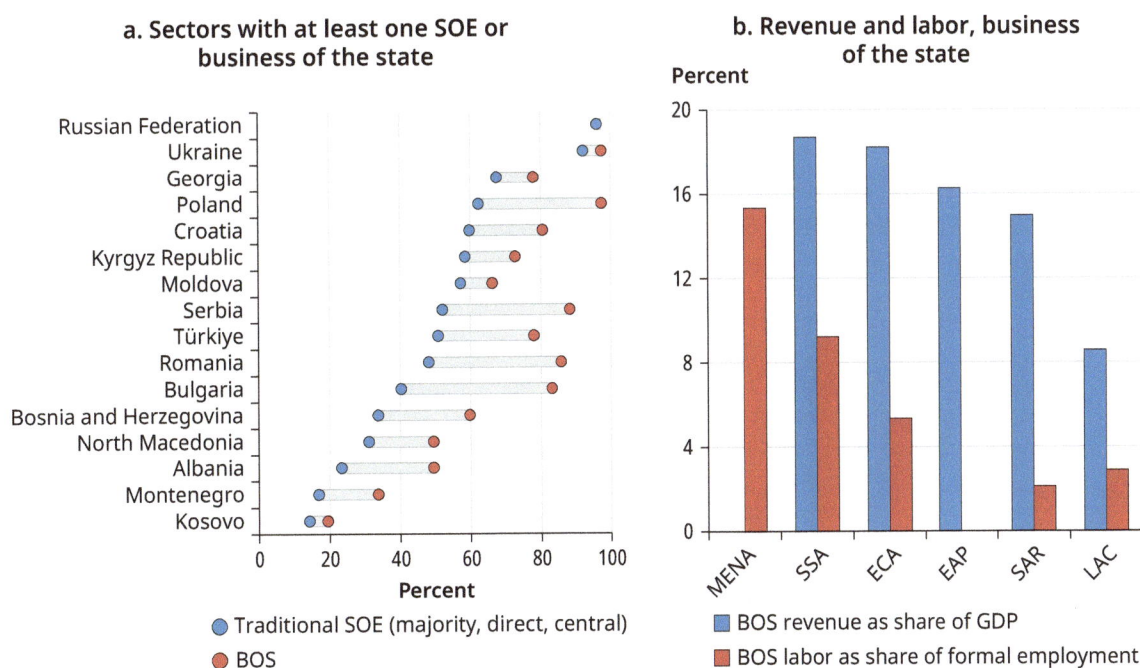

a. Sectors with at least one SOE or business of the state

b. Revenue and labor, business of the state

Source: Global BOS (Businesses of the State) database (internal database), World Bank, Washington, DC.

Note: Traditional SOEs are SOEs in which the central government holds direct, majority ownership. BOS = businesses of the state; EAP = East Asia and Pacific; LAC = Latin America and Caribbean; MENA = Middle East and North Africa; SAR = South Asia; SOE = state-owned enterprise; SSA = Sub-Saharan Africa.

SOEs account for a much larger share of investment in energy in developing countries than in advanced economies (OECD 2022). In 32 developing economies, one-third of energy investments were made by governments or SOEs in 2019. The SOE investment share in electricity networks, oil and gas supply, and fossil fuel generation was 73 percent in developing countries and 17 percent in advanced economies. For renewables and energy efficiency, it was about 27 percent and 3 percent, respectively.

For a successful energy transition, incumbent SOEs will be pivotal in decarbonizing electricity supply and electrifying energy demand. They will need to increase the share of renewable energy in their generation mix, modernize networks to integrate these variable power sources in the grid, and manage the ever-more varied and complex power needs of consumers. Utilities will need to be at the forefront of an accelerated push to provide electricity access in lagging areas. To meet these demands, ensuring reliable and affordable electricity service will require financially sustainable utilities that (1) can access inexpensive long-term financing, (2) are viable offtakers for private power investors, and (3) have the technological and management capacity to harness the opportunities created by an increasingly modern, distributed power system (World Bank 2024a).

Besides the large subsidies, a crucial obstacle to the transition to lower emissions is the profitability across energy SOEs in the region and their ability to scale up. On average, 29 percent of SOEs in this sector are unprofitable, which is a far higher rate than in other MICs (14 percent) or HICs (12 percent). This weak profitability is creating risks for private firms that seek to invest in clean energy generation in the region.

Market participants believe that most electricity transmission companies do not have the capacity to allow additional connections by independent renewable power producers in the region. In a recent survey among private companies in the region, 88 percent of the stakeholder respondents deemed grid access as a high or remarkably elevated risk (World Bank 2024d). Stakeholders expect most ECA countries to encounter issues in integrating the planned solar and wind volumes without substantial additional investment in transmission and distribution networks. The risk is greater in remote areas with small population densities and high renewable energy potential.

Nonetheless, the large state presence in sectors relevant to the green transition also means that governments can influence the trajectory of these sectors by helping turn SOEs into agents of change. One positive example is the United Kingdom, where privatized transmission and distribution companies that were once SOEs and new regulations that promote innovation competition have increased R&D activity and helped foster the adoption of modern technologies, such as smart grids (Ribeiro and Jamasb 2024). This has enabled a larger share of renewable energy to be incorporated into the grid.

Several studies have explored how climate action can be incorporated into the operations of SOEs. The main approaches involve integrating guidance and requirements on emissions reduction by SOEs within legislative documents; incentivizing SOE shareholders to prompt SOEs to respond to climate change; or supporting SOEs through various programs, alongside support for the private sector (Benoit 2019; De Kleine Feige 2021; Gonguet et al. 2021).

Economic Merit Order

Economic merit order is a method to determine which electricity producers will sell power to the electricity grid. It is based on marginal cost, starting with the lowest cost producer. The electricity price selected is therefore equal to the price of the most expensive dispatched producer, which, in the ECA region, is typically a coal- or gas-fired plant.

If the economic dispatch system is properly implemented, it should incentivize renewable producers and reduce the revenues of coal-fired plants. However, rather than selecting lower marginal cost generators, many ECA countries assign preference to generation by state-owned coal-fired producers with higher marginal costs to protect them from closure. Often, this preference also reflects the need to have backup generators given the slow progress in the installation of battery storage. Thus, while market distortions persist and shift the balance in favor of coal in the ECA countries in which economic dispatch is implemented (including Bulgaria, Poland, and countries in the Western Balkans), the original goals of merit dispatch cannot be met.

In Poland, the government introduced economic dispatch in the power sector in early 1990 as part of its market reforms. Today (and likely in the future), coal is generally the most expensive marginal resource in the Polish power system. However, the coal plants have remained dominant even if electricity prices are lower in neighboring countries and the unit cost of solar and wind has declined to levels below that of coal generation. This stems from limited interconnector capacity to access cheap electricity abroad in moments of system stress. Lignite plants also have must-run status that overrides merit order to ensure that these plants are working at least at 60 percent capacity, the cutoff for them to be profitable. Lower-cost renewable generation is curtailed during system stress because of the lack of flexibility of the coal-fired plants.

Cushioning the Impact of the Forces of Destruction

The transition to lower energy intensity and carbon emissions may create losses among some consumers, workers, and businesses as industries and sectors adjust and so may lead to resistance to the transition. If energy is costlier (say, owing to the introduction of carbon taxes or the costs of new infrastructure), vulnerable households may ration energy consumption, while energy-intensive firms may lose competitiveness. Many households and small firms may be credit constrained and unable to undertake the up-front capital spending that would allow them to benefit from the operating cost savings of low-carbon energy. The affected groups will push back against well-intentioned reform, with possibly destabilizing consequences. This may lead voters to elect governments that promise to maintain the forces of preservation, entrenching dependency on fossil fuels and making subsequent reforms even more difficult.

Protecting Vulnerable Populations

Addressing these political economy concerns requires careful policy sequencing so that reforms impose no unbearable burdens on any group. There is a trade-off: unambitious reforms that are unlikely to create a backlash may not lead to the emergence of new firms and the destruction of the old. In Kazakhstan, for instance, the level of the carbon price is so low, at slightly above $1 per ton of CO_2 emitted, that it does not force hard choices on major actors.[10] Nor does it shift the economy away from fossil fuels. Identifying more ambitious, but nondestabilizing policies can better serve the purpose of creative destruction.

An important way to make the forces of destruction acceptable to vulnerable groups is by accompanying them with compensatory policies. Reductions in fossil fuel subsidies can be balanced among vulnerable groups by income support that leaves the groups with higher effective income, while saving the government money (because most fossil fuel subsidies apply to all population groups, including the most affluent). And because destruction also involves job losses, as in coal mining, cushioning policies must go beyond income transfers and create new opportunities for workers in affected sectors.

One example is the coal phaseout in Poland agreed to in 2021. The destruction of mining jobs for a complete phaseout by 2049 is to be cushioned with a "social contract" in which workers losing their jobs could elect to continue to receive 80 percent of their salary if close to retirement or receive a severance payment and retraining. In addition, investment in transforming the structure of the most coal-dependent region, Silesia, would be financed through the EU Just Transition Fund.

A Just Transition

Countries such as Bulgaria, Poland, and Romania will benefit from the EU Just Transition Mechanism. Other non-EU economies, including the major fossil fuel exporters in Central Asia or the South Caucasus, need to ensure sufficient fiscal space to fund their just transitions as global demand for fossil fuels declines.

The EU Just Transition Mechanism was unveiled in January 2020 as a regional development initiative. It aims to deliver specialized assistance to EU regions that will face significant adverse impacts from the shift toward a carbon-neutral economy. In Bulgaria, Poland, and Romania, the mechanism will fund just transition–related activities in 13 geographic areas and emphasize the development of small and medium enterprises. Other focus areas are the rehabilitation of industrial sites and coal mine–contaminated land and developing renewable energy, while emphasizing job creation.

Although the current just transition initiatives in the region are still at an initial stage, lessons can be drawn from previous coal phasedowns during the second half of the twentieth century in Eastern Europe, Germany, and the United Kingdom (World Bank 2021). The region has around 450,000 direct coal jobs. A key difference between the historical phasedowns and the current transition is that the former were driven by the declining competitiveness of coal, whereas the latter is associated with the dual challenge of replacing power capacity and creating jobs.

The first lesson is that the scope of just transition support needs to be as holistic as possible, covering entire supply chains of directly and indirectly affected jobs and vulnerable households. This may mean a stark broadening in the scope of the supported population. In Poland, the indirectly affected jobs from a coal phaseout range between 57,000 and 130,000 compared with 158,000 directly affected jobs (Christiaensen et al. 2022).

A second lesson is that there is a trade-off between periodic and lump-sum income support. While lump sums are initially attractive, evidence from Poland and Romania shows that they are often rapidly used up and can lead to wide income shortages absent new employment opportunities. In 1998, Poland introduced the Mining Social Package, which provided options for the voluntary departure of mining workers. Of the people who took the package, most selected a one-time payment (Szpor and Ziółkowska 2018).

The third lesson is that skills, preferences, and wages—key factors in reemploying affected populations—need to be aligned with newly available jobs. The skills and preferences of workers may not be aligned with alternative jobs with the highest overlap in tasks and skills (Christiaensen et al. 2022).

The Role of Government as an Enabler

The primary role of government in the energy transition is to provide certainty in policies, incentivize the private sector, and provide any necessary public investment. The government also has to ensure that transition costs are palatable to all segments of the population that are impacted by the transition, This can be accomplished through social assistance and support in the development of human capital. These tasks require coordination across government, industry groups, and the affected segments of the population.

Conclusions and Policy Recommendations

The transition to lower carbon emissions and, ultimately, net zero has the potential to support higher growth in productivity and output among the ECA MICs. But this link is not automatic and will require deliberate, well-sequenced steps to facilitate technology adoption; the infusion of foreign capital, knowledge, and management expertise; and for some, opportunities for frontier innovation.

A few essential prerequisites are more evident. The first is to create or complete markets for energy, while enabling prices to reflect the true economic and social cost. Governments need to phase out explicit and implicit fossil fuel subsidies that tilt the playing field in favor of high-carbon emission and energy-intensive technologies. This is a priority among the countries of the South Caucasus and Central Asia because of their larger subsidies. Introducing a carbon tax or instituting an ETS also needs to be considered. EU candidate countries are focusing on this at present. Maintaining subsidies while imposing carbon taxes will be hugely inefficient and needs to be avoided.

The political economy challenges are formidable. Many ECA MICs have neither a carbon tax, nor an ETS. The imminent launch of the EU Carbon Border Adjustment Mechanism is likely to have only a modest macroeconomic impact in most countries, although the impact on certain emission-intensive sectors or certain areas or income groups may be more significant (World Bank 2022a, 2024e). Countries may consider a more palatable set of measures, at least initially, by increasing energy taxes. These taxes already cover a significant share of global emissions and send much stronger carbon price signals than their direct counterparts. They also raise much-needed revenue, which can be used to fund vital government services and support vulnerable groups in adjusting to higher energy prices.

The second prerequisite is for governments to help sustain the economy's structural transformation to allow enterprises to integrate more tightly into global markets and value chains. Structural transformation should be aided by stepped-up energy efficiency measures in housing, transport, and other economic sectors. Upgrading enterprise technologies should help raise productivity, while reducing energy use, thereby improving energy efficiency. Institutional capacity in managing energy efficiency is the highest in the EU member states and Türkiye, while there needs to be more efforts in Central Asia, the South Caucasus, and the Western Balkans. The need for standards and regulations is greater in the first two. All ECA countries must strengthen financing mechanisms.

The most crucial step in the transition to lower emissions and more rapid economic growth will require enterprises to participate in global value chains that produce cleaner technologies. Many ECA MICs will find leading on clean innovation challenging. The experience will be at least as difficult as the adoption of other new technologies in the past; most MICs are now consumers of such technologies. Most ECA countries spend little on R&D and receive few patents relative to China, the advanced economies of the EU, and the United States. And innovation is a path-dependent process not only globally, but also nationally. It depends heavily on the availability of previous innovations, markets, institutions, and talented workers.

This is where the recommendations in the previous two chapters come together. Speeding up the market transition of the ECA region, reinvigorating private enterprise, and dramatically improving the quality of education and mobility are essential to achieving stepped-up innovation, tighter links with global markets, and participation in global value chains, all of which will drive the transition to lower emissions and more rapid economic growth.

Given the prevalence of SOEs, realizing secure and affordable energy while reaching high-income status must involve policies to discipline incumbents. New competitors need to be able to enter the market without hindrance. Policies to facilitate this approach include both ex ante regulation, such as the streamlined design of interconnection charges and strict adherence to economic cost dispatch, and ex post regulation, such as efforts to detect and counteract abuses of dominance. The competition framework, including auctions, access to network connections, and grid integration, are more advanced in the EU member states and Türkiye.

The appropriate mix of policy recommendations depends on the context faced in each country. For this purpose, countries are sorted into four groups, given the heterogeneity in terms of energy that the ECA MICs grouping encompasses (refer to table 4.2): (1) ECA EU members states (Bulgaria, Croatia, Poland, Romania); (2) EU candidates (Georgia, Moldova, Ukraine, Western Balkans); (3) Türkiye, which is also an EU candidate but has a different energy profile and merits presentation separate from (2); and (4) Central Asia and South Caucasus (Armenia, Azerbaijan, Kazakhstan, Kyrgyz Republic, Tajikistan, Turkmenistan, Uzbekistan).

- *For ECA EU members, the key priority areas* revolve around ETS implementation and preparedness for the ETS2 by 2027, disciplining incumbents, removing barriers to entry created by authorization processes and network issues, and dynamically leveling the playing field to nurture innovation and new technologies as they pass through R&D, demonstration, and pilot phases toward commercial viability. This is in addition to the long-term strategic priorities of energy efficiency and the reduction of fossil fuel use, where there has been remarkable progress. For instance, the EU demand for natural gas fell by 18 percent between August 2022 and May 2024, enabled by efficiencies and the scale-up of renewables and supported by a just energy transition (World Bank 2021).

TABLE 4.2 Energy and emissions: summary of recommendations

Recommendation	ECA EU	EU candidates	Türkiye	South Caucasus	Central Asia
Get prices right, fully reflecting economic and social costs					
Phase out explicit subsidies	Medium	Medium	High	High	High
Phase out implicit subsidies	Medium	Medium	Medium	High	High
Introduce CTs and/or ETS	High	High	Medium	Medium	Medium
Create energy markets for renewables					
Support entrants	Medium	Medium	Low	Medium	Medium
Investment framework	High	Medium	Low	Medium	Medium
Regulatory environment	Low	Low	Low	Medium	High
Competition	Medium	High	Low	High	Medium
Economic merit dispatch	Medium	Medium	Medium	High	High
Discipline incumbents	High	High	High	High	High
Energy efficiency across the board					
Standards and regulations	Medium	Medium	Medium	High	Medium
Introduction of more stringent energy efficiency standards for appliances	Low	High	Medium	High	High
Financing	High	High	High	High	High
Reduce fossil fuel usage	High	High	High	High	High
Research and development spending	Medium	High	Medium	High	High
Protect the vulnerable during the transition	High	High	High	High	High

Source: World Bank.

Note: Central Asia: Kazakhstan, Kyrgyz Republic, Tajikistan, Turkmenistan, Uzbekistan. ECA EU: Bulgaria, Croatia, Poland, Romania. EU candidates: Albania, Bosnia and Herzegovina, Georgia, Kosovo (potential candidate), Moldova, Montenegro, North Macedonia, Serbia, Ukraine. (*Türkiye* is mentioned separately. See text for details.) South Caucasus: Armenia, Azerbaijan, Georgia. The priority ranking of low, medium, or high should be viewed relative to the progress already achieved and relative to other priorities. CT = carbon tax; ETS = emissions trading system.

- *For EU candidates*, the key priority areas revolve around the facilitation of private investments and integration with EU markets (including power and gas markets, ETS, and the carbon border adjustment mechanism), together with strengthening competition and disciplining incumbents to provide space for new entrants and start-ups, while protecting the vulnerable during the transition. Other high priorities include deepening financial markets to attract expertise and investments in highly efficient and low-carbon technologies, which typically offer essential air pollution co-benefits as well.

- *For Türkiye,* which is also an EU candidate, but has a different energy profile, the key priority areas revolve around the phase out of explicit subsidies, while protecting the vulnerable, disciplining incumbents, and attracting financing for the promotion of high-efficiency technology adoption and renewables.

- *For the countries of Central Asia and the South Caucasus,* the key priorities involve getting the foundations right by phasing down explicit coal, power, gas, and district heating subsidies, as well as implicit subsidies, while protecting the vulnerable. Additional priorities are facilitating private investments, reducing the state footprint, disciplining incumbents, strengthening competition through the development of domestic and regional power markets for increased power trade, and introducing economic dispatch for power generators. Improving incentives for high-efficiency and low-carbon technology adoption in building, transport, and industry are also key areas of priority to reduce energy and carbon intensity.

Notes

1. Data reported in 2022. Refer to GCPT (Global Coal Plant Tracker) (dashboard), Global Energy Monitor, Covina, CA, https://globalenergymonitor.org/projects/global-coal-plant-tracker/.

2. The Convergers are the formerly planned economies of Central and Eastern Europe that have achieved high-income status since the 1990s (refer to chapter 1).

3. The other form of an ETS is the baseline-and-credit system. Under such a system, "there is no fixed limit on emissions, but polluters that reduce their emissions more than they otherwise are obliged to can earn 'credits' that they sell to others who need them to comply with regulations they are subject to" (OECD 2021).

4. Refer to EU ETS (European Union Emissions Trading System) (dashboard), European Commission, Brussels, https://climate.ec.europa.eu/eu-action/eu-emissions-trading-system-eu-ets/what-eu-ets_en.

5. Refer to ISO 50001: Energy Management (dashboard), International Organization for Standardization, Geneva, https://www.iso.org/iso-50001-energy-management.html.

6. The California Solar Initiative has provided incentives for homeowners and large-scale commercial projects to install solar panels. According to another policy that took effect in 2020 under the California Solar Panel Law, the state mandates "that new single-family homes and multi-family dwellings up to three stories high install solar panels" (Lozanova 2024).

7. State Aid (dashboard), European Commission, Brussels, https://competition-policy.ec.europa.eu /state-aid_en.

8. Globally, fossil fuel subsidies amounted to $7 trillion (7.1 percent of GDP) in 2022 versus $5 trillion in 2020 (Black, Parry, and Vernon 2023).

9. In this chapter, SOE and business of the state refer to any enterprise with direct or indirect government ownership of at least 10 percent.

10. State and Trends of Carbon Pricing Dashboard, World Bank, Washington, DC, https://carbonpricingdashboard .worldbank.org/compliance/price.

References

Allen, Robert C. 2009. *The British Industrial Revolution in Global Perspective.* New Approaches to Economic and Social History Series. New York: Cambridge University Press.

Ananthakrishnan, Prasad, Torsten Ehlers, Charlotte Gardes-Landolfini, and Fabio Natalucci. 2023. "Emerging Economies Need Much More Private Financing for Climate Transition." *Climate Change* (blog), October 2, 2023. https://www.imf.org/en/Blogs/Articles/2023/10/02/emerging-economies-need-much-more-private-financing-for-climate-transition.

Arkolakis, Costas, and Conor Walsh. 2023. "Clean Growth." NBER Working Paper 31615 (August), National Bureau of Economic Research, Cambridge, MA.

Bellini, Emiliano. 2023. "Turkey Sets Minimum Price for Solar Cell Imports." *pv magazine*, January 30, 2023. https://www.pv-magazine.com/2023/01/30/turkey-sets-minimum-price-for-solar-cell-imports/.

Benoit, Philippe. 2019. "Engaging State-Owned Enterprises in Climate Action." Center on Global Energy Policy, School of International and Public Affairs, Columbia University, New York.

Black, Simon, Antung A. Liu, Ian W. H. Parry, and Nate Vernon. 2023. "IMF Fossil Fuel Subsidies Data: 2023 Update." IMF Working Paper WP/23/169 (August), International Monetary Fund, Washington, DC.

Black, Simon, Ian W. H. Parry, and Nate Vernon. 2023. "Fossil Fuel Subsidies Surged to Record $7 Trillion." *Climate Change* (blog), August 24, 2023. https://www.imf.org/en/Blogs/Articles/2023/08/24/fossil-fuel-subsidies-surged-to-record-7-trillion#:~:text=Fossil%2Dfuel%20subsidies%20surged%20to,economic%20recovery%20from%20the%20pandemic.

Brown, Stanley. 1971. "The Next 25 Years in the Electricity Supply Industry." Lecture, Institute of Electrical and Electronic Technical Engineers, November 16, 1970, Central Electricity Generating Board Information Services, London.

Christiaensen, Luc Jozef, Céline Ferré, Tomasz Janusz Gajderowicz, Maddalena Honorati, and Sylwia Michalina Wrona. 2022. "Towards a Just Coal Transition: Labor Market Challenges and People's Perspectives from Wielkopolska." June, World Bank, Washington, DC.

Daily Sabah. 2020. "Turkey Opens 1st Integrated Solar Panel Manufacturing Facility." *Energy* (blog), August 19, 2020. https://www.dailysabah.com/business/energy/turkey-opens-1st-integrated-solar-panel-manufacturing-facility.

De Kleine Feige, Annette Irmgard. 2021. "State-Owned Enterprises and Climate Action." World Bank, Washington, DC.

Dobrotkova, Zuzana, Aditya Lukas, and Jas Singh. 2018. "Energy Efficiency in Industry." Live Wire Brief 2018/96, Energy Sector Management Assistance Program, Energy and Extractives Global Practice, World Bank, Washington, DC.

Ernst, Iulian. 2023. "Turkish PV Panels Producer to Build Factory in Romania." *Energy* (blog), November 7, 2023. https://www.romania-insider.com/turkish-alfa-solar-factory-romania-2023.

ESMAP (Energy Sector Management Assistance Program), OECD (Organisation for Economic Co-operation and Development), GIF (Global Infrastructure Facility), and Hydrogen Council. 2024. *Scaling Hydrogen Financing for Development.* ESMAP Report. Washington, DC: World Bank.

Gonguet, Fabien, Claude P. Wendling, Ozlem Aydin, and Bryn Battersby. 2021. "Climate-Sensitive Management of Public Finances: 'Green PFM.'" IMF Staff Climate Note 2021/002 (August), International Monetary Fund, Washington, DC.

Hallegatte, Stéphane, Catrina Godinho, Jun Erik Maruyama Rentschler, Paolo Avner, Ira Irina Dorband, Camilla Knudsen, Jana Lemke, and Penny Mealy. 2024. *Within Reach: Navigating the Political Economy of Decarbonization.* Washington, DC: World Bank.

Hasna, Zeina, Florence Jaumotte, Jaden Kim, Samuel Pienknagura, and Gregor Schwerhoff. 2023. "Green Innovation and Diffusion: Policies to Accelerate Them and Expected Impact on Macroeconomic and Firm-Level Performance." IMF Staff Discussion Note SDN/2023/008 (November), International Monetary Fund, Washington, DC.

IDA (International Development Association). 2024. *Multiphase Programmatic Approach of the Scaling-Up of Energy Efficiency in Europe and Central Asia.* Project Appraisal Document PAD00193 (May 29). Washington, DC: World Bank.

IEA (International Energy Agency). 2021. "The Cost of Capital in Clean Energy Transitions." Report, December 17, IEA, Paris. https://www.iea.org/articles/the-cost-of-capital-in-clean-energy-transitions.

IEA (International Energy Agency). 2022a. *The Future of Heat Pumps*. World Energy Outlook Special Report, December. Paris: IEA.

IEA (International Energy Agency). 2022b. "World Energy Employment." September, IEA, Paris.

IEA (International Energy Agency). 2023a. *Net Zero Roadmap: A Global Pathway to Keep the 1.5°C Goal in Reach*. 2023 Update (September). Paris: IEA.

IEA (International Energy Agency). 2023b. *The Oil and Gas Industry in Net Zero Transitions*. World Energy Outlook Special Report, November. Paris: IEA.

IEA (International Energy Agency). 2023c. *World Energy Investment 2023*. May. Paris: IEA.

IEA (International Energy Agency). 2024. *Renewables 2023: Analysis and Forecasts to 2028*. January. Paris: IEA.

IRENA (International Renewable Energy Agency). 2023. "The Cost of Financing for Renewable Power." IRENA, Abu Dhabi, United Arab Emirates.

Juhász, Réka, Nathan J. Lane, and Dani Rodrik. 2023. "The New Economics of Industrial Policy." NBER Working Paper 31538 (August), National Bureau of Economic Research, Cambridge, MA.

Kesikli. 2020. "Renewable Energy Law Update: Amendments to the Local Content Support Regulation." *News and Insight* (blog), June 15, 2020. https://kesikli.com/news-insight/2020-07-18-renewable-energy -law-update-amendments-to-the-local-content-support-regulation/.

Kurmayer, Nikolaus J. 2024. "Three Countries Became Heat Pump Forerunners in 2022, Germany Did Not." *Energy, Environment, and Transport* (blog), September 29, 2024. https://www.euractiv.com/section/energy-environment /news/three-countries-became-heat-pump-forerunners-in-2022-germany-did-not/.

Lozanova, Sarah. 2024. "Understanding the California Solar Panel Law: California Solar Mandate 2025." *Greenlancer* (blog), January 22, 2024. https://www.greenlancer.com/post/california-solar-mandate.

OECD (Organisation for Economic Co-operation and Development). 2021. "Emission Trading Systems." Web archive, July 19, 2021. https://web-archive.oecd.org/temp/2021-07-20/213777-emissiontradingsystems.htm.

OECD (Organisation for Economic Co-operation and Development). 2022. "Climate Change and Low-Carbon Transition Policies in State-Owned Enterprises." OECD, Paris.

Ptak, Alicja. 2023. "Heat Pumps Boom in Poland, Europe's Fastest Growing Market." *Business, Energy, and Climate* (blog), April 28, 2023. https://notesfrompoland.com/2023/04/28/heat-pumps-boom-in-poland -europes-fastest-growing-market/.

Rhodes, Chris, David Hough, and Louise Butcher. 2014. "Privatisation." Research Paper 14/61 (November 20), House of Commons Library, London.

Ribeiro, Beatriz Couto, and Tooraj Jamasb. 2024. "Innovation by Regulation: Smart Electricity Grids in the UK and Italy." Working Paper 7-2024, Department of Economics, Copenhagen Business School, Copenhagen.

Rodrik, Dani. 2014. "Green Industrial Policy." *Oxford Review of Economic Policy* 30 (3): 469–91.

Rozenberg, Julie, and Marianne Fay, eds. 2019. *Beyond the Gap: How Countries Can Afford the Infrastructure They Need While Protecting the Planet*. Sustainable Infrastructure Series. Washington, DC: World Bank.

Stantec. 2021. *Stantec Annual Report 2020*. Edmonton, Alberta, Canada: Stantec.

Szpor, Aleksander, and Konstancja Ziółkowska. 2018. "The Transformation of the Polish Coal Sector." GSI Report, January, Global Subsidies Initiative, International Institute for Sustainable Development, Winnipeg, Canada.

Tiseo, Ian. 2024. "PM2.5 Emissions in the UK 1970–2022." *Statista*, February 15, 2024. https://www.statista.com /statistics/808071/pm25-particulate-pollution-emissions-united-kingdom-uk/#statisticContainer.

World Bank. 2021. "Supporting Transition in Coal Regions: A Compendium of the World Bank's Experience and Guidance for Preparing and Managing Future Transitions." World Bank, Washington, DC.

World Bank. 2022a. "Kazakhstan: Country Climate and Development Report." November, World Bank, Washington, DC.

World Bank. 2022b. "Türkiye: Country Climate and Development Report." June, World Bank, Washington, DC.

World Bank. 2023a. "The Development, Climate, and Nature Crisis: Solutions to End Poverty on a Livable Planet." World Bank, Washington, DC. https://www.worldbank.org/en/topic/climatechange/publication/the -development-climate-and-nature-crisis.

World Bank. 2023b. *Lessons from Korea's Energy Efficiency Policies in the Industrial Sector*. Washington, DC: World Bank.

World Bank. 2023c. "Scaling Up to Phase Down: Financing Energy Transitions in the Power Sector." April, World Bank, Washington, DC.

World Bank. 2023d. "State and Trends of Carbon Pricing 2023." World Bank, Washington, DC.

World Bank. 2023e. *Testing Resilience*. Western Balkans Regular Economic Report 23 (Spring). Washington, DC: World Bank.

World Bank. 2023f. *World Bank Group Support to Demand-Side Energy Efficiency: An Independent Evaluation*. Washington, DC: Independent Evaluation Group, World Bank. https://ieg.worldbankgroup.org/evaluations /world-bank-group-support-demand-side-energy-efficiency.

World Bank. 2024a. "The Critical Link: Empowering Utilities for the Energy Transition." World Bank, Washington, DC.

World Bank. 2024b. "Greening the Economy of Europe and Central Asia." Europe and Central Asia in Focus, Office of the Chief Economist, World Bank, Washington, DC.

World Bank. 2024c. "Net Zero Energy by 2060: Charting Europe and Central Asia's Journey toward Sustainable Energy Futures." Energy Sector Management Assistance Program, World Bank, Washington, DC.

World Bank. 2024d. *Scaling Up Renewables in Europe and Central Asia: Barriers and Opportunities*. Washington, DC: Energy Sector Management Assistance Program, World Bank.

World Bank. 2024e. *Western Balkans 6: Country Climate and Development Report*. October. Washington, DC: World Bank.

www.ingramcontent.com/pod-product-compliance
Lightning Source LLC
Chambersburg PA
CBHW050907210326
41597CB00002B/51